WITHDRAWN
TRACES

WITHDRAWN TRACES

TRACES

SEARCHING FOR
THE TRUTH ABOUT
RICHEY MANIC

Sara Hawys Roberts and Leon Noakes

Foreword by Rachel Edwards

1 3 5 7 9 10 8 6 4 2

Virgin Books, an imprint of Ebury Publishing,
20 Vauxhall Bridge Road,
London SW1V 2SA

Virgin Books is part of the Penguin Random House group of companies
whose addresses can be found at global.penguinrandomhouse.com

Penguin
Random House
UK

First published in the United Kingdom by Virgin Books in 2019

www.penguin.co.uk

A CIP catalogue record for this book is available from the British Library

ISBN 9780753545348

Typeset in 11/16 pt Bell MT
by Integra Software Services Pvt. Ltd, Pondicherry

Printed and bound in Great Britain by Clays Ltd, Elcograf S.p.A.

Penguin Random House is committed to a sustainable future for
our business, our readers and our planet. This book is made
from Forest Stewardship Council® certified paper.

MIX
Paper from
responsible sources
FSC
www.fsc.org
FSC® C018179

Contents

Foreword

I was 24 years old when I last saw my brother. Twenty-four years have passed since the day that he went missing. I have been without him for half of my life. I am almost the same age that my mother was when her son disappeared.

There are a great many things I do not understand in life. I do not understand why my brother Richard went missing. I do not understand how, in an area with some of the highest levels of CCTV coverage, he could apparently just vanish from the face of the earth. I do not understand how after so much searching, so many appeals, that not one shred of information about him has ever come to light. Surely someone, somewhere, knows what happened to him. I do not understand how I can grieve for him when there is always hope just around the corner that we will find an answer.

But there are some things I do understand. I do understand the impact of having a loved one go missing. I do understand that every moment is affected by the absence of those you hold dear. How every phone call fills you with anxiety. How potentially every e-mail and letter could provide you with the answer. How every walk through the crowded streets leaves you searching. Having a missing loved one is like having a candle that is never lit. There is a diminishing of light and of joy. And although I live daily with this loss, I find through sharing memories and prayer, I can rekindle the light through uncertainty, and find hope.

I want my brother to be remembered as more than just a member of a band. I want him to be remembered as an artist and as a person and as a dearly loved and missed family member. Although there has not been a shortage of writers keen to work on Richard's biography, it was not until my meeting with Sara, some ten years ago, that I felt able to entrust anyone with my brother's story and extensive archive. Sara 'got it' from the outset, seeing Richard as an artist standing in, yet outside, his creation – and not just a member of a four-piece band. That he should be remembered as someone who stands outside of this framework. This is the first attempt in any book to explore Richard in this way, in a sympathetic light. The authors reveal my brother as I knew him.

Sharing my recollections, many aspects of the private life of my family, and the contributions from people who both knew and cared for Richard has not been an easy undertaking for me. My parents, when alive, were quiet, dignified and the least likely couple to wish to have attention drawn to themselves. As the remaining living member of our small family, I feel that if I can reach out one more time to as wide an audience as possible, not only will Richard be remembered but the light from that candle may illuminate what became of him.

As for my thoughts about what became of Richard, I honestly don't know. People will ask me if I think he's alive or dead, and I have no answers. Without a body there is no certainty, and the only certainty I have is uncertainty. Richard was a highly intelligent, enigmatic and most of all complicated character. His very complexity sometimes makes it seem appropriate that his fate is shrouded in such mystery.

The book concludes with more questions than had previously been raised during the investigations into Richard's disappearance. Part of its legacy is to discover the story behind all of those other stories – not the soundbites, not the headlines – but the actual reality. Everything has to now be re-explored. I have felt a sense of burning injustice in the way the case has been handled by the authorities and various agencies, therefore being involved with this book has proved to be a cathartic experience.

We now know that the timeline of events has been wrong from the moment Richard went missing. Even though the police are aware of this, it is enormously frustrating that they have closed the case and will not reopen it.

Only new information can now change the situation. There have been Missing Persons cases which the public have solved before. Perhaps someone knows something but had their reasons to conceal it at the time? Or maybe they have some evidence but do not believe that it is important? From my perspective, any new information is valuable.

If the mystery of Richard's disappearance can be explained, then it is only you, the public that can help me. Please come forward with any information if you have it. Both my parents died without knowing what happened to their son; I don't want to die without knowing what happened to my brother.

Rachel Edwards, 2019.

Introduction

'You've got to reach out on a massive level. Once we've done
that we'll fade away. You'll never hear from us again.'
Richey Edwards, 1991

Over two decades have passed since the disappearance of Manic Street Preachers' lyricist and guitarist, Richey Edwards. A missing person since 1 February 1995, his car was found at the Aust service station overlooking the old Severn crossing. He has not been seen or heard from since.

This mysterious case is lodged in the popular consciousness. Even those unfamiliar with the Manic Street Preachers, or unable to match a face to Richey's name, have heard of the legendary missing rock star and his dramatic story.

As the years go by with no apparent progress, will we ever find out what happened to Richey Edwards? This book is an invitation to consider the issue anew, in the hope that something of the obscured truth of what happened to him may come to light.

In a 1992 interview, Richey stated, 'Whatever anyone thinks of me, whatever happens to me, at least I know that I tried to be a person. I set out to be something worthwhile that meant something real and valuable; to talk about ideas and attitudes that are important and real,

1

and that no one is saying or is too scared to speak of; to be the influence to people I never had when growing up.'

Since his adolescence, Richey dreamed feverishly of entering the pantheon of rock's greatest figureheads, aiming to contribute to that lineage. His devout mission was to become a pop-culture icon, and one that *meant something.*

Richard James Edwards grew up in the working-class town of Blackwood in the Welsh Valleys, a once thriving and close-knit community, now devastated by industrial decline. A teenager of the eighties, he spent much of his youth in his bedroom, listening to The Smiths and The Clash, reading the Beat poets and dreaming of escape.

With his fierce intellect, he initially believed academia would be his ticket away from a home town he later described as 'being a museum, full of rubble and shit'. Born to a generation mired in defeatism and hopelessness, he saw this new barrenness as a great opportunity, a blank canvas upon which to daub. He would join forces with three local friends and become 'Richey Manic' – a spokesman for a generation revered for his highly charged, polemic and politicised lyrics.

When the Manic Street Preachers broke into the musical mainstream in the early 1990s, their name became synonymous with a certain literacy and barbed rhetoric. Richey's acute intelligence and desire to deliver complex and uncomfortable truths, lyrically and in interviews, hit home hard.

His attempts to tackle head-on the existential questions of a post-Cold War world, and his strong knowledge of political history, offered music fans a whole new perspective. His mission was to follow the goal of all great art – to take us out of our commonplace reality and reveal alternative ways of seeing. Richey became the central focus for the band's core message – that magic could be found even in a disenchanting world.

Despite the band's pursuit of their own romantic escape from mundanity, they remained committed to understanding how modern society is constructed: politically, culturally, and economically. Their concerns and obsessions reached far beyond the set agenda of most rock bands.

'We'll never write a love song,' said Richey in 1991. 'If you wanna end up with gold discs on your wall, it's pretty easy to go that way. We don't care about that; it doesn't matter to us. You can maybe ignore our songs, but when we walk down the street and you see our song titles on our chests, you've got to think something.'

Masters in the art of narrative, the Manic Street Preachers brilliantly defined their own identity using the building bricks of rock mythology. They referenced, drew from, and alluded to a vast range of cultural texts to magically weave an involving narrative that was very much their own. This was rock music steeped in self-awareness.

Richey's perspective set him apart from his contemporaries on the music scene. Of a deeply idealistic and sensitive disposition, it was evident that the world he wrote about troubled him greatly, and as his time with the band progressed, his own troubles played out for the world to see.

More than twenty years later, he has become uniquely mythic among the tragic young rock heroes whose stars burned out rather than faded away. But it was a painfully premature departure for a man with potentially so much more to give.

We'll never know the true impact Richey Edwards could have had on the world, had he stayed around. In the annals of rock he stands alongside such beloved cult figures as Ian Curtis, Syd Barrett and Stuart Sutcliffe – rising stars whose creative genius was precipitately cut short, their legends transforming into something more alluring, and mysterious.

Richey's disappearance captures the imagination with its appalling ambiguity; for having no resolution. There are those who will believe that he took his own life, while others simply refuse to completely give up the hope that his vanishing was planned.

As far back as 1992, Richey publicly referenced *The Catcher in the Rye* author J.D. Salinger, famed for his life of isolation in self-imposed exile. In the last known year of Richey's life, this fascination with writers and characters in exile grew. His parting words to the British music press came in late 1994, when he told readers of *Q* magazine that Joseph

Conrad's *Heart of Darkness* would be his Christmas reading material. One of the central characters, Kurtz, is a renegade ivory trader and charismatic cult leader, hunted down while living off-grid in the heart of Africa.

Reading through Richey's personal archive and talking to those close to him a pattern emerges that suggests a possible life in exile. Scrutinised in detail, what appears to be an uncanny trail of puzzle pieces is surely enough to convince even the most hardened sceptic that Richey may have planned his disappearance.

For those who believe he took his own life, Richey's vanishing signalled his release from an extended period of suffering. A history of self-harm, anorexia and alcoholism, together with his own self-confessed inability to love, lead many to think Richey Edwards was a casualty of problems beyond his own control. Throughout his time with the Manic Street Preachers, his bloody-minded desire to confront life's harsh realities seemed to corrode him physically and his quest for truth appeared to weigh down on him heavily.

We wrote this book at the request, and with the help, of Rachel Edwards, who for years has been frustrated at unchallenged notions about her brother's life and disappearance. 'People seem to think there are only two outcomes when it comes to discussing what happened to my brother,' she says. 'One is that that he walked off into the sunset to go somewhere exotic and the other is that he jumped off the bridge. There are a million different scenarios between those two things.'

Only a partial version of Richey Edwards's story has ever been told. The many writings about Richey invariably approach him from the perspective of his position in the band and the music industry. There is more left to be uncovered, and a lot until now left unsaid.

We have interviewed many crucial people who knew Richey during different stages of his life. Most are speaking publicly for the first time – childhood friends; university housemates; former girlfriends; colleagues from the music industry and fellow patients from his time in rehab. It all helps to bring us closer to understanding the life and mysterious vanishing of Richey Edwards.

INTRODUCTION

In our research, Rachel Edwards has kindly granted us unprecedented access to an archive of Richey's possessions: letters, essays, artwork, unused lyrics, photographs and other intimate belongings.

We have followed every new source available to attain the truth – but we found that Richey's story is more complicated than we had imagined, and the narrative neither simple nor linear.

The disappearance had an enormous impact on Richey's remaining bandmates. The perspective of James, Nicky and Sean has fluctuated throughout the years when they have spoken about their old friend and colleague. In this book, Richey's private archive, and the recollections of new voices, offers fresh perspectives on his life and story.

Had Richey planned to disappear, and should he have survived, it would have meant an almost superhuman exertion of willpower, and the emergence of a very different kind of music icon.

Speaking to the press in 1991, he made abundantly clear the band's initial manifesto: 'We want a real classic purity, because we've never heard of a band that were perfect, that we could feel were the real deal. Because they've all carried on too long, and become so banal and uninspiring, you lost all faith in them. It's what we take from every generation of rock 'n' roll to become the perfect band which I don't think there ever has been.'

The appeal of the early Manic Street Preachers was their self-awareness, their willingness to submit to the world of rock cliché when the occasion demanded; from the very beginning they promised tragedy, suicide and disaster. Might Richey Edwards have become so immersed in the theatricality and the myth-making of rock super stardom that he felt compelled to adhere to the band's early manifesto, or was he so overtly aware of the clockwork machinations of shallow fame, that he consciously shunned what might have seemed the obvious outcome?

How far was Richey Edwards prepared to go to achieve his ambition of creating the perfect band, and to what lengths would he go on a personal level?

Richey radiated a rare and undeniable personal charisma, so captivating the hearts of his adoring fans that some music writers labelled him a 'cult leader'. His fans have suffered the accusation of being slavish disciples, and part of the 'Cult of Richey'. Writing this book, we met people who felt ashamed of expressing their admiration for him. As passionate admirers of a gifted lyricist and sensitive artist, they were fearful of association with only the more tragic aspects surrounding Richey's life.

Since 1995, Richey has not received the recognition he very likely would have following a confirmed suicide. This is possibly explained by people's unwillingness to contribute a critical opinion while his tragic story remains unresolved. There is reluctance to give a definitive verdict when there is still the possibility that Richey retains full authorship of his fate, and may yet walk back into our lives at any point.

In the two decades since Richey's disappearance, by far the most energy into the search for him has been expended by Rachel Edwards. Rachel has expressed profound frustration at her dealings with the police and the catalogue of errors that she believed followed the events of 1 February 1995.

Rock biographies do not usually aspire to affect matters in the real, wider world, but *Withdrawn Traces* may just be an exception. We hope that this book might stimulate renewed interest and perhaps even a fresh commitment by the authorities to treat this case with all due seriousness.

We are grateful for the generosity of Rachel and those who knew Richey for sharing their precious memories. Without their contributions, and without Rachel giving us access to his personal archive, this book would not exist.

Ultimately, *Withdrawn Traces* is a tribute to the life of Richard Edwards, to celebrate him as a unique artist, visionary, friend, son, brother and profound human being. It is also, of course, for the fans who have never stopped worrying for his safety, hoping for a revelation as Richey continues to occupy their minds. This book is for those who miss him.

Chapter 1

I Accuse History

'The Welsh are the most melancholic people in the world. Where we come from, there's a natural melancholy in the air. You've got the ruins of heavy industry all around you, you see your parents' generation all out of work, nothing to do, being forced into the indignity of going on courses of relevance. Everybody, ever since you could comprehend it, felt pretty much defeated.'
Richey Edwards, 1991

Dusk is falling when we pull up outside 2 Penmaen Villas in Oakdale, Blackwood. The lights are on, and there are new occupants in the modest, terraced home that directly faces the local comprehensive school. The two-storey property is not dissimilar to any other Valleys house in any other Valleys town in South Wales. Serried rows of dwellings are interspersed with the ubiquitous local pubs, post offices and boarded-up chapels. But the colliers and their families who once resided in them, and the mines where they toiled, are now but a distant memory.

Constructed in 1906 to house a mining family, 2 Penmaen Villas would gain a reputation when one of its original residents became known as the local hermit. Bethones John moved into the property as a young girl, with her parents and siblings, including her older sister Kezia. For Bethones it was not a happy home. Following the death of most of her family members over the years, she became notorious in the area as a recluse, a 'shut in'. She shunned everybody, even her remaining relatives, and stayed in her childhood home, mostly alone, for more than eighty years. She was Richey and Rachel Edwards's great-aunt Bessie.

'Richard was obsessed by her story,' remembers Rachel. 'He was fascinated by the way she lived her life, and that she existed within our family. Growing up, he'd keep asking Mam and Dad to tell him Aunt Bessie's story over and over again. Nobody ever saw her, and she was this big enigma to us and everyone else in the area. I do sometimes wonder about the significance of it all ...'

It was 1992 when Richey Edwards said, 'We're the sad victims of twentieth-century culture. The cinema in our town, which is the poorest and most boring town in the country, closed down when we were eight, so what do you do? You go out and get pissed and have fights, or you stay in and get on with your boredom. We were happier to go along with the boredom.'

Twenty-five years on in Blackwood, we are given a guided tour by Mark Hambridge, Richey's close friend from his adolescence, and the Manic Street Preachers' driver in their early days. He walks us around Blackwood High Street, now as homogeneous as any in Britain with its takeaways, chain stores and Wetherspoon's. And, finally, a new cinema, which opened in 2014.

'Blackwood used to have an identity. Local businesses. A proud work force. Political movements. A sense of community,' he says. 'But that had nearly all died out by the time Richard and I were teenagers. Shops were boarded up, and industry was closed down. Unemployment, violence and defeatism were all around us. All that was left were betting shops and pubs.'

The Blackwood in which Mark and Richey came of age was a microcosm reflecting new realities across South Wales. A distinct and fiercely autonomous region of the British Isles, once steeped in community values, political radicalism, social solidarity and its own unique popular culture – it had now been attacked and abandoned.

South Wales had been the bedrock of socialism in Britain; the place where Karl Marx suggested interested parties should seek seeds of revolutionary change. His remarks reflected a time when Britain was witness to the rising Chartist movement for greater democracy, and the South Wales branch was particularly militant.

On 4 November 1839, over ten thousand Chartists marched on the coastal town of Newport, overlooking the Severn Estuary. It was the last ever native armed insurrection against the British state. On the night before the conflict, revolutionaries gathered in the valleys north of Newport – and Blackwood was the epicentre.

As the history books record, South Wales never did spark a violent revolution. Nonetheless, the nineteenth century saw the rise of the South Wales miners. Their organisation into a powerful trade union was another potentially revolutionary crisis for imperial Britain.

Over a century later, the South Wales miners wielded their democratic power in industrial strikes that would topple a prime minister. In 1972, miners across Britain went on strike, with 135 pits closed across South Wales alone. Dock workers in nearby Newport and Cardiff refused to offload coal imports in a show of solidarity. The strikers' victory resulted in miners enjoying the highest pay among the working class.

However, their success was short-lived. Another strike, in 1974, resulted in a coal shortage for the nation's power stations. The ensuing crisis prompted Prime Minister Edward Heath to call a snap General Election. Expecting the country to be behind him against industrial militancy, he was ousted from power.

Such was the democratic potential of proletarian South Wales, it took the rise of Margaret Thatcher, who came to power in 1979, to tame the threat that the Valleys posed to imperialism, and to capitalism. Decades of deliberate de-industrialisation, coupled with the replacement of coal by oil, saw the long, slow depression that became South Wales's beaten and prostrate future.

This class war, the climax and death knell for industrial South Wales, was all that Richey Edwards and the young Manic Street Preachers had ever known. As teenagers in the mid-eighties, they were witness to the falling away of one kind of society, and the horrible birth of another.

'Richey was right,' says Mark. 'When all the industry and everything left, there was nothing but frustration. People would go out and pick a fight. Defeated individuals who should have been a collective were left to take it out on each other.'

He points down a boarded up alleyway. 'There's a common misconception about the Manic Street Preachers' first single, "Suicide Alley". It wasn't a place to go and die by your own hand – it was about the fact that if you walked down there it'd be full of despairing, aimless people dispersing from the pubs, and you'd get your head kicked in. It'd be suicide to walk down that alley.'

The economy and society of South Wales were once dominated by coal. The historic concentration around one industry meant a remarkable unity of experience, thought and feeling, and real social-political solidarity. This society, in which most of Richey Edwards's recent ancestors lived, came with its own powerful narrative.

The pre- and post-war Valleys were defined in the public imagination by clichéd images of male voice choirs, rugby union, radical politics and religious revival. These have been the predominant icons of modern Welshness, perpetually rolled out in cosy depictions of the recent Welsh past; an exportable view of Wales, seen famously in the John Ford film *How Green Was My Valley* (1941). The Welsh coalfield was a living narrative, steeped in idealism, struggle and illusion.

The harsh realities impacting South Wales, and its people's precarious position in the face of social upheaval, are written into the story of the Edwards family. For hundreds of years, Richey's family, on both sides, lived in the cluster of towns and villages surrounding Blackwood. Richey's grandmother, Kezia Edwards – with whom Richey and his family would later live during his formative years – was born in 1896, towards the end of the Victorian era. She was raised just outside Blackwood in the rural hamlet of Rhiw Syr Dafydd, and lived there with her seven siblings, her mother Rachel John, and her coalminer father, Thomas John.

The young John family was deeply affected by a new era. The first decade of the twentieth century saw an increase in demand for Welsh coal from the expanding industrial economies of mainland Europe and North America. Among the many entrepreneurs, eager to increase their fortune in 'black gold', were the Tredegar Iron & Coal Company, composed of local wealthy industrialists.

In 1906 that company executed its plan to exploit the rich seam of coal under the Sirhowy Valley, directly beneath where Kezia and the John family called home. Its mission was to create several new mines in the area – one of which was Oakdale Colliery. It gave its name to the new village and in turn, almost sixty years later, to Oakdale Comprehensive School. For the new village of Oakdale to be built, however, Rhiw Syr Dafydd and other areas of the Sirhowy Valley needed clearing. What had been a Welsh-speaking community would soon be inundated with English-speaking mineworkers and the ancient tongue and associated cultural memory all but eradicated within a few years. It was to be a pattern repeated across South Wales.

The John family was moved from Rhiw Syr Dafydd to the newly built 2 Penmaen Villas in 1906. Kezia was ten years old at the time. Such huge upheaval inevitably had a profound and lasting impact. The effect upon the family is impossible to measure, and would doubtless have hit each individual differently depending on their sensitivities and propensity to soak up violent change. However, what we know from official records is that in 1907, one year after the upheaval of being moved from her home, Kezia's mother, Rachel John, was dead at the age of 41. Her death certificate states that she died from 'Chronic alcoholism: Heart failure.'

Her passing left her husband with seven children to raise. Kezia was only 11 and it is highly likely that, being now the eldest female, she was tasked with caring for her younger siblings. But this wasn't her only commitment to the family's survival. In the 1911 census, now 15, she was listed as a 'coal-miner/hewer' in the nearby pit of Waterloo. Women and girls worked 'surface' jobs well into the twentieth century; however, it had been illegal for some decades for any females to work underground. Kezia's role as 'hewer' involved the dangerous task of digging coal at the seam, during a period in history when mine owners were happy to flout the law for profit.

> *'All developing economies abuse their young. When Britain was a developing economy we sent our children up chimneys and down coalmines and out into the street to steal.'*
> Richey Edwards, Bangkok, 1994

Three of Kezia's brothers were packed off to fight in the First World War. The oldest brother, John Richard John, served as a lance-corporal with the 1st Battalion South Wales Borderers. From May 1916 he was stationed at the small coalmining village of Philosophe in Artois, northern France.

Four months later, John and his battalion were digging a new trench on the front line, when his 'D-company' came under fire from German machine guns. Twenty-three-year-old Lance-Corporal John Richard John (13208) was among the fallen. Less than three months after that, his younger brother Private William Charles John (3137) of the Monmouthshire Regiment was killed by German shelling.

In Oakdale, a memorial to those who died in the Great War of 1914–18 occupies the most prominent position in the village's Central Avenue. The monument commemorates the 22 local young men who gave their lives, including J.R. John and W.C. John, Richey's great-uncles. *With Everlasting Honour We Keep Their Memories Green.*

The loss of the family's two eldest brothers had a terrible impact on those back home in Blackwood.

'My Great Aunt Bessie was never the same after her brothers died. I think that could have affected the way she came to be,' says Rachel Edwards. 'I heard she used to be sociable and outgoing. She was learning to be a seamstress and was engaged, but it all fell through and along with losing her brothers, she just shut down physically and mentally. She spent all of her time looking after her brother, David.'

CHAPTER 1

David John was the only brother to return from war. He was relieved from his duties and discharged due to poor health. 'He came back from the war very paranoid, and was obviously mentally ill,' Rachel explains. 'He lived with Bessie and she cared for him, but he died long before her.

'My parents used to tell Richard and me that if they ever saw Bessie, she'd still talk about David as though he were in the room, even though he'd been dead for decades. It was just the two of them for a while, and then just Bessie all alone in that house for a long time.'

With Oakdale Comprehensive just across the road from 2 Penmaen Villas, every school day must have reminded the young Richey of his strange, reclusive and now very elderly great-aunt Bessie. Did he sit in his history class absorbing the facts of the First World War, knowing that Bessie was just across the road, still deeply traumatised and reliving the cataclysmic events that tore her family apart?

Bessie passed away in late 1994, mere weeks before her great-nephew himself mysteriously vanished. Her death was close enough to the time of Richey's disappearance to suggest that it may have affected him. Although they were not in contact, he was certainly conscious of her. 'Nobody ever saw her, she was this big enigma, and when she died, I guess her life was up for scrutiny again,' says Rachel.

That one of Richey's blood relatives found solace in seclusion and safety in isolation draws instant analogy with Richey's own disappearance. Here was a precedent example of a recluse in his family, and somebody who clearly fascinated him.

When the two John brothers were killed in France, Richey's grandmother Kezia, who was slightly older than Bessie, had already started a family of her own. In 1914 she married Thomas Edwards, a coalminer from nearby Cwmcarn. Thomas's father, Ivor Edwards, a deacon at the local chapel, bought Thomas and each of his siblings a house of their own. One was 12 Church View, Blackwood, where Thomas and Kezia set up home.

Six children soon followed, of whom the youngest was Graham James Edwards, born in 1935. He was seven years younger than his closest sibling. 'There was quite an age gap,' says Rachel. 'Being born later than the others, it definitely resulted in my father being closer to my nan.'

Graham attended Pontllanfraith Junior School, but by his early teens he was working first as a baker and then, for a time, as a coalminer. He was later called up for compulsory National Service, and at 18 served with the Parachute Regiment in Egypt, prior to the Suez crisis.

Considering the impact the First World War had on Kezia, with the deaths of her brothers, deep anxieties about seeing her youngest son deployed to the Middle East would have been all too understandable.

'My dad never really spoke about his time in the Red Berets,' recalls Rachel. 'There's a photo he had and he wrote underneath it, "Egypt – never again", but we never knew why. He told Richard and me that the training was harder than average army training, and he did mention the paratroopers were made to do milling exercises – where you would stand for 60 seconds and take punches without blocking them.'

During Graham's time in military service, he lost his father, meaning Kezia was widowed. Returning home after his 18 months' service, he moved back in with his mother. With his siblings now independent of the family home, Graham and Kezia's bond grew even stronger.

Following Graham's time in the military, he trained to be a women's hairdresser in Cardiff before starting his own business just outside Blackwood in nearby Crumlin. In the spring of 1961 he met his future wife, then called Sherry Davies, at a dance at Blackwood Miners' Institute. An apprentice hairdresser at Sutherley's Hair Fashions on Blackwood High Street, Sherry was still living at home with her parents and two brothers in Cefn Fforest.

Sherry Kayron Davies was born on 24 May 1943. Her mother, Lily May Cole, had worked at Cefn Mably Hospital, a chest sanatorium near Caerphilly, before herself contracting tuberculosis. Following her recovery, Lily worked at an upmarket clothes shop on Blackwood High Street. Sherry's father, Horace Davies, worked as a foreman carpenter for the local health authority.

CHAPTER 1

Both of Sherry's brothers, Robin Lorne and Christopher Shane, taught at local secondary schools, before Shane embarked on a voyage to America in the early 1960s to gain his professorship at the University of Austin, Texas. His life story is another that fascinated the young Richey.

'That was another story Richard used to like hearing,' says Rachel. 'He'd ask my parents to tell him Uncle Shane's story a lot. About how he left Blackwood for America, and how he ended up living out there for the rest of his life.

'But what he found most fascinating was that, when Shane first went out there, he didn't visit home for five years. Of course, it was harder to make contact in those days, so essentially to the family he was living off the grid. He became another mysterious figure in the family for a while, until he started visiting us back home again.

'Maybe Richard liked that story because it showed there was a means of escaping a place like Blackwood. Either way, it fascinated him that his uncle could go off the grid like that – and my dad always thought Richard would come back after five years, just like Uncle Shane did ...'

Sherry and Graham married on 28 August 1966. They set up home at 12 Church View with Kezia Edwards, and with Graham now owning two successful businesses – Graham's Hair Fashions in Blackwood and another branch in nearby Crumlin – the future was looking bright.

By the following spring, they were expecting their first child; it was to be a boy.

Chapter 2

A Fixed Ideal

'A happy childhood ... is the worst possible preparation for life.'
Texan singer and satirist Kinky Friedman
– quoted in Richey's archive, 1994

Richard James Edwards, Graham and Sherry's only son, was born at County Hospital, Pontypool, on 22 December 1967. His parents brought him back to his grandmother's at 12 Church View, and photographs of the infant Richey show him wide eyed and responsive to the world around him.

In November 1969, he was joined by a younger sister, Rachel. Also on Church View lived two sets of aunts, uncles and cousins. Graham's brother Clifford, his wife and son Nick were a few doors down, and Graham's sister Ceridwen, her husband and children Paul and Graham were at the end of the street.

'The neighbourhood had a really old-fashioned village atmosphere, and everybody knew each other,' remembers Rachel. 'It's a bit of a cliché to say it was that olden days mentality of leaving doors open and popping back and forth to one another's houses, but there was a sense of community that's hard to find these days.'

Being near to extended family gave the young Richey a real sense of belonging. He would later reflect on that time in a 1994 interview.

'I was ecstatically happy. People treated me very well, I lived with my nan and she was beautiful.'

Richey and Rachel would spend their formative years with their grandmother, Kezia, an important and consistent figure in their lives. 'Nan was always there when we'd get back from school,' explains Rachel. 'Mam and Dad would be at work until five or six, so she'd cook us egg and chips and look after us.'

Richey was deeply influenced by Kezia, later describing her as 'the wisest person I've ever met'.

'She was certainly an unpretentious woman,' remembers Rachel. 'Very warm and down to earth. Both Richard and I were very close to her growing up. In a sense, it was like having a third parent around. She was very genuine, and things like that meant a lot to Richard. And all five of us lived in Church View very happily.'

'All I remember is green fields,' said Richey in an early interview, 'blue skies and Clarks shoes with the compass at the bottom.' According to what we heard from Rachel, and those who knew Richey at the time, freedom, innocence and enjoying the surrounding countryside were significant features in his young life.

Richey would spend time with his cousins and neighbours, making friends with brothers Andrew and Richard James who also lived on the street. Rachel tells us that the brothers now run a gym, nine minutes away from Church View. She suggests we call them for a chat.

Richard James is happy to hear from us and is enthusiastic about the chance to reminisce. 'We were both the same age, and both had the same first and middle names so we had nicknames on the street. Because of our stature, he was Little Richard and I was Big Richard. He was a bit of a goody two shoes in some senses. We'd all be doing naughty things like knocking on doors and running away and trying to get him to join in, and he'd be shaking his little head.

'But I do remember him standing up vehemently for his opinions and for what he believed was right, which would sometimes lead to pushing and shoving. I'll never forget the time he brought out an antique Bowie knife. To this day, I don't know where he got it from.

He traded it to me for a pack of stickers. I always wondered if his parents found out.

'A lot of the things said and written about him, I just can't relate to. All this doom and gloom and rock star behaviour was at odds with the Richard I grew up with.'

It was in this close-knit, village atmosphere of Church View that the first stirrings of an obsession with music emerged. Richey's love of the world of rock and roll could be attributed to his cousin Nick Edwards, seven years his senior.

'Cousin Nick played guitar in a local band called Dark Star,' says Rachel. 'He had the rocker look of that time: long hair, big boots and a motorcycle. Every Saturday morning, when Richard and I were little, we'd go to Uncle Clifford's where Nick lived and go up to his room and listen to Black Sabbath and Status Quo.'

By the age of ten, Richey had amassed an impressive vinyl collection, with The Police, The Skids and Blondie lined up in the bedroom he shared with Rachel. They would come home from school and use the turntable in the lounge when their parents were still at work.

'During primary school, the first band he became a real fan of was the Boomtown Rats,' remembers Rachel. 'He bought all their singles and albums. Then through comprehensive he'd listen to a variety of music – he'd have Squeeze, Sham 69, Altered Images, Echo & the Bunnymen, Joy Division, Big Country, Nick Cave and The Smiths. Cousin Nick was an influence in terms of turning him on to rock at a young age – we wouldn't hear that kind of music when we listened to the radio at home.'

Cousin Nick was also the first of the Edwards family to attend Swansea University, where Richey would later study. 'I remember the summer of Nick's A-level results really well because it's when Richard broke his leg,' recalls Rachel. 'He was running out from Big Richard's house and my Uncle Clifford ran him over. My uncle was devastated! When Richard came home from the hospital, he'd be screaming in pain some nights, reaching for my nan's knitting needles to scratch an itch under his cast.'

Richey's possessions include a piece of homework documenting this event and its aftermath. He recalls in detail the accident, which happened three days before his tenth birthday, just before Christmas 1978.

'He was like Tiny Tim from *A Christmas Carol* on his crutches that year,' Rachel recollects. 'He was off school for six weeks, and I imagine that brought him closer to my nan. When everyone on the street was in school or at work it was just the two of them. It was one of the rare times his school attendance wasn't a hundred per cent, but he'd have the teachers send the classwork home and he'd complete it from his bed, which I think he enjoyed.'

Richey began his formal education at Pontllanfraith Primary School on Penmaen Road, and his reports describe a pupil who excelled across the curriculum.

'I think he got the thirst for education and learning from my father,' says Rachel. 'My dad had the whole *Encyclopedia Britannica* collection, and bought Richard and me the *Junior Encyclopedia Britannica* when we were little. He never stopped educating himself and learning new skills.

'Growing up, we'd see my father enrolling in night classes at Oakdale Comprehensive. He'd learn Spanish, Welsh and attend painting and drawing classes. Even up until he was 60 he was trying new things like tai chi, skiing and creative writing.'

At primary school, the nine-year-old Richey completed a project entitled 'Shops in Blackwood'. Sherry and Graham were told at the subsequent parents' evening that their son had gone above and beyond what any other pupil had submitted, and that the attention to detail for one so young was meticulous.

At the end of his time at Pontllanfraith Primary, Richey and two other high-performing pupils sat an examination to compete for a place at Haberdasher's Monmouth School for Boys, a private boarding school 30 miles from Blackwood. Richey passed the exam and was offered a scholarship. He declined, claiming he'd rather stay with his friends in Oakdale. To this day Rachel ponders how different life might have been if he'd taken up the opportunity.

'I often wonder what would have happened if he went to Monmouth school. Would a place like that have made him more positive about the future? Would it have made any difference at all? My parents never put any pressure on him to go and respected his decision, but he wanted to stay with his friends, and at the time, he felt life here was too good to give up.'

'We had a fantastic childhood,' recalls Richard James. 'We'd always be out playing football or cricket or playing tennis in the lanes thinking we were Borg and McEnroe. We spent all our time outdoors building rope swings, dams and camping out.'

During school summer holidays, between the ages of 11 and 13, Richey had his first paid job, joining the James brothers and spending six weeks picking potatoes at nearby Williams Farm in Woodfieldside. When they'd finished their working day, they'd head down to another farm and spend their wages on glass bottles of cola.

Richey and Rachel also enjoyed traditional seaside summer holidays in Blackpool, Bournemouth and Tenby. However, the highlight for Richey must have been when he was 11 and he and his family went to Texas to stay with his Uncle Shane – a journey seldom made by families from South Wales.

'When Richard joined the band, there was a big deal made about these boys from Blackwood who'd never left the British Isles, and the band made a point of telling the press none of them had ever owned a passport before – but that's a myth,' states Rachel. 'Richard had a passport ever since he was little. We'd have holidays in Spain. When we went overseas, they were always big holidays because about 14 of the family and friends of the family would go. They were the best of times.'

When we ask about Richey's childhood years, Rachel shares plenty that has previously remained private. Among the archive of papers and ephemera is a childhood Christmas list. Comics and *Doctor Who* annuals are among Richey's requests, as is the table-top arcade game Astro Wars.

Richey's love of comic books from an early age is confirmed by a clipping from the British publication *2000AD*, most famous for its character Judge Dredd. In 1981 he entered his drawing of an alien into a nationwide competition and won first prize.

'He was always very creative,' remembers Rachel. 'He'd keep a dream diary when he was younger and elaborate on his dreams by turning them into longer fantasy stories. One of the last times he came up to the house in Blackwood was to paint an old silver dustbin black, then he started decorating it with Joy Division lyrics. It's still in the garage, half painted, still unfinished.'

When Richey was ten, there was a new addition to the family, a Welsh springer spaniel, which Richey named after the character from one of his favourite childhood cartoons. 'We had Snoopy when he was tiny, the youngest you can take a pup away from their mum,' says Rachel. 'We picked him out from a big litter, choosing him because he was so bouncy and spritely, and took him with us back to Church View.

'Richard was besotted with him, and we'd take him for long walks after school. Sometimes he'd escape from the house when it was raining, and Richard would have to go chasing him up the fields to get him back. Both would come back absolutely drenched. He was the family dog but he and Richard were particularly close.'

Other family pets included two goldfish who, according to Richey's diary jottings from the time, daily ran the risk of being devoured by Snoopy. Their gerbil was named after Field Marshal Bernard Montgomery, who during the Second World War commanded the Desert Rats in North Africa, where later Graham Edwards was stationed during his National Service.

Richey's interest in his father's military experiences crops up again in his first year at high school, when his class's set homework was to write to the BBC television programme *Jim'll Fix It*. A 12-year-old Richey asked to jump from a plane during a paratroop raid, and requested 'if possible to begin the raid' – which was ironic, given his later political beliefs regarding the dominance of the British Empire.

Richey's own verdict on his pre-teen years was that they were happy and problem-free, a theme which runs throughout his personal correspondence and archive.

The Manic Street Preachers made plenty of controversial statements in their early career, but Richey delivered arguably the most shocking. Speaking to teenage music magazine *Smash Hits*, Richey famously declared: 'Our manifesto is kill yourself on your thirteenth birthday!' The interview was never published, but the journalist involved, Sylvia Patterson, stated that Richey went on to explain at length that unless you did, you were doomed to an adult life of exploitation and bitterness forever.

> *'I don't want to go through puberty,' I cited my sister. She's already*
> *acting like a nut. I see myself standing on a hill above a lonesome valley*
> *I'll never be able to cross – I'll probably never be this calm again.'*
> *A Boy's Own Story*
> – quoted in Richey's archive, 1994

When Richey was 13, the family left the house where he had spent his formative years. With only three bedrooms at Church View, Richey and Rachel had shared a room. Now, with Rachel starting high school and Richey already a teenager, it was time to find somewhere more spacious. Making good money from their hairdressing businesses, Graham and Sherry bought a plot of land and employed a local architect to design their new house from scratch. The bungalow on St Tudor's View was the centre of Richey's world throughout high school, university and his time with the Manic Street Preachers. It has remained the family home to the present day.

'There's that interview Richard gave, where he says, "Then I moved from my nan's and started a comprehensive school and everything started going wrong,"' says Rachel. 'I can see where he's coming from, because when we left Church View we lost that sense of community, and we also left behind my nan, who we loved so dearly.

'It was a big change, the start of coming home from high school and being by ourselves, and really the start of growing up. But, without meaning to sound belittling, it's also that time when your hormones kick in, so I'm not really sure how different Richard would have felt if we had stayed at my nan's.'

During this time, Richey decisively disengaged himself from attending the chapel where he had been a member since he was five years old. Speaking in 1994 he said, 'I was made to go to church when I was young. You're a little kid and you're five minutes late or you miss a Sunday, and some appallingly fat old man in his eighties is screaming fire and brimstone in some little Welsh Elim Chapel. I could never reconcile that with what I'd read in the Bible.'

In 1994, bandmate Nicky Wire elaborated on Richey's misgivings about the Church, commenting, 'He's always had this thing about it [religion]. I've never really talked to him about it, but he's always made out that it really pissed him off and fucked him up.'

Rachel confirms that Richey attended chapel until he was 13 but never observed any signs that it visibly bothered him at the time. 'Neither of my parents were religious but they sent us to chapel, as most parents would send their children back then. It was more a social thing and something for us to do on a Sunday morning. We did have a minister who was very evangelical, and over the top, but that's how many ministers were in those days.

'We'd then go to Sunday school and we'd write and draw our own interpretations of Bible stories. Richard never made a fuss about attending, and he was always very questioning, very agnostic. He may have not liked organised religion and certain doctrines within it, but he was open to the idea of a concept of something bigger, and of spirituality beyond how the Church presented it. For him, it was a more complex issue than being a believer or being an atheist.

'For his last Christmas in 1994, he asked me to buy him wisdom literature – the book of Ecclesiastes – and shortly before he vanished, he bought the Gospel of John, which is why I wrote to all the British monasteries when he disappeared.'

When Rachel thinks back to Richey's pre-adolescent years, she is unable to pinpoint with certainty any particular incident that might have changed the carefree young boy into such a troubled adult. 'I'm aware something could have happened to him, a trauma he didn't tell the family about. Some people keep those things to themselves. There's only one incident and even then I don't know if it *was* an incident, but it sticks in my mind to this day.

'Richard was about ten at the time, and playing by himself in the woods. All of a sudden he came careering out of the trees screaming his head off, with tears running down his face. I'd never seen him in such a state. I looked into the woods and saw a boy who was in his late teens at the time but was known as a local oddball. Being so close to Richard, I felt inside of me something particularly bad had occurred because I'd never seen him so shaken. He refused to tell me what happened, but it was something obviously distressing that made him have such a reaction.'

On the surface Richey remained an entirely normal pre-teen. He was a keen footballer, and it was on the Gossard factory playing fields that he was to encounter his future bandmates – Nicholas Jones (aka Nicky Wire), and cousins Sean Moore and James Dean Bradfield – for the first time.

'I first met him playing football when we were little,' recalled Nicky Wire in a 2008 interview. 'I lived on the different side of the street and we'd go on the field and play for this little crappy trophy my dad had found in a skip. He was a decent right winger. That's my first memory of him.'

Nicky bestowed on Richey the nickname 'Teddy Edwards' after a cuddly character from children's television. Richey was a school year older than James and Nicky, but in the same year as Sean, and all were pupils at Pontllanfraith Primary School. Yet Rachel recalls there was no notable interaction between them until her brother's later adolescent years.

'Richard, James and Nick used to play football together but they were more acquaintances than friends because of the age difference. Sean was the same age, and highly musically gifted, always carrying his trumpet around and hanging out with the school band, so he mixed in a different crowd to Richard.

'I do remember the interviews when the band first came out and Richard and the three of them saying they'd all been best friends since they were five years old. Whilst I can imagine Nick may have been with James and Sean, I don't recall it being the case with Richard. It may be that they wanted to create that "Stand by Me" narrative that would make a good story for the music press? I don't know, but like Richard pretending he didn't have a passport, it got them the coverage they wanted.'

All four boys would later attend Oakdale Comprehensive. Richey started there in September 1979, and his devotion to academia continued. 'Whenever I do something,' Richey would later explain, 'I like to do it a lot. When I was 13, I did a Shakespeare project that was 859 pages long. Everyone else did six!'

Rachel shows us her brother's school exercise books, ranging from his first to his final year at Oakdale. Richey had covered almost every one in magazine clippings, pages and pictures from books and newspapers, or personal doodles. We pore over one of these, 'Richard Edwards – 4TB – Essays, Letters & Spellings', featuring his beloved Clare Grogan and early eighties pop new-wavers Altered Images. Straight away, startling content appears.

Inside is a story, 'My Visit to the Hospital', written in early October 1982. Set in 'Gwent Hospital', the narrator arrives and enters the 'Pneumatology Ward' (pneumatology being the study of spiritual beings, intermediaries between humans and God).

'Mr James, put Edwards down,' said Sister.

'Why, why, why sis-sister?' replied the mischievous patient.

The Trollies clattered along, nurses bleepers buzzed haphazardly, patients screamed and the ward seemed to be in chaos. On one of the patients bed was a bottle of usquebaugh. All of the patients seemed to be listening to a lecture by a tall, erect man. Then I remembered, this was a mental ward and lectures were part of the treatment. A black man had a tegument wrapped around his arm and he looked to be in pain. I hurriedly left the ward because a man was about to have his stitches removed.

I decided to go to the café for a cup of tea … waited in the queue behind a man with a big tarboosh on his head.

'Cup of tea, please, luv,' I asked. I sat in a corner table. The tea was foul. It tasted of dish water. I tipped it into a plant pot and I almost expected the plant to die. I sat there for a few minutes admiring the well grown plants, in particular the pennyroyal.

I was wondering whether I should check if the man was alright but decided that it was uncongenial to my timetable.

'That hospital is busy,' I thought as I walked down the road.

Usquebaugh, tegument, pneumatology, tarboosh, uncongenial? What really jumps out at us, though, is such an early use of subject matter that would arise again in the early nineties. 'Pennyroyal Tea' was a Nirvana song covered by the Manics on their last tour with Richey. The mention of pneumatology is very apt, considering Richey's late obsessions with matters spiritual. Likewise the fact that there is a man having his stitches removed – presaging the scene, known to anyone familiar with Manic Street Preachers history, when Richey attended hospital after the '4 REAL' incident. The bottle of booze. The lectures inside the mental ward, conjuring images of his stay at the Priory 12 years later. Reading it has a startling effect, and there is plenty more.

Time and again, a page is turned and content pours from his early-teen mind which seems to link with his later life. Were these premonitions of what would follow? Or do these pages more likely give testimony to Richey's authenticity, in showing that themes repeat throughout his life to the end?

One 1982 exercise book contained a list of words for Richey to look up in the dictionary. It's remarkable how many later turned up in Manics lyrics – cauterise (from 'Ifwhiteamerica …'), transitory ('Removables'), opulent (*Journal for Plague Lovers*).

Half of one exercise book was dedicated to 'Poetry & Novels of Personal Choice', wherein Richey wrote about James Herbert's *The Spear*, a horror novel set in London involving a neo-Nazi cult. Also, two books from Alan Sillitoe – *The Loneliness of the Long Distance Runner*, and

Saturday Night and Sunday Morning. A list of recommended authors includes J.D. Salinger, Mikhail Sholokhov, Alexander Solzhenitsyn, Ernest Hemingway, John Wyndham, John Steinbeck, Dylan Thomas, William Golding and H.G. Wells.

A Richey composition, 'The Rebel', involved a geneticist, Dr Blake, who is bitter at the government withdrawing funding for new research. He is kidnapped by a mysterious man in black.

'Good evening, Dr Blake. I am sorry to hear about your operations being cancelled. I think that I will be able to help you ... a sparkling new hospital, all the latest technology, massive kennels for animals, nurses and a choice of the finest doctors available ... all yours! Yours, Dr Blake!'

'Yes, I'll do whatever you want. I want to get revenge on society and the government,' Dr Blake said angrily.

'There is an important MP in the Blackthorn Hospital. He has a private ward and he is suffering from syphilis. He is Martin Foot, the Labour Party's chief whip. Imagine the publicity ... Dr Blake, leading genetic engineer, holds an MP hostage. After two or three days you could let him go and I would have a helicopter waiting for you. I could fly you to South America where you would be safe, rather like Ronnie Biggs,' shouted the man.

Dr Blake carries out his mission, and enjoys reading the front-page headlines from his secret hideaway. The story ends with a daring rescue by the SAS, and the revelation that the 'man in black' was in fact the Labour Party's previous chief whip, sacked and replaced by Foot. Themes firmly place Richey's imagination in the early eighties but what shouts most loudly is the act of social transgression culminating in a plan to escape and live on in freedom abroad. And this, in Richey's mind at the age of 14.

Another assignment saw Richey having to write the first chapter of his autobiography. His story plan read: 'Listening to records – friends arrive – take me to woods – meet two teachers – conversation (blackmail) – sent for by headmaster – teacher tricked us – in big trouble – run away – get caught – taken home – on trial – convicted for blackmail – detention centre – get out – find job in newspaper – get sacked – regarded as martyr – become rich and famous.'

Again, those prescient themes. Richey's tale begins, set in 1981, when he is ushered into the world of action and intrigue by a group of local boys, all with a musical accompaniment:

David Bowie was blasting out 'Ziggy Stardust' from the stereo when I noticed flashes of light through my bedroom window. Quickly I ran to the window and peered out into the gloom and smog of the night. Below, at the entrance to our house, stood John, Tich, Echo and Peter, my school friends. I dressed quickly and ran outside to meet them without telling my mother.

What follows must have sent a shiver through the staffroom at Oakdale Comprehensive. The boys discover their teacher and a school secretary having sex in a clearing in the woods, and attempt to blackmail them. As their plan falters, they face possible jail, and Richey considers his options:

That evening I thought about my future. There was no doubt in my mind that we could be sent to a Detention Centre. I thought through every possibility of tricking myself out of the situation and realised there were none. I decided to run away.

As we make our way down the page, Rachel points out to us a passage she found particularly chilling. In this short piece of fiction, a 13-year-old Richey describes escaping over the Severn Bridge, without leaving a note for his family.

That evening at two p.m. I left home without leaving a note and headed for the Severn Bridge. I thought that in Bristol I might be able to find a job. I set off, hopes high, and followed the M4

for about three hours. It was hell. I couldn't see anything expect
for car headlights bursting forth from the dark void that lay ahead.
Gradually it became lighter and I saw the bridge in the distance.

'The fact he always had the image of the Severn Bridge in his head
at such a young age is quite something,' says Rachel. 'That even then,
when things got tough, he saw crossing the Bridge as a means of escape.'

School reports describe Richey as a stable, intelligent pupil who
excelled at history and art. He ranked among the top of the class for
most subjects – but not, interestingly, for music, where he was placed
eighteenth.

However, among the glowing comments was one from his English
teacher, Mr Bartlett: 'In his essay work, Richard needs to be careful
not to let his sense of humour run away with him. He also needs to be
more careful in the way he puts his work together – his choices of
words and expressions are often inappropriate.'

It's not hard to see how Richey's English teacher may have found
some of his work 'inappropriate'. His story about finding his teachers
fornicating in the woods hardly bothered to conceal the identities of
the individuals he wrote about – half-heartedly turning his Maths
teacher into a French teacher, and identifying another member of staff
as being 'as old as Stonehenge'. This cheeky humour and sense of
provocation would become apparent throughout his time with the Manic
Street Preachers.

Mr Bartlett might well also have taken offence at 14-year-old Richey's
response to a piece of English homework on the subject 'Why I find it
hard growing up'. Richey answered that it was because of the homework
assigned to him by this very teacher. Asked to write 'My Encounter
with a Strange Animal', he described coming face to face with another
person: 'Alas, a human being is an animal. Don't believe? Check with
the biology department.'

Nicky Wire recalled Richey's sometimes provocative nature mani-
festing on a school coach trip to France. When the pupils took turns
to put on tapes, Richey's choice was Einstürzende Neubauten's

avant-garde post-industrial screeching and noise. It lasted ten minutes before a teacher ordered, 'Let's get this off!'

Rachel feels Oakdale Comprehensive had little positive impact in helping Richey to facilitate his dreams. She says the stultifying atmosphere sought to iron out individuality. 'I never understood why Nick sang the praises of Oakdale Comprehensive,' she says. 'It was not a nurturing school in terms of talent, it's written down in Richard's school reports, telling him to give up his dreams of wanting to be a writer and to go and work in a bank instead.

'He came in once for prize day and on that occasion you could wear what you wanted. He'd done his hair high like Ian McCulloch from Echo & the Bunnymen. He was called up to receive a prize from the footballer John Toshack, but prior to that, a teacher had approached Richard and said, "Don't come back with your hair like that. You're not welcome here looking like that!" And she wasn't joking. I remember him telling me at the time that nobody inspired him there.'

In 1998, three years after Richey's disappearance, childhood friend Jonathan Medcraft gave an interview to *Melody Maker* in which he spoke about Richey's time in Oakdale Comprehensive. 'I remember Richey's gothic phase, when he was wearing eye-liner and Oxfam coats. Image-wise he was kind of androgynous even then, and there were early signs of anorexia. I mean, in Wales you don't find that high cheekbones occur naturally – you need to starve yourself.

'At one point, he befriended this boy whom nobody else would talk to and this boy was universally ignored. Richey got to be really good friends with him.'

The boy's name was Richard Fry, and he and Richey grew closer and spent time together outside of school, walking their dogs around Pen y Fan Pond and taking photos of themselves in the surrounding countryside. The photographs show two 16-year-old boys in various carefree poses, outside in the rugged outdoors and at one with nature. One could interpret this as Richey trying to emulate and re-capture the innocence of his fading childhood.

'I was the youngest in the year, and Richard was one of the older ones,' recalls Fry. 'I only had one other friend in the whole school, so when Richard sat next to me, I was really surprised but mostly grateful.

'My home life was difficult. I was adopted and shortly after my adoptive mother passed away, her partner re-married and I never found a place in that new family. I was a teenager who didn't have any sense of who I was or where I came from, and I never felt wanted by people in any way. The other pupils in Oakdale picked up on the negative things about me, but Richard saw something that nobody else did, and we became really close friends.'

The two boys would spend their weekends taking the train to Cardiff, where Richey would buy vinyl from Spillers Records and spend hours browsing the city's bookshops.

'I wasn't very much into music or as voracious a reader as he was,' says Fry. 'In fact my main memories are of him sitting outside on the grass in high school reading Marx, Lenin and books about the history of Russia, but we connected on a level beyond that. We had very similar senses of humour and we spent most of our time laughing. I remember our first joke was calling the Chemistry teacher Badger, because she was this big matronly woman with black and white hair, who was always baring her teeth and shouting.

'Richard had quite a surreal sense of humour, quite abstract, he'd send me a single biscuit and teabag through the post and tell me to treat myself, but of course the biscuit was crushed to bits by the time it was delivered to my place. He'd be really daft sometimes too, typical teenage boy stuff like picking up my deodorant stick and licking it like an ice cream just to get a reaction. He'd like to get a rise out of people, he'd enjoy shocking people, and making them laugh.

'He was a natural performer, and when he'd come over my stepmother would always comment on how camp he was. He'd talk about being a successful writer or musician and he knew I was a keen photographer, so he'd always tell me, "When I'm famous, you can come and take pictures of me next to my swimming pool in LA."'

Towards the end of their time at Oakdale, Richey and Fry went to stay at Fry's aunt's house in Ebbw Vale for a weekend. For the first time his friend noticed anxiety in Richey's behaviour. 'We'd gone up to the mountains because Richard asked me if I'd take some photographs of him for posterity. He told me he wanted to document his life before he became famous and so people could see his origins. "I want to remember where I came from" is something he'd always say. I think at that age he was proud to be Welsh.

'We had a really good time and headed back to my aunt's cottage. As the place was so small, we had to share a bed. He seemed really nervous about it and when it came to bedtime, he left his jeans and jumpers on and put his pyjamas on over the top. We were sleeping in the room with the boiler and it was a really warm night, but rather than take a layer of clothing off, he went to lie on the floor halfway through the night and slept there. I thought at the time it may have been something to do with his skin. He had terrible acne on his face, and I imagined he was self-conscious and trying to hide the marks on his back.

'This behaviour continued on to college. We took an A-level Geography trip to Hilston Park in Monmouthshire, and walked and surveyed the landscape. When everyone got back they were expected to shower before dinner. I was quite shy so I'd wait until last before going into the shared cubicle, but Richard would wait until the middle of the night and go down and shower alone.

'At the time I didn't think much of it, he was always unique in his own way, but as time went on I wondered about his problems, and his hang-ups and where they could have stemmed from. In one interview Richard said he identified with victims, and I've always had so many problems in my life. I spent a long time in my early twenties coming to terms with my sexuality, so I always wondered if he could relate to me because of something he'd experienced or was experiencing.'

Richey is not remembered for having any major disastrous moments or traumas during his time at Oakdale. Reports show an integrated pupil who became class monitor for his form in the first year, and would later attend computer club, soccer practice and cross country during lunch breaks. Most notably during his time there, he won a prestigious national art prize which was submitted through his art and design class.

Rachel's one worrisome memory is that her brother would sometimes faint in school assemblies. 'It happened two or three times, and we never got to the bottom of it. I'm not sure if there was an underlying illness, because by his twenties he was having problems with his thyroid, but at the time we were baffled.'

During his final school year, Richey was taught Economics by his own uncle, Sherry's younger brother Robin Lorne Davies, who also taught History at the school. 'My uncle never taught us History, but growing up Richard would sometimes say he'd like to be a History teacher, if he was asked,' says Rachel. 'But I don't think that was his main passion, it was more of a safety net as he'd obviously been discouraged by teachers when he'd told them he wanted to be a writer.'

Richey gained ten O-levels in the summer of 1984, including A grades for Economics and History, and B's for Art & Design, English Language, English Literature and Geography.

The year that Richey left Oakdale Comprehensive coincided with the end of an era for mining in Britain, signalling the death of South Wales's identity as a place of class solidarity, miners and their unions, and socialist values.

People from towns like Blackwood had known for decades that the coal industry was in chronic decline. What had been by far the dominant industry, defining the society and political life of the Valleys, was being obliterated; and by now most locals had only ancestral links with mining. The Thatcher-led Conservative governments of the eighties sped up the decline process as the show-piece in an aggressive ideological conflict – dismantling the post-war consensus, privatising industries, reducing greatly the power of trade unions – and all accompanied by a very public hollowing out of the Labour

Party. In 1983 Welsh MP Neil Kinnock would become Labour's new leader. His constituency of Islwyn included Richey's home town of Blackwood.

'Everything Neil Kinnock and the Labour party stands for is everything that my grandfather would have spat at,' Richey told the music press in 1992. 'His desperate craving for power at any cost. Labour were told by a right-wing press to move towards the centre. But they should have gone more extreme.'

Early eighties Britain, rejecting the drabness and industrial strife of the seventies, went in hot pursuit of brashness, consumerism and individualist self-reliance. Working-class people were now encouraged to cultivate selfishness; greed was good; there was, claimed Thatcher, 'no such thing as society'. All of which laid down something of an existential quandary to working-class towns across Britain. And, in truth, people in places like Blackwood were as susceptible to the shiny new epoch, to personal ambitions and material delights, as voters elsewhere.

Embracing Thatcherism in South Wales was, however, markedly different to doing so in south-east England. A whole identity was at stake. South Wales had been synonymous with mining, trade unions and Labourism. Suddenly, communities and families and friendships were tested to breaking point.

With the conflict dominating the headlines, and Britain's future trajectory at stake, people were compelled to choose sides. For young people coming of age in a former mining community in the Valleys, it was a pressing, immediate issue, in Blackwood as much as anywhere. Such matters were certainly upfront in the minds of young music fans. The Smiths' song 'Margaret on the Guillotine' was just one of many emphatic statements marking the era in pop.

In such an atmosphere, any hint of ambivalence was pounced upon. Was there a pressure on Richey, the son of two business-owners, to make clear his political persuasion? Rachel says that one reason her brother favoured Church View was that it was seen to be more working class. 'He didn't like what he felt was the suburban bubble of St Tudor's

View. He preferred where we were before. That older, slower pace of life, where what you saw was what you got.'

Richey witnessed first-hand on the streets of Blackwood the year-long miners' strike of 1984–5. If upcoming generations were to avoid being left on the scrapheap, education had to work for them like never before.

Chapter 3

Crosskeys

'There's an awful lot of white British kids that have never really gone hungry, always had a roof to live under, but at the same time are desperately unhappy. It's not total poverty, just a poverty of ideas.'
Richey Edwards, 1993

In September 1984, the 16-year-old Richey Edwards enrolled at Crosskeys College. A seven-mile journey from Blackwood, the college had a student body mainly drawn from the local comprehensives. Rachel recalls Richey being optimistic about starting college, despite fretting about his severe acne. He would join his sister in applying homemade yoghurt facemasks and steaming his skin before his first term commenced.

Richey was to study for A-levels in Economics, Geography and History. Five days a week, he would regularly make the trip from Blackwood to Crosskeys campus on the number 156 bus. It was at the bus station that he caught the eye of Mark Hambridge, two years his senior.

Among Richey's possessions that we examine are address books spanning the years from 1988 to 1995. As time went on, he filled them out less and less, and his 1995 address book – a special John Betjeman edition – contains only a very few names. In his final address book, under the heading 'IMPORTANT DATES', Richey also listed the birthdays of his nearest and dearest: his mother; his sister; his then girlfriend 19-year-old Jo from the East End of London, whom he met while touring with the band in the summer of 1991; and the name 'Den'.

We ask Rachel about Den, who has appeared in the address book consistently from 1988 to 1995. She says it is Richey's close friend Mark Hambridge, who still lives in the Blackwood area.

When we first contact Mark online, he is reluctant to talk without first making sure of Rachel's involvement in the project. A few days later he suggests we meet at his local Weatherspoon's on Blackwood High Street.

On arriving, Mark produces photographs of himself and Richey as teenagers, together with letters from Richey during his time in college and university. He tells us about the first time he saw Richey at Blackwood bus station. 'Richard was sat at the end of the bench alone and away from the more typical rugby boys. He had his head in a book and really stood out because he was wearing this dark trench coat with this big Echo & the Bunnymen quiff. He had a quiet grace about him, a magnetism that made you want to go and talk to him.'

Mark and Richey were both cripplingly shy, and the two didn't manage to speak until over a year later. Mark was walking home when he spotted Richey up a ladder in a pair of overalls. 'I saw him painting the walls of his grandmother's house. I decided to bite the bullet and made a comment about his hairstyle and then he came down the ladder and we started talking music. We quickly found out we were both obsessed by Morrissey and The Smiths.'

In the eighties, Morrissey became a figurehead, and brought a new perspective on life in Britain for a particular kind of person not readily represented elsewhere. The introverted, bookish aesthetes of teenage suburbia suddenly had a voice speaking directly to their experience.

'When you like bands like The Smiths and the Bunnymen, it's for a reason,' says Mark. 'You hone in on the words, and the messages are there for you to decipher.

'As we got closer, I remember Richard spoke about his life before reaching adolescence a lot. In all his letters to me, he's talking about his innocence. We'd both talk at length about how much better it was when you're young and oblivious. You grow up and there are so many factors ruining your life – jobs, money, relationships – and you're constantly wishing it could go back to how it was.

'I think he had such a lovely childhood, and there was no way you could carry that on into later life. Even an innocent thing like our friendship was picked apart when we got older because we'd spend so much time together. We got called gay or benders by the rugby lot because of the way we looked. We'd even be hanging around with girls and the boys would still call us gay. We could never reconcile that.'

Richey would allude to these times in 1992: 'The worst thing about the Thatcher years was that gender barriers were re-established. You had to either be laddish or Sharon-ish. The whole Happy Mondays thing was so sad. All the beer-swilling, lager lout, football fans were suddenly ultra-cool.'

The miners' strike, and the high point of Thatcherism, were the very public death of what American Marxist theorist Fredric Jameson has diagnosed as socialism's master-narrative, and its replacement by post-modernity, the cultivation of infinite more localised and personalised narratives. If Richey and the future Manic Street Preachers have a core meaning or explanation, then it is here in the excruciating crossover from one era to another, as their home community and the very iden-tity of South Wales straddles an older sensibility and the future. And Richey arguably embodied that tension.

Richey would likely never have enjoyed a traditional male role in heavy industry, let alone donned the miner's helmet and worked under-ground; and for him, as for a generation of young working-class males growing up in the eighties, the new era posed something of a paradox. They might regret and mourn the defeat of the socialist narrative and the collapse of a viable working-class movement, but the new era was also, undeniably, a time of new opportunities, exciting possibilities. Particularly as regards gender roles and new masculinities.

Traditional male roles, probably best embodied by the figure of the coalminer, were disappearing fast. So, while many young men embraced the prevailing lads' 'lager lout' culture, it was a time that also presented new opportunities for previously marginalised identities to come to the fore – through a new tolerance of male femininity and non-macho maleness.

'Richard had an androgyny about him,' remembers Mark. 'He was simultaneously one half male and one half female in the way he acted. You could talk to him about sports, girls and have a pint, but you could also talk about things boys in the area didn't really talk to each other about – anxieties, insecurities and whatever was getting you down. I had hang-ups about being overweight and he had hang-ups about having bad skin. It was something I think we both found hard to talk to other people openly about at the time.'

The two boys spent their time in their rooms at home, even dropping letters through each other's doors describing what they termed their 'bedroom culture'. Like many Smiths fans, they took great pride in bunkering down indoors, developing their intellectual and artistic palettes. They rarely ventured out, shunned pubbing and clubbing and pursued instead the lifestyle embodied by Morrissey – an introvert's odyssey deep into books, films and music. They eschewed the adolescent stereotypes of the day in favour of Ken Kesey and William Burroughs, Rimbaud and *Rumble Fish*.

'You can see how he contributed to the band's early aesthetic from the letters he'd send me. Every inch would be decorated in these photographs that would make an amazing collage. Sometimes he'd go overboard, and the postman would have trouble reading the address. He'd encourage me to send him my poetry I was writing, so I'd sit inside a lot scribbling away, whilst he'd be doing the same down the road.'

'I wish I never had to leave my bedroom, then you just have yourself. I've compromised over so many things since I've left my bedroom. I wish I could enter Dostoyevskian Underground and stay in my bedroom forever.'
Richey, letter to Mark Hambridge, 1986

'You just felt extremely lucky that he chose to spend his time with you because he was so nourishing in terms of all the information and knowledge he shared,' says Mark. 'He wasn't pretentious about it. He seemed more interested in talking about your day and your problems than talking about himself.'

In the 24 years since Richey's disappearance his influence still looms large in the lives of those he knew in Blackwood. Adrian Wyatt met Richey at Crosskeys College in 1986. When we contact him online, he suggests we talk in the Edwards family home. When we arrive at the bungalow, Adrian and Rachel are reminiscing in the kitchen. A frequent visitor in the eighties, Adrian looks back on this time in his life with great fondness.

'Richard and I both took A-level History, but he was better than me, better than the teacher in fact,' says Adrian. 'I can remember the first lesson we had together, and there was Richard looking like Ian McCulloch, and I was quite intimidated by him. But I sat down next to him and he asked what music I was into, and then he started picking apart every band I liked at the time. I was into The Jam in a big way, and he quoted some lyrics back to me and said, "What's that about? What's that even supposed to mean? That's just rubbish!"

'He was good-natured about it, though, not judgemental, he'd just point out things and try to change your mind. I admired how insightful he was, and we became really good friends.'

Richey, Mark and Adrian would spend time with two other boys they met at Crosskeys College – Stephen Gatehouse from Blackwood and Byron Harris from nearby Risca. They would occasionally drink in the Red Lion pub on Blackwood High Street, but Adrian admits it was a challenge to get Richey out of the house.

'Stephen and Byron were into drinking and going out to the pubs,' recalls Adrian. 'A bit more laddish. For a long time, every Saturday night, Richard and I would just stay in and listen to records at mine when my parents were out. We'd lock ourselves indoors and be really comfortable doing it, but we acknowledged that at our age we should be out drinking and enjoying ourselves. We'd have this long-running joke where we'd go "Shall we go down the Red Lion?" … and then we'd look at each other and say "Nah … maybe next week?" I remember him even spending his eighteenth birthday inside, watching *Coronation Street*. But during college, on the rare occasions we both ventured out, it was the gang of five of us who hung around together.'

The five boys would buy bottles of San Miguel at the Spar on Blackwood High Street before pub crawling until closing time. During these rare drinking sessions, Richey would get into heated debates about anything from the merits of The Smiths versus Echo & the Bunnymen to the politics of Northern Ireland.

'He was out one night, and me and my cousin were there,' remembers Mark's ex-girlfriend Joanna Haywood. 'Richard and her were arguing over the divide in Northern Ireland. She was shouting, so Richard calmly said, "If you don't shut up … I'm going to pour this pint over my head." She went on and on trying to pick a fight, until in the end he stood up and poured the pint over his head. I remember the whole pub just stared in total silence and amazement.'

Richey's adolescent political instincts were unfailingly radical. Rachel remembers him, at the age of 13, being captivated by IRA hunger striker Bobby Sands on the news. Richey would later say, in a 1994 interview, that what Sands did was 'a better statement than anything else that was going on at the time, because it was against himself'.

In 1981, a year after Sands died from his hunger strike, Richey wrote a short fictional story entitled 'The Intruder' in which the protagonist sets out to become a poet who would highlight political injustices. After ridicule from his parents, the writer flees his home and makes his way to the Marquee Club in London in the hopes of performing his poetry. When he arrives at the venue he meets the comedian and actor Craig Charles, who steals his poetry, and performs it as his own. Eaten up by rage and injustice, the writer sees no option but to martyr himself, and plunges a dagger deep into his own side. However, he wakes up in hospital, and is now extremely pleased to see that he has become a *cause célèbre* among the British media.

In Blackwood, Richey's peers viewed his passionate stance on current affairs as eccentric. 'He would talk at length about everything – international affairs, local governmental issues, cultural politics – knowing the most tiny, minute details and most obscure theory,' remembers Adrian. 'I remember other students saying, "He just talks about politics all the time! What's the point?!"'

During his time in Crosskeys, Richey would excel in his studies of modern political history. He received A+ grades in topics as varied as the Irish Act of Union to Partition, the role of nations in the Treaty of Versailles and post-war foreign policy analysis.

One essay on nineteenth-century parliament was graded a B+, much to Richey's dismay. The examiner noted: 'Richard – a very lengthy effort with far too much detail. Perhaps you should be more selective at times.' This assessment was greeted by Richey scrawling his own, rather less considered retort on the paper: 'FUCK OFF CUNT.'

One afternoon, walking through the college corridors, Richey was suddenly asked to stand in front of the neighbouring class by the college's History professor, Mr Copely. The teacher extolled him to the class as an example of a stellar student, telling the pupils, 'Everybody should expect great things from Richard Edwards in the future.'

'He never told us about this incident,' says Rachel. 'I only found out about it from a friend a few years ago. Apparently Richard was blushing and looked like he wanted the ground to swallow him up. But I think he really enjoyed his time in Crosskeys, and felt his work and critical thinking was more appreciated there than it was in Oakdale.'

'He genuinely enjoyed all that academia entailed,' recalls Adrian. 'You could tell in political debates he'd sometimes hold back, not to show the full extent of his understanding or knowledge on the issue, because it may be a bit full-on or in-depth for some people. He'd like to play games and voice an opinion that wasn't his own – because he liked nothing better than to get a reaction. He'd give me a nudge under the table.

'I saw those nudges in his later lyrics. They were challenging, with so many undertones and a lot less obvious messages so that if you were similarly well educated you could pick up on them. It's a bit like that mentality of "go off and do your own research".

'At college, he was very principled and very idealistic in wanting to open up other pupils' eyes to a deeper understanding of how the world worked. Whilst a lot of students adopted their parent's political point of view, or had none, he was unique because he had opinions outside of what you'd read in the papers or hear on TV just by watching *Newsnight*.'

Richey was to reflect on his time in college in a 1988 letter to a girlfriend called Claire Forward:

Take college. Most people hated me from day 1. Which is good. I said from day 1 that I'd get three A's cos I knew I would. Copley told the class to read Norman Stone so I'd read Asa Briggs. Mr Bevan told the class to learn 'weather' so I learnt statistics. Mr Vaughn told us to learn 'demand' so I learnt 'supply'. I hope you see. If people want to close their eyes and be blind that's their problem. I don't know if you saw me very often in my college days but if you did you would have seen I hardly spoke to anyone. That's cos I hated them all. One boy (a friend – Rhydwin) said once that he hated everything I stood for, despised everything I said and sometimes felt like hitting me. Then he said he knew what I said was true and that's why he sometimes hated me. Everyone longed to see me fail but the problem was that they knew immediately, from day 1 that I'd get three A's. The teachers knew it as well. Look, in my year 2 people out of 25 passed Geography—I got an 'A'. Someone else (Rhydwin) got a 'C', and the rest failed. Don't you think it's significant that the one person who befriended me did well??? They all thought I was a big headed arrogant bastard. Only Rhydwin could see it was all a fraud – he saw my shyness. He saw my vulnerability. I was gonna say 'I hoped' I would get three A's but it would've been a fucking lie. I will not come down to some stupid level just to make them feel better. I told my Economics class to stay in one weekend to revise cos they were holding me back. They hated me but if they could have been bothered maybe they've been passed. Same in Geography – I told them all they were stupid but they believed they would pass from their notes. Everything in that exam I did myself. I even got information from a bus poster, and they kept learning the same stupid arguments. I just want people to think for themselves. They never do. On my last exam I wrote about inner city riots for a 'Richard III' essay and still got an 'A'. It was totally irrelevant but if you think you can make anything apply. This girl and her friends asked to borrow my essays and I told them to fuck off. They just missed the point. You cannot learn from someone else's arguments. Do it yourself. In Economics the teacher photocopied all my essays and gave them to the class. So in the exam I developed a completely new argument from my own essays. They all failed and I passed. Now if I'd written my original essay before it got circulated around the class I'd have still got an 'A'. Do you see, the argument was not wrong, but the people who wrote it were. They missed the point, they learnt the work, but did not understand, did not breathe with its lungs, did not see with its eyes, did not feel its emotion. They knew every material detail but they did not know its soul. It's the same in music. They all know The Wedding Present words but they do not understand its soul. Just like economics, I have to find a new band and when the mammoths discover it they'll kill it dead. Stone dead. Absolute killers. Do you know what it's like to cherish beauty and then see so-called people come and crush it? It burns my skin.

The letters show a passionate commitment to learning, and the importance the adolescent Richey was now beginning to place on the world of music. Throughout college Richey's files and paperwork were adorned with lyrics from his favourite bands, cartoons of his favourite musicians and musings about the rock stars of yore.

'I remember in our final year of High School we went to see [Visage singer and 1980s New Romantic pop star] Steve Strange together at a record fair in the old Oakdale Miners' Institute,' says Richard Fry. 'We were meant to go to Cardiff afterwards, but Richard refused to leave because he wanted to meet Steve Strange.

'He wanted to get his CDs signed and try to strike up a conversation with him. You could see that music really mattered to Richard. I kept telling him my dad was outside ready to give us a lift to the station but he kept fobbing me off, so in the end I left him to it, and went home in a huff.'

As Richey's time in college progressed, he would go to more and more gigs, seeing bands such as The Wedding Present and Wire, and travelling alone as far afield as Nottingham to see The Jesus and Mary Chain. He was at an infamous Smiths concert in Newport in 1986 when the gig was cut short after Morrissey was dragged into the overzealous crowd and treated for concussion at the A&E department of the Royal Gwent Hospital. However, one concert Richey didn't attend was an early Manic Street Preachers headline gig in Blackwood's Little Theatre on 4 October 1986.

'Richard was back from university for the week, but didn't seem particularly interested in going,' says Rachel. 'I went along myself and left him at home watching TV. I don't think the boys in the band really figured in his life closely until his time in university.'

James Dean Bradfield and Nicky 'Wire' Jones joined Crosskeys College as Richey entered his second year in September 1987. The two quickly gained a reputation as an inseparable duo, impenetrable to the world around them.

'James and Nick went through this phase where they decided that they didn't like anybody else,' recalls Adrian. 'People would try and talk to them and they'd blank them. They were building up their own little aura, trying to create an image for themselves. They were very dismissive of everybody around them, but I guess that's a phase some teenagers go through.

'Richard was always quite playful when he was interacting with people, never aloof. He may have had his reservations about people but he was always outwardly very polite, and always very engaging.

He was good at bringing you out of your shell and making you feel considered and appreciated.'

Towards the end of his time at Crosskeys, Richey was encouraging those around to him, specifically Mark, to pick up a guitar and channel their written poetry through music.

'He'd talk about creating an ultimate band,' remembers Mark. 'But at the time I never took him seriously because he was more studious and academic than suited to the world of rock and roll. He'd always buy the *NME* and write letters to them about the gigs he'd been to and his opinion on upcoming music. I don't think it was until university he started to entertain the notion seriously about becoming a rock star. He'd try encouraging others to take the stage, and I think that was because of that shyness he had, and because he was so self-conscious when it came to his skin.'

Yet the adolescent Richey was eager to find a vehicle to channel his maturing frustrations. Growing up, he would speak of the apathy surrounding him following the miners' defeat – pointing out in letters how life for those around him could be vastly different if only there was a way to 'inject passion into the sick wrists of youth'. His voracious reading habits led those around Richey to think he would become writer, as he constantly cited the Beat Generation of authors whose writing explored and influenced American culture and politics in 1950s America. He also began reading the works of the Situationists, a group of French avant-garde intellectuals whose ideas led to the social and political revolution of Paris 1968. He would frequently lend friends the works of Jack Kerouac, William Burroughs, Guy Debord and Raoul Vaneigem.

'He was desperate to find something to believe in, to find a vehicle for his voice, and the group of us imagined he'd discover this in the world of writing,' says Adrian. 'He always had a pen and paper with him and was forever scribbling things down.

'He had the point of view that the community was a collective, it was class warfare, and he supported the ideology behind the miners' strikes. He didn't see politics as a side issue to discuss over a pint, he saw it everywhere, he saw it as a world view. I think when he went on to join the band he applied more political theory to the music, and elevated it to an academic form, rather than an art form, so it made more sense to him.'

Like the Sex Pistols manager Malcolm McLaren, who applied critical theory and the discussion of socio-economic issues to the birth of punk, Richey would state in an early interview that he'd always wanted to be part of a band that 'sang about politics, a culture that said nothing, a culture that made him feel like a nobody and treated him like shit'.

Richey's final report from Crosskeys College included a comment from one of his lecturers suggesting that his mind may already have been on other things. 'Richard often appears not to be paying too much attention this final year, but his exam result clearly shows that he is an able and perceptive student.'

It was also during this time that the public attack on the industrial communities reached its zenith, with the final miners' strike of 1984–5. Coinciding with these momentous events, Richey edged into adulthood, leaving college and taking his much prized three A grades with him.

Chapter 4

Student Body

'Born. School. Work. Die.
Born. School. Work. Die ... but to live?
I don't want a life of what ifs.'
Richey's archive, 1987

Days before Richey Edwards vanished in 1995, he acted out what many now believe was a practice run for his later disappearance. He went missing from his Cardiff home, only to turn up two days later, maintaining that he'd simply needed some time alone. It later emerged in a brief diary entry that he had driven down to Swansea on the South Wales coast. This seaside city where he lived and studied for three years, and where his career with the Manic Street Preachers had begun, was obviously at the forefront of his mind in those last known days.

Richey arrived at Swansea University in 1986 to study Political History. With his older cousin, Nick Edwards, having already passed through its doors, it seemed like the ideal choice for Richey at the time. Yet in a 1993 *NME* article ('Manic Sheep Teachers') that focused on musicians and education, Richey looked back on his time at university, and berated his fellow students' obvious disinterest in academia and learning.

'I thought it would be full of people who wanted to sit around and talk about books and it wasn't like that at all,' he said. 'It was full of people who wanted to sit around and do as little as possible other than have as much fun as they could. I never equated university with fun. I thought it was about reading and learning but, for most people, it was about getting laid. Big fucking deal!'

Rock and roll cliché has traditionally tended tacitly to promote turning off one's brain, to mentally drop out, in order to muddy the perception of life's harsh realities. Richey's sensibility turned this equation on its head; only the misguided took learning for a joke, and wasted further education as mere rites-of-passage. James Dean Bradfield recalled Richey saying, 'My mam and dad worked really hard to get me here, and I'm not going to piss it up in the Uni bar.'

There is no doubt that Richey's time at Swansea University is of particular interest – a crucial turning-point, in which he explored and was exposed to material that influenced his thinking, lyrics and vision for the Manic Street Preachers.

In early October 1986, fresher Simon Cross arrived at the ten-storey Mary Williams Halls of Residence in Swansea. He entered his room on the fourth floor, to hear a favourite tune blaring from room 207 next door. He decided to knock on the door to meet his new neighbour.

'I didn't know a soul there at the time, so I was really excited when I heard The Smiths coming through the walls,' he says. 'Growing up, I was utterly obsessed with Morrissey. I took a deep breath and knocked on the door not knowing what to expect. When his door opened, this big haired, big brown-eyed head popped out with a little smile. I complimented him on his music taste and he invited me in to show me his room. He'd only been there a few weeks, but there were posters and fantastic collages all over the walls – Ian Curtis and Debbie Harry, and films like *Taxi Driver* and *Rumble Fish*.

'I thought I was shy, but he was *really* shy in every sense. I remember seeing him going to the shared bathroom, which about twenty of us used, with his toilet paper wrapped in a Sainsbury's carrier bag. The rest of us would just carry it outright, but it seemed he had this really girly embarrassment about his body, which I thought was quite sweet.'

Simon had spent his first fortnight living in a B&B in the town centre due to a lack of accommodation on campus. However, the room next to Richey became available when its first inhabitant left after two weeks, citing acute homesickness. Richey often mentioned him and wondered what became of him. Simon recalls that homesickness was less of a problem for those higher up the social ladder. Describing his own background as 'very middle class', he had attended a boarding school in Kent. Privately educated youths like him were well-acquainted with life away from home, and fending for themselves.

During his first few weeks at Swansea, Simon noted a marked variety in the social backgrounds of students. He perceived Richey as coming from a 'very working-class background'. If Richey had expected Swansea to be a wholly meritocratic environment, he would be disappointed. Many of his fellow students, including some Richey considered close friends, came from what Simon Cross himself calls 'privileged upbring- ings' but were far from sharing Richey's commitment to 'working first, and partying later'.

Class consciousness famously permeates the Manic Street Preachers' and Richey's lyrics and interviews. Throughout his private papers, viewed for this book, he refers to things as working class or middle class often enough to abbreviate them to 'wc' or 'mc'.

By the mid-eighties the Edwards family, despite being descended from generations of coalminers, may have felt that their lives differed somewhat from the experiences of many in their small town, particularly during a time of growing poverty, and the closure of traditional indus- tries. Graham and Sherry Edwards had run not one but two successful businesses, as well as renting out property as private landlords. Although Richey's parents could never be described as seriously wealthy, the perception among those back in Blackwood is that Richey Edwards stood out, even from the other Manic Street Preachers, as being from a relatively bourgeois background.

'I remember when Richard used to come back from university and you'd have some of the boys around here, including James, Nick and Sean, saying Graham Edwards was in the Freemasons,' remembers Mark Hambridge. 'It was totally untrue, Graham had a really strong work ethic and nothing was handed to him on a plate. They weren't flash at all, and Richard never perceived himself as better than anybody else because his parents ran a business. His friends never changed, his attitude never changed, and he was the same Valleys boy right up until the end.'

Yet while their home-town peers may have perceived Richey as relatively socially rarefied, some of the students around him in Swansea University came from the Home Counties, were privately educated, and were properly and unmistakably posh. In comparison he appeared very working class.

Simon Cross recalls how significant this whole issue was to Richey. 'I think he was perhaps a bit self-conscious about where he came from, because of the whole Welsh bashing that was popular in the media at the time, thanks to people like Neil Kinnock. I don't think it was the class thing he was ashamed of, but a certain shyness that he may be judged for being a bit of a Taffy by other people.'

'At the start we never went around wearing Welsh credentials.
Richey was really paranoid about ever coming across as Welsh.
He always called it the Neil Kinnock factor.'
Nicky Wire, 1997

One group of friends were close to Richey throughout university, and stayed in touch long after graduation. Hampton-born Dan Roland and Nigel Bethune had known each other since childhood and arrived at Swansea together. Richey was also close to Simon Cross's girlfriend, Sorelle White, who lived on the floor below. The three would often pass the time in each other's rooms drinking and listening to music.

At the end of 1986, Richey and Simon went to their first gig together as friends – or rather attempted to. The Smiths were scheduled to play in London, and the plan was to drive there. By now Richey had a driving licence, but the family car he shared with his parents and Rachel was back at home in Blackwood. Simon went on to introduce Richey to a fellow student called Melissa, who volunteered to drive the three of them to the gig.

The trio turned up to find that the show had been cancelled due to Morrissey's sore throat. To Simon the whole episode is memorable for its chastening mix of social classes.

'We ended up going back to Melissa's parents in Surrey for the night,' he says. 'When we pulled up outside her house, Rich's eyes popped out of his head because she lived in a real mansion. I don't think he'd ever really seen how the other half lived. He went into the house and was pointing out all the chandeliers and gasping at the size of the bathroom. I'm not sure if he was impressed or disgusted by it.

'I always saw that trip as a sign that music could transcend those barriers. A working-class, middle-class and upper-class trio on a road trip bonding over The Smiths.'

Music brought out another side to Richey, and as a member of the Entertainment Society he indulged his passion by organising trips to venues away from Swansea. He travelled with fellow students to see the Psychedelic Furs at Newport Leisure Centre and ex-Clash guitarist Mick Jones's latest group, Big Audio Dynamite, in Bristol.

'At the gigs, Rich really let loose,' recalls Simon. 'He jumped up and down; which was a nice change as he was normally very self-conscious and quite reserved in how he came across. In his final year I have a memory of him and Nicky Wire on the dance floor in Cinders on the end of Mumbles Pier. The DJ was playing The Clash and they were pogo-ing up and down, and Rich banged his head on Nicky's face. There was blood everywhere and Rich thought this was amazing. He was saying, "Blood on the dancefloor – what an image! That's what we need!"

With Richey studying Political History and Simon doing joint honours in English Literature and Politics, the two had some classes in common. Simon recalls the specific times the pair sat next to each other in Philosophy.

CHAPTER 4

'At Swansea there was a very famous philosophy lecturer, D.Z. Phillips, who had written many well-regarded books. In the lecture theatre, where we sat, carved into the wood on the bench in front, someone had written, "Ian Curtis R.I.P. He Died For Us." Rich thought that was really cool. We sat there every time because he was such a big Joy Division fan. In the lectures, Richey, like the rest of us, was taking notes, but he'd always add a line of his own questions at the bottom of the page, or be doodling away in the margins.'

When Rachel passes us Richey's lecture notes and essays, their volume and content are at the level of postgraduate research. There are lever-arch files bursting with captivating content, including lecture notes, submitted essays, and un-submitted work which would approach an essay's title question from every conceivable point of view.

When we start opening the pages, we sense most haven't seen the light of day since the late eighties. Some are yellowed with age, particularly those covered with sellotape. Other pages open crisply and appear brand new. There are also the personal touches: a thumb-print; a hair from Richey's head stuck in the margin; splashes of coffee, and what might be blood? There are no typed scripts. All Richey's work is handwritten in his instantly recognisable scrawl.

He was taught History modules by Welsh historian Prys Morgan, brother of Rhodri Morgan, the former First Minister of Wales. One of the topics covered was the Rebecca Riots of the 1840s, where Welsh agricultural labourers, incensed by rises in tollgate taxation, stormed rural tollgates dressed in women's clothing to hide their identities.

For those familiar with the Manic Street Preachers' lyrical output, it's easy to spot historical figures and moments later name-checked in lyrics and interviews. Essay titles such as 'From Marxism to Leninism', 'Stalin: Ally & Victor', 'Mussolini and the 'Development of Italian Nationalism', 'Kennedy and the Cuban Missile Crisis' and other references which permeated Richey's later writing with the band.

Richey took advantage of any opportunity in his essay work to doodle references to his favourite bands. The heading 'Irish Nationalists' saw him scribble 'Alternative Ulster – Stiff Little Fingers.' Nazi Germany's

53

invasions of its neighbours were a trigger for The Ramone's 'Blitzkrieg Bop'. Work on Wat Tyler's Peasants' Revolt is dotted with the words 'fascist regime' courtesy of the Sex Pistols' 'Anarchy In the UK', while work on US foreign policy was accompanied by lines from the The Clash's 'I'm So Bored with the USA'.

When they weren't in lectures, Richey and Simon could be spotted in the campus refectory, where they would eat their daily lunch and dinner. 'We'd have the same Monday to Friday – pie, chips and beans for 62p,' recalls Simon. 'It was really cheap, greasy horrible stuff, but we couldn't be bothered cooking.'

Richey would also call in favours from his friend Richard Fry, who was working at the Pot Noodle factory in Crumlin, near Blackwood. He would take the family car, pick up hundreds of discarded Pot Noodles that couldn't be sold due to being over or under the official weight specification, and drive them back to Swansea.

'I had paternal feelings for him,' says Simon, 'and remember quizzing him about how he was going to eat in his second year if he was sharing a house, and away from the main campus canteen. He told me, "There's a microwave there, so I can eat baked potato and baked beans every day." I wouldn't be surprised if that's what he did.'

Richey developed a signature dish that he would cook for others. He called it 'WHITE NOISE' or 'WHITE TRASH' and wrote the recipe in the margins of 1987 lecture notes. The name of the dish itself may have derived from Don DeLillo's novel *White Noise*, which Richey was reading at the time. The book critiques modern society's rampant consumerism and the shortcomings within latterday academia. Life for students in the 1980s tended to be a hand-to-mouth existence, and Richey's signature dish highlighted this. Sparse and frugal, it contained three basic ingredients – potatoes, rice and sweetcorn.

University was when Richey began fending for himself. It was also the time he ventured into the world of girls and dating.

'He was a bit of a late developer,' says Mark Hambridge. 'Throughout college, girls came secondary to academia and music, but was that down to choice? Before university he was so painfully shy around the opposite sex, and really believed nobody would accept him because of how he perceived himself to look. He had a very old-fashioned view of dating, almost like courtship. I remember when he liked girls he'd start buying them flowers and cuddly toys even though all the other boys took the mick.

'I'll never forget when I visited him in Swansea and we went to the pubs on the Mumbles Mile. Two girls pointed him out and one said, "Oh my God, he's fucking gorgeous. My fanny is dripping for a fucking tonight!" Richard was absolutely appalled. Me and Simon and Dan were laughing and could see the funny side of it, but he just couldn't. It really upset him that people, especially girls, would lower themselves to that base, animalistic level.'

Mark shares a letter written on a mock exam paper from an innocent sounding Richey, where he describes the best night of his life watching indie band The Primitives, and his joy at meeting one of his biggest crushes – the lead singer, Tracy Primitive.

During his first year at Swansea, Richey became fixated on a petite, red-haired English girl named Clare. He would often speak of his unre-quited love for her. She was dating a tall, leather-jacket wearing boy named Dominic, viewed on campus as the archetypical cool guy. The exact opposite of how Richey viewed himself.

'Rich reminded me of boys in high school when they'd just discovered girls at 13 or 14,' says Simon. 'He'd put them on pedestals like they were a different species. He'd always use the word classic to describe girls. He'd tell me I was lucky to have Sorelle as she was "classic girl-friend material".

'He'd go on about Clare being his first love and how he was the total opposite to Dominic, because he saw himself as short and ugly. He'd spend a lot of time styling his hair every morning, parting it over the spots on his forehead. I remember him having a giant can of hairspray and never having a single hair out place, but it didn't help his confidence at the time.

'There's a great photo I had of Rich and Dan on my bed together, when Rich was blind drunk and Dan had written this sign to put in his hands saying "I love Clare". We always joked that one day we'd show her.'

When Richey started university he told his fellow students he'd never drunk before, a statement that he stood by until his later years with the Manic Street Preachers. Simon remembers taking Richey down to the Union bar and buying him what was meant to be his first alcoholic drink.

'I sometimes look back and feel guilty because I remember buying him his first pint,' he says. 'I recall thinking it was mad at the time – an 18-year-old who'd never had a drink before. I do sometimes feel guilty that I introduced him to alcohol by buying him that first pint.'

Yet Blackwood friend Adrian Wyatt dismisses the notion of Richey being a naïve teetotaller on arrival in Swansea. 'That's Richard all over,' he laughs. 'He had a charming vulnerability that he could play up to at times. He knew how people reacted to it, and that's one thing he did do quite well around the age of 18. He was good at it with girls too, they'd find his innocence charming. I think he'd say certain things to endear himself to them. He knew how people would react to the things he said and did.'

In the late spring of 1987, Richey's infatuation with Clare ended, when she cut her hair into a style that he didn't like. He also finally plucked up the courage to talk to her, and discovered that her voice was 'too nasal' for his liking.

'It's like that Billy Bragg lyric,' says Adrian. "She cut 'er hair and I stopped lovin' 'er" – it was something that simple that ended this almost year-long infatuation. He got over it pretty quickly, and said he could justify it because he was always only looking from a distance anyway.'

Something far more significant was to happen only a month later, when Richey received an unexpected visitor on the evening of 8 June 1987. Graham Edwards had driven all the way down from Blackwood to deliver the heartbreaking news that Richey's beloved grandmother Kezia Edwards had died earlier that day.

Richey had continued to visit Kezia in Church View until just before her death. When he returned to his devastated family home late that summer evening, he heard the sound of his father breaking down in tears through the bedroom walls.

Graham Edwards was an old-fashioned man, displays of such raw emotion were rare and, of course, there was the need to stay strong for his grief-stricken wife and two teenage children. However, this incident of hearing his father cry for the first time, and realising that Graham Edwards felt he needed to do such a thing privately, is something Richey would spend a lot of time deliberating on in his later life. By contrast, Rachel recalls Richey's outpouring of grief at Kezia's funeral.

'It was the first time he'd set foot in church in years, and when the service was ongoing, he was crying his eyes out,' she says. 'We were all obviously upset, but he was inconsolable. I don't know if with the death of our nan, he perceived that as a loss of his youth and innocence. I think of the lyrics he wrote for "Die in the Summertime" and how then, such an integral part of childhood had, for him, been extinguished forever.'

Soon after Richey returned to university following the funeral, Adrian Wyatt visited him for the weekend. He was to witness Richey self-mutilating for the first time.

'We were sat in his room and he was at his desk, and he started drawing and stabbing on his leg with a compass through his jeans,' he says. 'I asked him what he was doing and he made some throwaway remark to me about needing to feel in control. The blood was spurting out of his jeans, and I found it odd, but it wasn't sinister. The way he explained it away made me think it was more of a quirky, punk thing to do. The idea of self-harm as a way of coping was totally unknown to me.'

This demonstration of self-harm coincided with his nan's passing. During his later, turbulent years with the band, one counsellor diagnosed his need to self-harm as stemming from this period in his life, and the grief he experienced at her death.

The statistics for self-harm and its link to unresolved grief are high. Psychologists view grief as an energy which, when unresolved, is sustained inside the mourner. Self-harmers go to great lengths to disperse this energy, and Richey learned to deal with his unresolved emotions in one of the most destructive ways.

'Despite his intellect,' says Richard Fry, 'there was something at the heart of him that ate him up. That first year of university changed him somehow, he wasn't the laid-back person I used to know. I don't know whether it was the inability to cope away from home, or what happened to his nan, or because as time went by his internal problems began to amplify inside of him.'

'As so often with unusually intelligent people, Edwards had a simple side, so pronounced it was tragicomic. He couldn't work out how to use the washing machine in his Cardiff flat, so he took his dirty washing to his mum's. Talking to him was like chatting with a mini Rain Man. He could be describing in minute and obscure detail the corruption of Winston Churchill, only to become distraught at the prospect of missing his favourite television soap opera ... As a student, Edwards discovered that if he cut himself, it helped him concentrate. That's how he got through university, and that's how he got through life.'
Emma Forrest, 'Cut and Run', *Independent*, 1996

In September 1987, Richey began his second year at Swansea and moved into a six-bedroom house at 3 Mirador Crescent in the Uplands area of the city, with friends Dan Roland and Nigel Bethune. Brighton-born Greg Noble, one of his History class-mates, also joined them, bringing along two others from the Home Counties, including his childhood sweetheart, zoology student Jemma Hine, who would occupy the room next door to Richey's.

'When we were making living arrangements I remember Greg telling me this really, really clever bloke was going to be living with us,' she tells us. 'So I was expecting to be greeted by a bit of a geeky, bespectacled type, but when I met him I was surprised to see Rich was this very good-looking boy. He was totally unaware of it too, which made him that much more endearing. When we'd all go out together, it was Rich that all the girls would look at.'

Jemma's fond memories of living with Richey are typical of many students who co-habited during that era. Lunchtimes were spent watching *Neighbours* and evenings viewing *EastEnders*, with Richey sitting on the couch eating tinned beefburgers in onion gravy.

On special occasions, the housemates would visit Martha's restaurant in the city centre and treat themselves to a four-course meal for £5. Jemma's photographs show a birthday celebration, with the housemates sharing a Mississippi mud pie by candlelight. Another photo captures Dan Roland washing dishes after a rare, shared celebration at the house, marking the end of the term before their Christmas break, as a smiling Nigel in a Christmas cracker crown photobombs the picture. The last of her photos shows Richey on the house landing, hovering between his and Jemma's bedroom doors, dressed in an ill-fitting suit on the evening of Swansea University's Christmas Ball. Jemma stresses this is not representative of how Richey looked during his time at Swansea.

'Oh gosh, I remember him getting a pudding bowl haircut after he moved in! We were teasing him about it the whole time, saying he looked like something from the first *Blackadder*. Thankfully, he got rid of it soon after that.'

Despite these photographs showing his more sociable side, housemate Greg Noble recalls Richey missing out on the bigger events on the student calendar, preferring to spend his time alone in the house.

'He was quite insular and isolated most of the time,' he says. 'He and Nigel didn't always come out for meals with us. He wasn't a natural friend-maker. It didn't come easy to him like it did to someone like Dan. It took a while to get to know him, because he wasn't very extrovert or very public, which was the same for Nigel, and that could be why the two got on so well.'

At Mirador Crescent, Richey grew closer to Dan and Nigel, and the other housemates often called the trio 'The Three Musketeers'.

'If you met Dan alongside Richey,' says Jemma, 'Dan was always centre-stage, chatting 19 to the dozen, and I'd wonder if Rich had such an extroverted friend because he was so shy and it helped bring him out of himself. You could see why Rich got on with Nigel, because he was another very shy character. But Rich was much more optimistic about the world, whereas Nigel was quite a glass half-empty guy.'

The housemates' memories of Nigel are of an intelligent and insular young man with a dry sense of humour. He rarely bothered with his appearance and met most situations with an apathetic shrug of his shoulders. Jemma, who now works for the Royal College of Psychiatry, feels Nigel may have been clinically depressed at the time.

'Rich's skin was clearing but Nigel's was terrible,' she recalls. 'We'd go to the chippy and Nigel would eat greasy chips and gravy and I'd be telling him how bad it was for his skin, but he would say he didn't care about his appearance. Nigel would never speak about family at all or anything going on back home. He didn't seem to have any passion about anything and was normally quite flat. But when you got to know Rich, he'd be really passionate about missing his family, especially his sister and his dog, Snoopy.'

All of Richey's university friends recall that he would often mention his family life in Blackwood. Could this apparent emphasis on looking to home suggest that Richey failed to throw himself into student life and all its extracurricular possibilities? Did his drinking begin as a way of adapting to a new way of life, away from the family home?

In later interviews, Richey told the music press that he began drinking at university, especially alone before bedtime to aid sleep. Those around him remember a different version of events. Richey getting drunk was such a rarity that Jemma recalls a striking image of him waking up with a hangover after a heavy night out drinking.

'I'll never forget opening the door and seeing he'd been sick in several of his record sleeves. They were his pride and joy, and they were all arranged neatly on his shelf. He'd taken the records out, tossed them on the floor and used the sleeves like a bucket. He felt so awful, he had such a headache the next morning. He was like, "Jem, I just ruined my albums. You know how much I love my albums, and I've been sick in them like envelopes." He had no recollection of doing this.'

Was Richey adept at hiding his drinking habit from his housemates, or did he simply play up these aspects of his university life to the press? There is an undeniable disparity between the statements he gave to the media over the years, as Richey Manic, and the Richard Edwards known to people in Blackwood and Swansea.

Richey's archive includes two large, glass-plated collages documenting his time in the first and second years at Swansea. Two photos stand out: a selfie of Richey taken during RAG week in 1987 showing him dressed as a sperm, wearing white face paint, and a ginger Richey posing for the camera after an unsuccessful attempt to turn his hair blond with Sun In Lightener. Surrounding these pictures are many others of himself, Dan and Nigel – everywhere from the beach to the pub – frozen in time, a poignant demonstration of the affection he felt for his two close friends.

Back in Blackwood, Richey would continue to drink with his old Crosskeys college friends, while also developing new friendships that would shape his future. Nicky Wire joined Swansea University after transferring from Portsmouth Polytechnic in 1987. Described as a ghostly figure around the campus, and rarely seen at lectures, he preferred to spend most of his time back home in Blackwood. 'I never saw him actually spending much time up here,' remembers Simon Cross. 'A lot of people thought he'd dropped out at one point.'

In the summer of 1988, Richey, Mark Hambridge and Stephen Gatehouse would travel 20 minutes to Risca, between Blackwood and Newport, where Nicky also went to visit his girlfriend, Rachel Bartlett.

'Richard would come back from university and Stephen, Adrian, Richard and I would go up to see Byron Harris in Risca,' remembers Mark. 'Rachel Bartlett knew Byron, so we all hung out in a pub called The Cuckoo. Rachel had a friend also from Risca, called Claire Forward, who Richard developed a crush on. They eventually started going out, and I think that was what he considered his first proper relationship.'

Mark puts us in touch with Claire, now living in Derbyshire. When we speak on the phone, she reminisces fondly about the boy she considers her first love.

'We knew each other back in college, but we were both so shy we never spoke to each other,' she says. 'I remember thinking he looked so different to other boys in Blackwood. He had a natural androgyny that really appealed to me.

'In the summer of 1988 he plucked up the courage to talk to me in The Cuckoo, when he'd had a drink. I used to wear this floaty, flowery vintage dress on nights out, and once Richard noticed I wasn't wearing it, so he came up to me and asked me where my lovely dress was. I remember thinking it was so sweet because he must have known that dress made me feel pretty.'

Richey and Claire began dating in the summer of 1988, and he would buy her cuddly toys and literature, including Kerouac's *Big Sur* and a book of Shakespeare's love sonnets. He introduced her to the works of his favourite poets and writers: William Burroughs, Arthur Rimbaud and Remy de Gourmont. During their brief three months together, she viewed Richey as the ideal boyfriend, except for wishing he could overcome his intense self-consciousness which became more apparent as their relationship went on.

'He was so passionate about everything. The world, his ideals, but most of all a real passion for me, which I'd never experienced from a boy before,' she says. 'He'd write me these long letters with all this energy jumping off the page. I'd only got letters like "today I went to the pub" from boys before that. Rich's just blew me away at the time, and still do when I look at them today.

'The only thing was his self-esteem. It crippled him. He used to talk about not being as good as the other boyfriends I had, and how I deserved better. He had trust issues, and thought I was looking at other boys all the time. It really wasn't in a nasty or brute-ish way, it was more of an inward, almost masochistic thing that just made him hang his head low and want to go home. He would always say I was going to break his heart.'

One evening Claire and Richey were joined in The Cuckoo by Nicky and his partner, Rachel. Nicky had biked there from football practice, changing from his football kit into the tightest of cycling shorts. Richey was horrified at his friend's show of immodesty, and accused Claire of 'checking out' Nicky's crotch.

'Once he got an idea into his head it was hard to convince him otherwise,' she says. 'I kept telling him I wasn't interested in Nick, but he'd made up his mind. He left really upset and I remember thinking how prim and prudish he was. I guess it made sense as he'd grown up with a grandmother who was from the Victorian era, and that's maybe why he was quite old-fashioned in a lot of ways.

'He was still a virgin when we were dating, and although we were both very passionate together, we never consummated our relationship. He'd always stop it before we could go all the way. He'd tell me all he had left was his innocence and he couldn't just give it away unless he was sure about it.'

Claire never visited Richey's house, and had the feeling that Richey preferred to keep his family and love life separate. However, he would often visit Claire at her family home in Risca. Her sister Alice, a keen photographer, took some photographs of the couple together on the front porch.

'Getting him in the pictures was like pulling teeth,' recalls Claire. 'He kept telling us he believed it when the Native Americans would say photographs would steal your soul. We finally got him to do it because I told him I wanted a photo of us together before I went off to au-pair in France for two months.'

Claire had planned to do a gap year in Paris, where she would au-pair for the children of a wealthy family. Before she left, Richey tried to break up their relationship by telling her she'd only grow tired of him eventually, so it was best he protected his fragile feelings by ending it first. Claire reassured him that she would never do anything to hurt him, and the two began a long-distance relationship via telephone and letters.

Richey's letters to Claire during this period show how much he missed her. 'Look,' he once humorously suggested, 'why don't you suffocate the children, or kick them about a bit so you'll be sent home early and we can be together?' His many letters and calls, declaring his undying love for his 'Babey Claire', were so passionate and persuasive that after only four weeks Claire decided to pack in the au-pair job and come home to reunite with her pining boyfriend.

'When I came home I was so excited to see him, and couldn't wait to pick up where we left off, but when we actually met up, he ended it on the spot,' recalls Claire, who was broken-hearted at the time. 'I begged him not to and he had tears in his eyes and kept repeating "I can't, I can't, I can't" over and over without much explanation. But I knew it was because he couldn't deal with the inadequacy and jealousy that relationships made him prey to.

'Those themes and issues in those letters to me are apparent in his later lyrics. When I would read things in the press about him being anti-love, it just didn't sound like him at all. He was trying to be cold-hearted and denying that other layer of himself, that of a true romantic. It wasn't his essence; it wasn't his true heart, and denying that must have made him really unhappy.'

> *'Girls – I dunno, what a pile of shit. But they also look so fucking beautiful. I mean sometimes I see a girl I've been obsessed with and it makes me feel brilliant all day. Claire made me feel brilliant but I couldn't let the things she said not bug me. Even on a really low level of importance – say music. They just like a tune – I want more. On Saturday this really horny girl came up to me and just as I thought "Fuck, she's horny" she asked me to dance to the Cult! Stupid ain't it? And they think I'm stupid for wanting too much.'*
> Richey, letter to Mark Hambridge, 1989

Earlier that year, before Richey had started seeing Claire, he'd attempted some dates with a few girls, but with limited success. We speak to some of them and learn that he was invariably the perfect gentleman – opening car doors, paying for their drinks and walking them home at night.

In October 1987, however, Mark Hambridge received a letter in which Richey detailed one of his disastrous forays into the dating world. Richey was then nearly 20, yet his tone suggests someone much younger.

It has often been said, when people have been describing him, that it appeared he was missing a layer of skin. In the bulk of Richey's letters to Mark, his main grievance is with the opposite sex and the dating world. He doesn't hold back in expressing what he thinks about the disappointing ways of 'girls'. An overly idealistic and sensitive teenager comes to the fore in this autumn letter.

It shows Richey beginning the night positively, enjoying himself as he emerges from his usual introversion, but the episode soon transforms into what he feels is public humiliation – once the males in the party start highlighting Richey's alleged naïvety and inexperience with women. They take the mick and happily neglect him – and his date Karen goes along with the peer pressure and walks away with the gang of males.

Richey's reaction to how others perceive him is one of confusion, disarray and hurt. He also conflates his idealised take on love with his equally idealistic appreciation of guitar-based music, neither of which he claims those around him can match, nor understand.

Within this letter, composed well in advance of his fame with the Manic Street Preachers, are the basic elements that would make Richey such a magnetic figure to many. Surrounded by boorish reactions to his awkwardness and sensitivity, rather than give in to peer pressure, he stands his ground, brandishing his differences as something dear and worth keeping.

We get an early glimpse of Richey's formula for beating the odds, and surpassing his peers. 'Kris', of the now largely forgotten Cardiff indie group Papa's New Faith, might have had all the girls and the attention then, but by deploying greater intellect and sensitivity, Richey would trump them all, in his own bid for fame and recognition – a personal success rooted in his superior love of music and truth. It was the world that would have to change, and come around to *his* unique way of thinking and perceiving.

'I will bring the whole edifice down on their unworthy heads.'
John Morlar in *The Medusa Touch*
– quoted in Richey's archive, 1994

Waiting on the horizon was the vehicle that would facilitate his transformation and become his salvation. With their anti-love credo, the Manic Street Preachers' musical aspirations would provide the perfect way out of Richey's relationship impasse.

'Forget girls, they are too complex,' wrote Richey in late 1988 to Mark Hambridge. 'Don't know about you but I've just about given up. I think you must concentrate on going to America, as I must my guitar. We must both have complete blinkered vision and not allow anything to interfere in it. If we fall in love … we will have given up the chance to affect any kind of change.'

As Richey's second year in Swansea drew to a close, former house-mate Jemma Hine shares a memory which has stayed with her over the ensuing years. 'It was late at night and I could hear ping, ping, ping coming from the room next door. It was a really horrible noise, so I got up and knocked on the door and saw Rich sitting on the edge of the bed in total darkness, with a new guitar he must have bought. So I said, "What are you doing?" and he said totally sincerely, "Jemma, I'm going to be in a rock band …"'

Chapter 5

Drop Your Life and Pick up Your Soul

'Imagine just driving into towns, flinging open cold mechanical
van doors and outpouring the energy of youth. A band: a belief – a
feeling – of energy – of hate and war – of love and peace – of attitude.
Rickenbackers and Les Pauls diving onto stage, capturing bodies
tricked by acid house, re-establishing the bonds of youth, accentuating
generation gaps, vital and burning. Go on stage and kick their
zero whiteness into submission – make them feel like you did
when you saw your best ever concert.'
Richey's archive, 1988

Richey's entry into the Manic Street Preachers is not quite so shrouded in mystery as was his departure, but the facts vary, depending on who you talk to and what you read and would like to believe.

'I'm not 100 per cent certain myself as to when Richard became a fully fledged member,' admits Rachel Edwards. 'He was on the periphery for a while, and it seemed he had one foot in and one foot out when the band was in its infancy.'

Ever searching for that 'perfect band', Richey was constantly on the lookout for new artists locally and any seeds of potential greatness emanating from South Wales itself. Having waited in the wings, watching for encouraging signs that the Manic Street Preachers were the band to back, by 1989 he had fully aligned himself with three friends from Blackwood.

'Down in Swansea, he was *the* music aficionado. He'd always have heard of a band before anyone else, and always had their records first,' remembers Simon Cross. 'He'd talk about Birdland before anyone had even heard of them. He had a love of music, its theory and the message it could convey – which was much more passionate than the average person. He'd be down the university shop first thing on a Wednesday morning buying all the music papers. It was an obsession. He knew everything about every band.'

Richey knew that he carried inside him something precious; a vision of what might come true given the right formula. He sought a band who could share his principles; political and aesthetic. Nothing but the best would do.

James Dean Bradfield was born on 21 February 1969 to Monty and Sue Bradfield of Pontllanfraith. His arrival created a degree of disharmony between the couple when they were unable to agree on a name for their newborn son. As an avid moviegoer, Monty threw Hollywood names into the ring, with the proud father initially opting for Clint Eastwood. Sue refused point blank, and Monty compromised, with James Dean making it onto the birth certificate.

Sue Bradfield's sister, Jenny, had given birth to Sean Anthony Moore, seven months previously on 30 July 1968. More than blood ties would bond the cousins, when Sean moved into the Bradfield household during his parents' divorce. Each an only child, the boys were like brothers, sharing bunkbeds throughout their time in primary school and high school.

A mile down the road in nearby Oakdale lived Nicholas Allen Jones. Born on 20 January 1969 to parents Allen and Irene Jones of Park Terrace, Nicky had an older brother, Patrick, born in 1965.

All four future band members attended Pontllanfraith Primary School. Richey and Sean were in the same academic year, and Nicky and James in the year below them, but it was the latter pair, who were in the same class, who formed a strong friendship from the outset.

Nicky reached a height of six foot three during his teenage years, and his gangly frame and long legs led to his nickname of Nicky Wire. Built for speed, it seemed a football career beckoned him, and at 14 he captained the Welsh Schoolboys XI before going on to be offered trials by both Tottenham Hotspur and Arsenal.

At senior school James became the victim of a bullying campaign which mainly focused on his small stature and his lazy eye, for which he earned the nickname 'Crossfire'. By his own admission, he was a 'Woody Allen-esque little nerd'. To compensate for his short stature, he began to turn himself into the archetypal stocky Valleys male. With his dedication to weight-lifting and a natural flair for running – especially the steeplechase – James went on to develop considerable athletic prowess. Assuming a 'hard man' image and spurred on by the Falklands War, an early dream was to enlist in the military.

During his adolescence, Sean participated far less in sport. His enthusiasm was reserved for music. His considerable musical talent led to involvement with the South Wales Jazz Orchestra, where he played the trumpet and cornet. During the 1984–5 miners' strike, he played while marching alongside NUM strikers down the streets of Blackwood.

Nicky's hopes of a future in football were dashed by injuries to his back and knee. He began writing poetry and lyrics instead. The first he named 'Aftermath', which he later described as 'a real doggerel diatribe against Margaret Thatcher'. James, too, had changed direction, transferring his energies into music after an increasing interest in punk rock – especially The Clash – overtook any dreams of a military career. Behind closed curtains in his parents' front room, he taught himself guitar and developed the skills required to be a lead singer.

'The way the miner's strike ended had a massive effect on us,' James was to admit. 'At that point we hated words like "sincerity", "passion", "ideology", "belief" – we just wanted to turn all those words into something else. We wanted to be so intelligent that we'd never get bludgeoned – as our history was bludgeoned and beaten into the ground.'

James Dean Bradfield, Nicky Wire and Sean Moore formed the Manic Street Preachers in 1986. In the years before Richey, others were tested out. One was bassist Miles 'Flicker' Woodward, who played nine gigs with them before departing amicably in spring 1987. 'I left because they were going more pop – I just wanted to go more hardcore,' he would say in a later interview. 'We used to like a lot of the same groups, but the others were also into indie while I liked a lot of heavy metal and American punk.'

Another incarnation saw them adopt the indie trend for female-fronted guitar bands set by the likes of Altered Images, The Primitives and Talulah Gosh. They recruited Nicky Wire's then girlfriend, Jenny Watkins-Isnardi, as lead vocalist, changing their name to Betty Blue, after the French art-house film based on a chaotic woman's descent into madness. After three months, the trio dropped Jenny and became the Manic Street Preachers once again.

For James, staying a three-piece was never an option, it was 'too much like The Jam' for his liking. He would later say, 'It was always meant to be four; the two gorgeous wingers, the stalwart in the middle and the drummer.'

*'We're haunted by the way we looked – the symmetry –
the four of us – everything was perfect.'*
Nicky Wire, 2004

As James was front man and lead guitarist, many saw the band as his baby. After Crosskeys College, he and Sean remained in Blackwood. James worked nights behind the bar at local rock and metal hotspot Newbridge Memorial Hall, while Sean took a desk job at Islwyn Borough Council.

After Nicky Wire made his way to Swansea University, the band took a brief hiatus then regrouped the following year. Mark Hambridge remembers 1988 as the time when Richey formed more concrete ties with the band. 'Richard and Nick got to know each other better when Nick arrived at Swansea University. Nick knew James and Sean well, so when the two came home, we'd all hang out together, drinking, laughing and talking about the world around us, but most importantly how to change it.'

Richey, Mark, the three Manics and a couple more local boys in Blackwood set up a movement called The Blue Generation. It was an attempt to get something artistic, creative and political happening in the town. Taking inspiration from the Beat writers – Kerouac, Ginsberg, Burroughs, Kesey – the new collective began to write fiction, poetry, plays and journalism.

They had all seen a Channel 4 documentary celebrating the tenth anniversary of punk two years earlier. Directed by the founder of Factory Records, Anthony Wilson, it inspired an ambition in them to ignite a punk-rock music revival, which they gave the name 'Bluebeat'. (In their provincial innocence, they didn't know they shared their moniker with a famous Jamaican record label of the 1960s.)

The Manic Street Preachers were firmly at the forefront of this movement. Mark and Richey were part of the writing division. They called themselves 'Denny Blue' and 'Ritchie Vee', and set out with an all-encompassing and purposeful attack on the world at large.

'I want kids to look at Bluebeat and wish they could have been around when this generation takes off. And it will. To change something, to change people you either have to antagonise or energise them. Make them want to start a band, quit their job, cut their hair even. If you don't do that you fail. I hate clubs, I hate dancing to dance records. I hate those words that say nothing. God it was brilliant seeing the press. We can substitute all that Gothic bullshit for a beatific crescent of awareness, of choice. We are a suburban cut too deep to heal, a strait-jacket too tight to breathe. People will try to write us off, put no faith in us, laugh at us. We are a state offence cos we care. We can substitute all this acceptance / apathy for positivism. Ok I know there's nothing worthwhile happening in the world but we can take it down and make it happen.'
Richey, letter to Mark Hambridge, 1988

'Before he joined, Richey was a fan of the Manic Street Preachers, or the MSP as he used to call them,' Simon Cross recalls. 'I remember going over to his house and he'd carved "I'M GOING DOWN

TO SUICIDE ALLEY" into his desk. He thought they had great potential.

'He came home from a weekend in Blackwood once, really upset because the boys had decided to turn their backs on rock music and form a hip-hop band. Apparently, James was really into Public Enemy at the time. Richey was gutted because he didn't think people would take the band seriously if they were rapping.'

By late spring 1988, The Blue Generation's musical division was beginning to gather momentum. Judging by their first piece of public press in Cardiff listings paper *Impact* in May 1988, Ritchie Vee was very much a part of the band.

'The Blue Generation' is a definite body of ideas and people, we are: – Seany Dee, Jamie Kat, Nicky Wire, Ritchie Vee (The Manic Street Preachers), Rusty Blueheart, Stevie-boy Gee, Tariq Tennessee, as well as these names we have a posse of howl-spirited bluebeats cruising the zero sidewalks of Blackwood, dropping their lives and picking up their souls and declaring that, this is the groove! Dig it kats or buy a body bag. So you want us to put our money where our mouths are. We will, but for a short while we will proceed to protrude our tight arses and heroic bulges on deep blue nights. Brahms And Liszt, Newport (town centre) 2nd June, is one of these nights. Come and watch the Manic Street Preachers and witness us kickstart the youth into the purest state of ignition ever seen. See the wave crash into Newport and replenish the burnt out adrenalin reserves of a zero generation. Steal a car, hitch a cloud and motor on down to the beat of the street.

Seany Dee & Jamie Kat, Blackwood

Despite Richey being listed as a Manic Street Preacher, their self-financed debut single 'Suicide Alley', released weeks later, showed only James, Nick and Sean on the cover. The three posed in the alleyway in leather jackets, tight white T-shirts and jeans. Richey got a photographer's credit, and the chance to freeze-frame the band before he impacted them fully.

'I think he was a silent member at the time,' remembers Adrian Wyatt. 'In the background contributing with some lyric ideas here and there, and helping them out practically – like hiring vans and driving them to gigs, because he was the only one with a licence.

'He was a bit like an unofficial manager. He would get to the venues early and plaster the tables with black and white photocopies of his collages, and the band's Bluebeat manifesto about inciting revolution and burning down the House of Lords. I do think the band wanted him on stage with them, but he hung back a bit for whatever reason, maybe because he knew he had his final year of university coming up, or maybe because he felt his guitar playing wasn't up to scratch at the time?'

During Richey's final academic year, with graduation and the world of work looming, he wrote to Mark: 'How's the job hunting going? Fuck knows what I'm gonna do after university. I hope to get a van and tour this shithole country, driving Le Preachers to fame and fortune.'

Having played driver, promoter, designer and photographer with ease, Richey soon learned that becoming a bona fide guitarist was not so simple. He became discouraged by his lack of progress, later telling the music press: 'I can't understand bands who like practising. I'm a pretty sad person, but anybody who practises guitar in their bedroom is a fucking sight sadder than me!' In another interview he claimed he disliked his guitar so intensely, that 'I can't even be bothered to smash the fucking thing. It doesn't deserve death.'

'He was always the first to admit he wasn't very good at playing guitar,' says Rachel. 'So maybe that did add to him having one foot in the band, and the other one on the outside in the beginning.'

Regardless of Richey's lack of guitar virtuosity, the nascent Manics soon realised he was essential to the mix. 'We didn't know how,' Nicky would later say, 'but we knew Richey had to be a part of it.'

'Today is a cold miserable pissing down Friday night in Swansea.
Everyone has gone down to the pub but I can't see the point anymore.
I don't want to get pissed, I don't want a girlfriend. I just want to
be a guitar hero in a new music-social-political revolution. Anyway,
seeing as my future depends to every extent on my guitar ability
I've got to do lots of practice and I love the prospect of it.
Of achieving something worthwhile.'
Richey, letter to Mark Hambridge, December 1988

In September 1988 Richey, Dan and Nigel moved into what they called a 'squat' on Swansea's King Edward's Road. Along with Dan's course-mate, Mark, the three also co-habited with two live-in landlords, a couple who claimed they had psychic powers.

This pair neglected the property and its tenants to such an extent that the environmental health department paid them a surprise visit not foreseen in their crystal ball. The house was declared uninhabitable, so the 1989 term started with a move to halls of residence in Hendrefoelan, a student village, where Nicky was also living. Dan christened it 'nightmare city' in an article for the campus magazine, describing it as 'like living inside the noisiest cardboard box, where French students all drink and yell'.

Richey's verdict was the same: 'I used to get woken up constantly by pissed-up students coming home thinking it would be really funny to rampage up and down the corridors knocking on everyone's door, or deciding to have a party in the kitchen at 1am. Pathetic. It reminded me of my first year of comprehensive, all these little idiots whose idea of a good time involved sitting round reciting *Young Ones* sketches to each other.'

With Richey's finals looming, and pressure mounting, he took to booze as the only remedy for sleepless nights.

'Obviously he was drinking before university,' says Rachel. 'But I remember when he came back for the holidays, there'd be some nights after going down the Red Lion, where he'd be up all night vomiting and lying down flat on the bathroom floor. He'd get in such a state that my mam would have to get him up and sort him out. I don't think he could tolerate alcohol very well, and if his uptake went higher in that final term, I don't think it would have been productive for him in any way.'

At the end of Dan's article, he describes his friend Rich, 'the nutter that he is', joining a 'raw spirit, anti-nihilist band', and it was during this time, by now living under the same roof as Nicky in Hendrefoelan, that Richey's involvement with the band accelerated.

Still a part of The Blue Generation, the two began co-authoring lyrics for the first time. In 1998, Nicky told *Esquire* magazine: 'Sitting in a room writing lyrics together. It was an unbelievable sensation. I was having a bit of a rough time women-wise and we'd just sit around listening to dodgy records and writing songs together.'

These rough times were alluded to in a summer 1988 letter from Richey to Claire Forward, wherein he described his admiration for the way Nicky dealt with his heartbreak following a (temporary) split from Rachel Bartlett – a grief-stricken Nicky joyrode a car drunk, being let off with a police caution after 'rolling the car down the street a few paces' and then abruptly falling asleep at the wheel. 'When Rachel finished with Nick – he stole a car. Look – here's the difference, Rachel did nothing. When girls and people in Risca finish, do they care, does it hurt them?'

With Richey feeling unable to commit to a relationship and Nicky's year-long romance ending, the two bonded. Pouring their energies into the band, they committed to shunning romance altogether and would empower themselves with a combustible cocktail of poetry, politics and rock. One of their first lyrics, 'Anti-Love', expressed the new credo with the fervour of a freshly minted manifesto.

'Forget Girls. They are too complex/Manic Street Preachers have next to no songs about girls and they will never have another one. From now on there will be no romantic lyrics of love or unrequited love, no personal statements just direct, hard statements about the state machine. About the repression of violence, of the oppression of disaffected youth,

of stupid idiots who beat each other up, of a government that sells misery
as if it's a commodity that we need (and makes a million while doing it).'
Richey, letter to Mark Hambridge, 1989

It was clear that for Richey rock music was a personal saviour with the potential to effect social and political change. The crucial turning point, and his decision to align himself with the Manic Street Preachers is seen in correspondence with his college friend Stephen Gatehouse. What emerged in his letters, as evidenced in Jenny Watkins-Isnardi's book *In the Beginning: My Life with the Manic Street Preachers*, was that the way forward was on his doorstep all along.

'When the majority think of "punk" they think of that Oaf in Sid 'N Nancy/To me Punk is ISAAC NEWTON. Ok – MANIC STREET PREACHERS – I don't know why everyone HATES me for associating with them. I really don't understand it (or maybe I know only too well). You know what NIETZCHE says about pathological hatred. Whatever you think of them it's obvious that they got the songs to smash this fucking apathy.'

Gatehouse was then drumming for Blackwood band Funeral in Berlin. Every town in Wales had its own goth-metal punk outfit who played a few gigs but never managed to break beyond a small home-town following. Before Richey joined the Manic Street Preachers, Funeral in Berlin were the bigger local band. Richey gave several people the impression of sitting between both camps.

'I remember when Funeral in Berlin were playing gigs and they were the headline act,' says Mark's ex-girlfriend Joanne Haywood. 'They were the ones who were going to be famous and the four-piece Manics with Flicker used to support them. Not many expected the Manics to eclipse them.'

Despite Stephen Gatehouse originally being a part of The Blue Generation as 'Stevie-boy Gee', it wasn't long before he had his Blue membership revoked. 'There was an animosity between Stephen and the band after he wrote into *Impact* magazine under the pseudonym David Geary,' says Mark Hambridge. 'In his letter he did praise the band for their ideas, but slated Nick for being "full of shit", saying how annoying it was to see him getting coverage. It seemed to me, after that, like Richey may have felt he was being pulled in two directions, what with knowing Stephen from college and now having the Manics as friends.'

When Richey came back from Swansea for the holidays, he spent more time with Nick, James and Sean, even choosing to spend his twenty-first birthday with James on a night out in Newport. The night was to end in violence at the town's newly opened McDonald's.

'It was to do with a gang of lads mistreating an employee there,' Adrian Wyatt recalls. 'James and Richard stepped in and said something, and were assaulted. If you're a certain kind of person, and quite sensitive, I think a violent attack like that is bound to have some sort of effect on you.'

Rachel remembers hearing from her parents that her brother was visibly shaken after the incident. However, James suffered the worst of the injuries, having to undergo surgery at the Royal Gwent Hospital to wire his damaged jaw. The band's progress and James's singing were put on the back burner over Christmas, and the following six weeks.

After the festive period, Richey returned to Swansea and chose to study the module 'German–Soviet Relations in the Inter-War Period', specialising in fascism, the rise of Nazi Germany and Russian foreign policy. It would contribute to a large portion of his overall mark, and the pressure began to weigh heavily on him.

James and Nicky noticed a marked difference in their friend. His weight plummeted as his self-harming became more evident. 'The first time I ever saw Richey cutting himself was in university, revising for his finals,' James told the *NME* in 1994. 'And he just got a compass and went like that (draws invisible blade across arm).'

Richey weighed just six stone when he sat his finals. He later described this time to the press: 'That was the skinniest I ever got, during my finals. But again, that was all about control. I suddenly realised that I can't go in to do my finals pissed. So the way for me to gain control was cutting myself a little bit. Only with a compass – you know, vague little cuts – and not eating very much.'

By this time Richey really was shunning nights out, preferring to stay in reviewing documentaries. These included 1989's *John's Not Mad*, which explored Tourette's syndrome through the eyes of its sufferers. He would later write about this in 1993's 'Symphony of Tourette' – echoing sentiments he had written about years earlier, that Tourette's was a modern disease, and due to an individual's reaction to a stifled, politically correct society.

He dedicated significant hours to earnest correspondence with music enthusiasts from around Britain. One was Alistair Fitchett, a Scottish fanzine writer he met through the publication *Hungry Beat*, created by a mutual pen pal, the Dartford-based Kevin Pearce.

Richey sent Alistair reams of letters eagerly putting across his views on the future of music and politics. He spoke passionately of his projected future with the Manic Street Preachers, while raging against the conformity expected of university graduates to acquire a nine-to-five job and his agitation at business companies looking to 'buy up eager young souls'.

Captivated by Richey's sales pitch of the band from the very beginning, Alistair was especially impressed by his rhetoric. 'Richey was much more about the art of being in a band, the art of popular culture, and of making more from music,' says Alistair. 'He knew how it all worked; he was willing to do the whole clichéd rock and roll smashing of his guitar if it meant getting his message across.

'A lot of our correspondence was recommending music and books to each other. I remember he'd quote Rimbaud to me a lot. It seemed like typical teenage stuff at the time, falling in love with the doomed poet and wanting to replicate that, but in his case it went on to be so much more. I remember a poem he sent me called "I am solitary" – it was about 19 pages, but there was a real heart to it, and a real drive to all his correspondence. I recognised that he came across as more of a great artist than a musician.'

Back in Blackwood, Richey was undecided on whether to pursue a life in music, asking those around him whether he should just 'go serious' and apply like his uncles to teach or become a postgraduate researcher.

Before his graduation, it was a real quandary for him. Should he continue in academia or take the road less travelled, a riskier foray into the world of rock?

'Apollo without Dionysus may indeed be a well-informed, good citizen but he's a dull fellow. He may even be "cultured", in the sense one often gets from traditionalist writings in education … But without Dionysus he will never make and remake a culture.'
Jerome Bruner

'It was like he purposely had two separate lives and two drastically different sides to him,' recalls Joanna Haywood. 'I always thought he'd go into teaching or something more studious, so when he told me, "I'm gonna be in a band and call myself Richey", I was like "Really?!"'

'He just didn't seem the type. He was so shy and more academic. I think he put on a persona to be in that band, just to be able to get up there and have the confidence to do it. I remember once he said to me, "I'm going to dye my hair ginger and shave my head because skinheads have power" – and the next day he did exactly that. It was odd how he could just add and drop parts of himself at times, like an actor dressing up to play a role.'

In June 1989 Richey received his degree result. Having been obsessed with getting a first, and after a tense final year where he'd dropped to six stone and turned to self-medicating in order to sleep, he was devastated to learn that he'd be leaving Swansea with a 2:1.

'We could have bet our lives he'd get a first, the way he was working in the second year,' says Jemma Hine. 'When we heard he'd got a 2:1 we thought there might have been some kind of mistake … but sadly, that wasn't the case.'

'We were all pleased for him,' says Rachel, 'but he was so upset. He kept going on about wanting to explore the examination process that determined the marks between a first- and second-class degree to find out where he'd gone wrong. He was particularly angry because someone else he knew got a first, and he kept telling my mam that he'd worked "much harder" than him and it didn't make sense. That to me was so Richard!'

Renowned and lauded for his work ethic and intelligence, to Richey this result felt like a setback. Barely masking his deep perfectionist streak, he later denounced his academic accomplishment as 'not a 100 per cent success'.

Richey would now immerse himself completely in the band. Breaking through to musical success and potential rock infamy would represent a fresh start, a new mission to throw his energies behind and whose inevitable triumph would surely reverse any recent defeats. From his initial contribution as de facto manager, and despite his limited guitar-playing ability, he was now a fully fledged Manic Street Preacher.

'After Rich hung on the periphery for a while, he really threw everything he had into it,' remembers Adrian. 'He told me that music wouldn't be a long-term career choice, because he found bloated, corporate rock like the Rolling Stones embarrassing. I recall Nick said that a 30-year career in music was disgusting, so they were all about stoking a fire, setting it ablaze and walking away at the height of it. Plus the fact Rich really didn't enjoy playing his guitar, so that was another reason to get in and out the music world fast.'

Rachel sees it differently: 'He turned not being able to play into his strength, it became his signature and he deliberately made a point of it to show how shallow the industry was, and how you could become a success if you had the right formula in terms of aesthetic, spirit and attitude.

'There were plenty of competent and talented guitarists and musicians in Blackwood and around South Wales trying to make it big on the scene, but it didn't matter, he knew that you needed something more if you were going to break the mould. The band always said that the music came second to their words, and that the music was there as the most popular means to carry that message.'

Years later, Nicky would share memories of Richey's increasing involvement with the band and his input into their future aesthetic, during their

80

time residing in Hendrefoelan. 'We almost poisoned ourselves,' he admitted. 'We were in this little room with only half a window open and we were spray-painting these white T-shirts for the band, and realised we felt really ill from the fumes.' The motifs on the DIY shirts included KILL YOURSELF ON VALENTINES DAY, CULTURE SLUT, AESTHETIC DEBRIS and another, USELESS GENERATION, which Richey would have tattooed on his arm two years later.

Richey understood that this forthright form of communication through uncompromising slogans would be the best way to spread the band's revolutionary spirit and convert the masses. 'We don't want to reach the music papers, we just want to reach the *Sun*, the *Star*, the *Mirror*,' he would tell Snub TV a year later. 'That's what most people read. We'd rather be sensationalised than just be another *NME* band and get critical respect.'

'Malcolm and Bernie were anti-intellectual ... That's why they went into Situationist politics. Situationist politics is merely sloganeering – second rate sloganeering at that – all pulled out of the 1960s dustbin.'
John Lydon, *Rotten: No Irish, No Blacks, No Dogs*

Returning home from Swansea, Richey funded his role in launching the Manics by taking a summer job mowing grass for Islwyn Borough Council. 'The council used to advertise seasonal work for students,' remembers Rachel. 'It was much easier to get a summer job back in those days. He did this a few times when he came back from Swansea. He'd get up early and a van would take him and a handful of other boys around the borough. He'd mostly work with the strimmers, and my mum remembers when he came back from the Showfields in Cefn Fforest saying he'd been strimming the ground and came across a pool of vomit that splashed all over him and his face mask!'

By autumn Richey was signing on for Job Seeker's Allowance, but staff at the local dole office failed to sway him from his main purpose.

'The band were practising at James's house a lot at the time, but occasionally they'd come over and use the garage at my mam and dad's,' says Rachel. 'I was in university in Cardiff during that period, but I remember my dad wasn't too happy about him joining a band.

'My dad was traditional in the sense that he expected Richard to get a respectable job. Richard felt he could apply theory with what he'd done with his degree to the world of arts, but my dad was old-fashioned and didn't think this was the best path for him to take.'

Evidence of Richey's dedication to the band is compiled in two quilted A4 pads dating from 1989 to 1991, documenting his role in busting the band out of Blackwood.

Glued into these books are vast lists of booking agents, promoters, solicitors, radio stations, music venues and recording studios, along with recorded delivery certificates for mailings to potential management companies. Also included are the names of London music journalists that Richey would target with personalised letters. He succeeded in striking up correspondence with several, including then *NME* journalist Steve Lamacq, who later commented, 'I'm sure they telephoned and wrote to loads of people around this time. I've got a letter from them and so has John Peel. Mine was scribbled on yellow A4, a scrawly note that savaged the shoegazers, the Madchester scene (including the Roses and the Mondays) and rejected the whole "trip out and tune out" mentality of the time.'

Richey added a personal touch; a photograph of Lamacq with the line 'Cheekbone Charisma' scribbled alongside it. Years later the band would describe their approach as 'quite clinical. We were like magpies, collecting information, keeping dossiers on journalists and learning how to manipulate them.'

Interestingly, also pasted into one of the books is a letter from Richey's bank manager in Blackwood, desperate to speak about his increasing overdraft. In keeping these small, minute details, you wonder whether Richey was already deliberately documenting the band's pathway to fame. As in the teenage mountainside photographs taken by Richard Fry, where Richey posed like someone who believed in his pre-ordained stardom, he clearly had a narrative for himself already mapped out in his mind.

Meanwhile, giving the band's shot at the big time all he had, he even wrote some of Nicky's final year essays to free up his friend's time to practise. He also applied for membership of the Musicians' Union on behalf of one Nicholas Jones.

'He used to do a lot in terms of organising the band,' Mark Hambridge recalls. 'I remember he'd come over mine and use my double tape deck to copy the "Suicide Alley" demos. He'd put them in a DIY album sleeve with glued-on newspaper cuttings and send them out to journalists, radio stations and management agencies.

'He'd add a photocopied press release or a letter when he posted them. We'd go out and have a drink after, and I remember a hilarious night when Nick wrestled Richard's shoes off him outside the Red Lion and hung them up on a street sign. Richard being much shorter than Nick couldn't reach that high, so he was drunkenly running and jumping through the air to grab them.'

Most pertinent was Richey's own personal transformation. He'd flirted with the idea of different names since he first became The Blue Generation's Ritchie Vee, then corresponding for a short time as Richey Zero. He knew the next step was to re-imagine himself in readiness for the quest ahead.

While in university, he studied the Situationists and Guy Debord's seminal work *The Society of Spectacle*. With Richey's knowledge of the construction of music mythology, he would have been acutely aware of how Malcolm McLaren applied Debord's ideas when he created the Sex Pistols, and the birth of British punk.

Richey knew the Manic Street Preachers would be a deliberate throwback to the Paris riots of 1968 and the punk movement of the 1970s, where youth culture and radical politics were intertwined. He sought to capture fans' imaginations by replicating the cultural influence that bands and writers wielded at that time.

'Punk didn't achieve anything, it was a brief flirtation with a youth movement,' Richey told the Welsh press in 1990. 'When they got tired of being punks, they quickly decided to move on to something else. The only difference is, we mean it.'

'Media stars are spectacular representations of living human beings, distilling the essence of the spectacle's banality into images of possible roles. Stardom is a diversification in the semblance of life, the object of an identification with mere appearance which is intended to compensate for the crumbling of directly experienced diversifications of productive activity. Celebrities figure various styles of life and various views of society which anyone is supposedly free to embrace and pursue in a global manner.'
Guy Debord, *The Society of Spectacle*

'When Richard was in university, and when he first joined the band, he used to tape bands off the television,' remembers Rachel. 'He'd sit and study their live performances and their interviews religiously. The main two bands he'd record were the young Rolling Stones and Guns N' Roses. He'd buy a leather case for the videos and put a collage on the front of the bands contained on the tapes. He'd sit and focus on them with the same concentration he'd study for his exams.'

'We all decided that from the start, me and Richey can't write music but we can write lyrics and look pretty tarty. Richey's the spirit of the band.'
Nicky Wire, 1991

Moved by The Blue Generation's spirit and Richey's enthusiasm, in 1989 Mark Hambridge took a trip to America with the intention of living the Beat dream. 'Richard inspired me to go,' says Mark. 'I wanted to do the whole Kerouac *On the Road* thing, and Nick's brother Patrick was already out there, so I decided to do it as I'd only be young once.'

Having graduated from Swansea University with a degree in American Literature, by the late eighties Patrick Jones was already living that dream. Writing and teaching literature in Tennessee, his pioneering odyssey to the Deep South, and later Illinois, was evidently of huge inspiration to Mark and the young Manic Street Preachers. Patrick's Blue Generation nickname was 'Rusty Blueheart' – after Rusty James, a character in Francis Ford Coppola's 1983 film *Rumble Fish*.

CHAPTER 5

From the very outset, the Manic Street Preachers advertised that they took as much inspiration from other art forms as from music itself. Novels and poetry were of great importance, but there is no question that a driving force powering them along their journey was their love of certain films – most of them American. After the public downsizing South Wales had just received, and the barely articulable yet deeply felt death of its previous identity and narrative, it fell to certain inspirational films to get hearts in the Valleys pumping again. As the young Manic Street Preachers discovered, great sustenance could be drawn from an analogy between post-industrial English-speaking South Wales and dramas portraying the tragedy and humanity of proletarian America.

Rumble Fish has been longer and more often associated with the Manics than any other film. It is clear how the young friends from Blackwood might see in it a glamourised reflection of their own lives. The story revolves around a group of adolescents stuck in the small post-industrial backwater of Sapulpa, Oklahoma. Caught in provincial hellish boredom, their entertainment comes in the forms of gang fights, or 'rumbles'.

The lead character, the Motorcycle Boy (Mickey Rourke), has legendary status among the youth, a former gang leader imbued with strange charisma. Local teens are fascinated by the fact that the Motorcycle Boy has successfully managed the impossible, and broken out of their dead-end existence; fascination in him is deepened by the fact that he is absent, having exiled himself to the relatively glamorous California. And the mythicising aspect of a sudden disappearance is a crucial component – the Motorcycle Boy has been gone for two months, leaving without explanation, or promise of return.

Sold as an existentialist movie for teenagers, *Rumble Fish* has as its main character an adult, contrasting with the youngsters popu-lating most of the action; he is world-weary, wise and broken. When the hero returns to Oklahoma, he has visibly changed, and is jaded by his former life and reputation. Of immense appeal to the young Manic Street Preachers was this character's objectivity, and what his father (Dennis Hopper) describes as his 'acute perception'. The Motorcycle Boy is a romantic figure; an enigma to those around him, and foredoomed.

Before Richey's disappearance in 1995, James Dean Bradfield knew well which reference to draw upon in fleshing out the mythic dimensions of it all. 'Richey was always much more into books and films than rock 'n' roll,' he said, 'and I think those art forms are much more idealised. I think they influenced the way he viewed life, and the way he thought it would be.

'Whenever I talk about Richey, I think of that quote from *Rumble Fish*: "He's merely miscast the play; he was born on the wrong side of the river; he has the ability to do anything he wants to do but he can't find anything he wants to do."'

There is little doubt that director Coppola worked on *Rumble Fish* very consciously as a film inspired by the recent punk/new wave movement in pop culture. The Motorcycle Boy was a hybrid of The Clash's Joe Strummer and the Sex Pistols' Johnny Rotten, an effect encouraged by the superb soundtrack created by The Police's drummer Stewart Copeland, and featuring vocals by Stan Ridgway of post-punks Wall of Voodoo. Locations used even included Cain's Ballroom, the Tulsa venue that hosted a notorious Pistols gig in 1978. For four punk fanboys in the blighted Blackwood of the mid-eighties, Coppola's masterpiece had tremendous pull.

Topping it all was the extremely seductive visual aesthetic. Coppola shot in black and white, drawing inspiration from European avant-garde cinema and literature. The South Wales Valleys could now easily be re-imagined as the set of an existentialist film noir drama; little wonder then that the Manic Street Preachers continued to reference this work for years, both verbally and visually.

As Richey told MTV in 1993, 'I think all great art is based on the politics of boredom, completely. When there's nothing around, you've got nothing in your life, you can just solely concentrate on what you're trying to say and what you're trying to do, which is definitely what happened with us.'

Graham Edwards and his Mother Kezia. Richey was deeply influenced by his grandmother, having spent his formative years living with her.

Bethones John (Great Aunt Bessie). Bessie passed away just weeks before Richey vanished. Her death was close enough to the time of his disappearance to suggest that it may have impacted him.

Graham and Sherry Edwards. Richey's mother and father.

CHRISTMAS   NOVEMBER 26TH

→ Christmas 1978. On December 19th after watching "TisWas" I went out to ~~not~~ play football but it started to rain so I went back into my house. About ~~10~~ ten minutes later I went back out to call for my friend Richard James but his brother said that he had gone out so I ran out onto the lane and my uncle was coming down in his car and it knocked me down. I was nearly unconscious so I ~~cannot~~ cannot remember much until I was in the ambulance. I went to the Royal Gwent. ~~They~~ They firstly took ~~x~~ xrays and asked me when I had had my dinner and I replied about "1.00 o'clock". The doctor told my parents that I could not ~~be~~ be operated on untill 5.00 o'clock because I would not have an injection untill ~~the~~ four hours had passed since I had my dinner. It turned out that I couldn't have my operation untill 10.00 o'clock because there had been a worse accident. The following morning I woke up to find that I had a plaster on my leg. Then I had my first taste of hospital food, it was horrid. For nearly all the morning I was having x rays taken. For most of the afternoon I slept but I couldn't sleep at all in the evening. The doctor said that I had to stay ~~I~~ in hospital

Homework, Richey's recollection of breaking his leg, Christmas 1978.
'He was like Tiny Tim from *A Christmas Carol* on his crutches.'

for three days. Then I realized that the day I would come out of hospital was the date of my birthday. On the third day I used crutches for the first couple of minutes I was very unsteady but very soon I mastered them. When I got home I found out that I had a Snooker Table for my birthday. pOn Christmas Day I was very ~~exerted~~ excited. I ~~was~~ wouldn't get out of my bed to wake up my sister, ~~&~~ I got very worked up about it, in the end I threw my pillow at her. She soon woke up. I then told her to pass my crutches and to tell my parents to help me down stairs. When I got ~~down the~~ down stairs I walked into the lounge and to my surprise there was a Music Centre, I just wouldn't believe it. It was very difficult that day ~~to visit my~~ because my sister kept hiding my crutches. I was very annoyed. The Christmas dinner was beautiful. There was only one thing that I missed this Christmas and that was not being able to play in the snow but all in all it was a very happy Christmas.

in a ~~so~~ beautiful place wi...
river to swim in, bu...

OAKDALE COMPREHENSIVE SCHOOL

Report for Period from 3rd SEPT. 1979 to 27 JUNE 1980

Name RICHARD EDWARDS Form 1EB

Actual Attendance	340	Comment
Possible Attendance	342	Most pleasing.
Punctuality		

Subject	Term Effort	Term Grade	Exam Result	Position	Remarks	Staff Initials
English	B+	B+	66	3	He has worked well and maintained a high standard during the year and in examinations.	
Mathematics	B+	B	58	5th	Richard is a capable pupil but must revise his work more thoroughly.	ART
Languages French	A-	A-	82	8	A very good examination result and year's work. Well done Richard!	ALP.
Sciences						
Chemistry	B	B+	71	7	A good result. Richard has worked hard.	JED.
Physics	B+	B	68	8	Richard has worked very well this year. A good result.	EMJ.
Biology	C+	C+	59	8	A good exam result	al
Humanities						
R.E.	B	B	73	4	A very pleasing year's work. Well done!	Ra
HISTORY	B	B	78	2	Excellent — has worked very well !!	RLD
GEOGRAPHY	B	B	71	5	Well done! A very good year's work	BJ.
Practical Subjects						
C/D Wood	C	C	42	4	Quite good, shows interest.	N.J.
METALWORK	C	C	48	4th	A good years work	GM
Arts MUSIC	B	B	88	6	Richard has worked well this year.	REJ.
ART	A	A	95	1	An excellent year's work. Well done Richard!	ABB
Physical Education	C	C-			Richard has worked well throughout the year.	ruf.

Activities I/H. C.C. I/H. Soccer. CLASS MONITOR.

General Attitude
A very pleasant & helpful pupil, who has proved himself to be a most able class monitor.

General Remarks A pleasing report. Richard has worked well throughout his first year. I am sure he will continue to do as well in future years. (Form Tutor)
Signed A Bolton
CH Turner (Head/D. Head) of School

Richey's high school report, 1980 – he excelled at art and history.

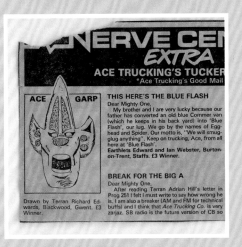

Left: Richey won a prize of £3 for his drawing of a character from the magazine 2000 AD. He loved comic books from an early age.

Middle: Richey's Christmas list, 1980.

RICHARD EDWARDS.   3RD NOVEMBER

CHRISTMAS LIST.

FIRST CHOICE. GRANDSTAND ASTRO WARS: An electronic table top game, featuring on screen colour with a special magnifying effect. Five lines of action with multi coloured invaders and futuristic sounds just like the real arcade game. 4 levels of play. Requires just 4 HP 11 batteries. (NOT SUPPLIED).

PRICE (APPROX) £30.00.

BOOKS. Whizzer and Chips, Jackpot, Tiger, Roy of the Rovers, Battle, Action, 2000 A.D and Judge Dredd. The books that I would like the most are 2000 A.D and Judge Dredd.

PAPERBACKS. Any Doctor Who books except for "The Day of the Daleks", and "The horror of Fang Rock", which I already have.

Richey's homework from the first year of high school, 1980. His devotion to academia was evident.

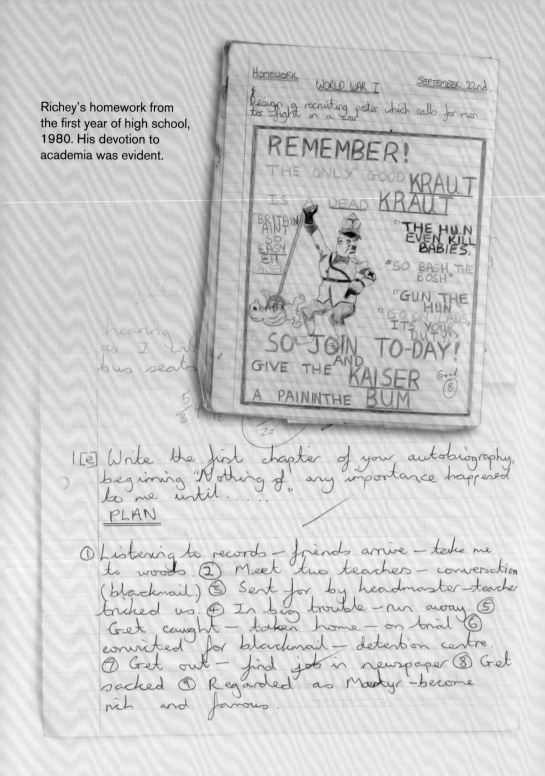

Richey's homework, 1980. Here he mentions escaping over the Severn Bridge in a chilling passage. Even then, when things got tough, he saw crossing the Bridge as a means of escape.

(4)

Nothing of any importance happened to me until August 24th, 1981. The day had started like any other; I attended school and came home. There was nothing spectacular about that.

David Bowie was blasting out "Ziggy Stardust" from the stereo when I noticed flashes of light through my bedroom window. Quickly I ran to the window and peered out into the gloom and smog of the night. Below, at the entrance to our house, stood John, Tich, Echo and Peter, my school friends. I dressed quickly and ran outside to meet them without telling my mother.

"What do you want guys?" I asked. "Never mind that," replied Echo, "follow us and we'll tell ya later." Without cause for concern I followed them through the park to the "Haven" as we called it. "Quiet," John whispered. They all got on their hands and knees and began crawling into a clearing and I followed. There, in the middle of the clearing on a big scarlet towel was Mr. Evans our French teacher and Miss Parkinson our attractive new secretary making love.

"Cooee, What do ya think you're doing then sir?" Peter yelled. In a quick burst of speed they both had blankets covering them. Before Mr. Evans could say anything Peter began talking, "I don't think your wife would be very pleased ~~is~~ if she found out would she sir." "No Peter, she would not!," he replied angrily.

"Now, Now sir she's not going to find out, is she?" Echo butted in.

"What do you mean?" he inquired.

"Well, if you make it worth our while, no one will find out. If you keep us out of detention, write us good reports, tell us examination questions and give us a little extra pocket money ~~the want~~ no one will ever suspect you ~~off g~~ this sordid little affair," Peter continued.

"But that's blackmail!" Mr. Evans shouted.

"I know, but would you rather your wife to find out," Tich answered.

"No, I suppose not," he replied.

"See you on Monday then sir," we all shouted gleefully.

On Monday morning we were all called to the headmaster's office where we meet Miss. Parkinson and Mr. Evans The headmaster explained that Mr. Evans had only been playing along with us on Friday night. ~~He~~ Mr. Evans explained that his wife already knew about his affair with Miss. Parkinson and had started divorce preceedings. We all knew we were in deep trouble. The headmaster explained that Mr. Evans ~~and~~ was ~~the~~ taking us to court for attempted blackmail. It was

only then I realised how serious a charge
blackmail was.

That evening I thought about
my future. There was no doubt in my mind
that we would be sent to a Detention
Centre. I thought through every possibility
of tricking myself out of the situation
and realised there were none. I decided
to run away.

That evening at two p.m. I
left home without leaving a note
and headed for the Severn Bridge.
I thought that in Bristol I might be
able to find a job. I set off, hopes
high and followed the M4 for about
three hours. It was hell. I could not
see anything expect for car headlights
bursting forth from the dark void that
lay ahead. Gradually it became
lighter and I saw the Bridge
in the distance.

A few hours later as I
was crossing the bridge a red mini
stopped infront of me. Mr. Evans stepped
out. I began to run but it was no
good, he caught and pushed me into
his car. I could have kicked myself.
I had not planned for teachers,
especially Mr. Evans, travelling to work from
Bristol.

The days passed by and the
trial grew ever near closer. During the
trial we had to sit next to our

Richard Edwards / 4 T.B. Set 1 English Language

wordprocessor

judge, Mr. Tindall, who was almost as old as stone henge. Tich, Echo, Peter and John pleaded innocent but I pleaded guilty, much to my present day disgust. Although I was mostly the innocent party [remember my friends had called for me] my so-called friends blamed everything on me. They got off with a warning but I was sent to ~~Burrlt~~ Norwich Detention Centre and believe me the film "Scum" is like a garden of roses compared to this place.

　　　　　After two years of ~~sheer~~ ~~hell~~ in the Detention Centre I ~~was sent~~ ~~free~~ for good behaviour, I continued with my education although I was two years behind everyone else. I ~~to~~ managed to get an interesting job with a national newspaper, "The Daily Mail," and began writing articles in it. My articles were mainly describing life in Borstal and ~~the~~ Britain's unfair Judicial System.

　　　　　After a few months the editor of the Mail sacked me. Since then I have been earning more money than I ~~t~~ ever dreamt of. Children in schools, borstals, prisons and the working ~~classes~~ regarded me as a Martyr. I ~~had did~~ no end of television and radio ~~appear~~ interviews and my future seemed rosy until ·····

Chapter Two.

Richard Edwards 4 T.B. Set 1. English

The Rebel. *Why no plan?*

"~~Plase~~ Plaster, please, Mrs. Jones," asked the weary Dr. Blake. (Dr. Blake is the worlds leading scientist on the use of genetic engineering in today's society.) "Do you know that this is our ~~hundreth~~ last operation on rats," he asked Mrs. Jones.

Paragraph Direct Speech

"Really Doctor Blake?" answered Mrs. Jones. "Are you sure about this?" she demanded.

"Terrible, isn't it? I've spent all my live working on genetics and now the government sees fit to stop supplying us with the money that we need for us to continue ~~f~~ our work. I feel very Bitter," shouted an irate Doctor Blake.

"I'm so sorry Doctor," ~~ask~~ answered Mrs. Jones.

"But mark my words, this isn't the last that you will hear of me. I can promise you that!" bellowed Dr. Blake.

Dr. Blake stormed out of the room. Through ~~the~~ a countless number of rooms he walked surrounded by the pungent smell of disinfectant. (Out through the hospital into the car park.) Just as he was about to ~~enter~~ ~~t~~ get into his car a

Not a sentence

Richey's homework, 1981: 'The Rebel'. A humorous story that firmly places Richey's imagination in the early eighties, but what shouts most loudly is the act of social transgression culminating in a plan to escape and live on in freedom abroad.

man approached him. He was very tall and was dressed all in black. He wore a black hat, black glasses, black donkey jacket, black trousers and black shoes. All Dr. Blake could see of him was a tiny scar on the left side of his cheek.

/Sp
Unnecessary repetition

"Good evening Dr. Blake. I'm sorry to hear about your operations being cancelled. I think that I will be able to help you. Imagine..... a sparkling new hospital; all the latest technology, massive kennels for animals, nurses and a choice of the finest doctors available .... all yours! Yours Dr. Blake!" whispered the man.

Suddenly his hand pulled a gun out of his pocket and it fired a sleeping dart.

"Good evening Dr. Blake. You have been asleep for three hours. Now have you thought about that hospital. It really could be yours if you take note of what I am about to say," the man said quietly.

"Yes, I'll do whatever you want. I want to get revenge on society and the government," Dr. Blake said angrily.

"Good, good," replied the mysterious man. You will know me as the man in black. If you are in trouble

Richard Edwards 4.T.B. Set 1. English.

just contact me at this address. There
is an important M.P in the Blackthorne Hospital. He has a private
ward and is suffering from syphillis.
He is Martin Foot, the ~~trade~~
Sp. ~~union~~ Labour parties chief whip.
Imagine the publicity..... Dr. Blake,
leading genetic engineer holds M.P
hostage because they put a stop to
his experiments. After two or three
days you could let him go and
I would have a helicopter waiting
for you on the top of the building. I could fly you to South
America where you would be safe,
~~Rather~~ rather like Ronnie Biggs," shouted
the man.
   "Yes, yes I see it now and in
South America I could have that
hospital and the people are so
stupid that I could ~~use~~ try out
Sp. my experiments on them," cryed Dr. Blake
He was almost hysterical.
   A few days later "Coronation
Street" was interrupted with a news
flash........ "Today at 1.00p.m,
Dr. Blake, a leading genetic engineer,
burst into Martin Foots ward in
the Blackthorne Hospital and is
holding him hostage. That is the end
of this newsflash." The following day

the man in black phoned ~~the~~ Dr. Blake. (Communications had been set up by the police on Dr. Blake's orders, they didn't know who was phoning or from where he was phoning)

"~~D~~ Blakely..... you've got you publicity allright dear boy. ~~Heres~~ Here's todays Daily Mail headline......

"Rebel" and all the other major papers have headings like this as well. They all ~~tell~~ tell of how the (govt) stopped your work," said the ~~man~~ ~~man~~ man in black.

Three days later Dr. Blake heard that he was to be picked up by helicopter at 2.00 pm the following day.

Meanwhile the S.A.S had been called in. Everybody thought that ~~Martin Foot~~ was to be killed.

"Go number one, two, three," shouted ~~a~~ a man.

Three helicopters took off carrying six S.A.S men. Suddenly, out of the gloom surrounding Blackthorne hospital three helicopters appeared, their phallic blades being thrust upwards. Two of them hovered over the roof while four men jumped onto the roof. The room ~~was~~ where Martin Foot was being held was right at the top of the building.

The four men threw ~~to~~ smoke canisters into the room. The other helicopter, with two men hanging from ropes ~~to~~ flew ~~stra~~ straight at the window and the men jumped through~~the window~~ ~~into~~ the window guns blazing.

The following day the headline of the ~~Daily~~ Mail read "Rebel Dr. Blake... Dead!" In the paragraphs that followed it told how the S.A.S rescued Martin Foot although a ~~s~~ stray bullet had grazed his arm.

"Disgusting" replied Arnold Wallace, ~~Sp~~ the Labour Parties ~~sa~~ Chief Whip who had been sacked from his job when Martin Foot arrived at the Labour Party. And if you looked closely at his left cheek you would notice a small ~~scar~~!

Good finish. However, the story is not too convincing. You use speech too much and the latter half of the essay is clearly a borrowed idea. Not true

1. The significance of the fact that ~~and the word~~

WHY I FIND IT HARD GROWING UP.

I cannot answer this question because I am already grown up but as I must I will. I am on the brink of insanity because when you are 14 you must pay adult price to see a AA but only childs price to see a A or U. Explain this please? When I am 14 I must pay full price on British Rail. You must be 18 to go into a pub and 18 to go to jail. Then they consider that you are an adult but in other other places you have to pay adult price at 14!! The reason I am on the brink of insanity is that I am not sure what I am? An adult or child? Could you please endeavour to explain this to me?

Another possible reason is that we have essay after essay given to us by a teacher named ? I think you guess.

Richey's homework, 1981. This cheeky humour and sense of provocation would become apparent throughout his time with the Manic Street Preachers.

With the power of great humanising and rousing works of art like *Rumble Fish*, the band's backwater beginnings could be transformed into a source of inspiration; a foundation for realness.

Just before Mark Hambridge's departure for America, Richey gave him an empty notebook, covered in his signature collage work, with instructions inside to 'Write a bluebeat novel. Write your soul.' Mark used the book to document his trip across the States.

Describing Richey as 'an encourager', Mark shows us another paisley-covered notebook, onto which Richey had etched the dedication 'Denny Blue'. Inside is an inscription: 'Happy Christmas 88# Den. Make this the best songbook ever, get your band going. Love, Richey x. BLUE TOO'.

Instead, Mark wrote 20 pages of diary entries and observations from life in Blackwood; a rare first-person testimony recording the atmosphere surrounding the early Manic Street Preachers – bleak, insular, yet hopeful and romantic.

We walked through the town, a cold town, an old town, my town. I felt a lot of affinity with it, but in a matter of two weeks things had begun to happen – sad town. The Council had opened their cheque books – dust threw everywhere – and decided to make it a new town, a modern town, a fast town, a moving town – no, a BULLSHIT town. Full of repression and money-grabbing bureaucrats. I've seen them already as I waited for the No. 6 bus. They speak with accents, and work like Robots – another towncentre-shopping precinctmarketsquare. No thought or care, 'thrown it up', 'the sooner it's up the sooner we can make more money and get fatter and have an heart attack' – Sooner the fucking better!! My town already has a reputation, but I really think the younger generation are going to have more places to fight, drink and generally enhance the reputation to a pitch where my town is going to be a battleground and my affinity will disappear. I was raised here and in years to come I don't want to frown when I talk of where I lived.

It was cold that night, although I wasn't complaining. As soon as I'd got some of that crisp fresh air into my lungs and I was side by side with my friends I felt as if there was a glow sheltering us as we walked through our town. We talked and laughed freely, walking towards the terraced house where Tea and Toast was plentiful, normally until 3am. Many times I had felt the need to talk and that terraced house, in which I had heard many songs that had cause to inspire me, was always where I headed and always where I felt wanted, and more importantly for me, a part of everything.

The drummers burned drumming. Makes of kits, 'hardware' and prices were swapped. The writers and musicians scored and talked about friends that had gone on trips to places near and far. The kettle didn't stop boiling and a third of a bottle of whiskey together with a large bar of chocolate also disappeared. I took a back seat and breathed-in both conversations, paying some attention to the music in the stereo.

The walk back to my house was exciting. J— was drunk and was mad and was burning. I retired to my bed in the knowledge that this was going to be the start of something good.

Well before they won recognition outside their immediate circle, the Manic Street Preachers and their accomplices had begun building the narrative later consumed by millions. Mark's up-close testimony offers a good outline of the self-mythologising, self-creating story that The Blue Generation and the Manic Street Preachers embedded themselves in. Immersing themselves in music, art and literature, they incorporated these sources to construct a world within which they could be the protagonists in a thrilling story, designed to eject them out of their dead-end existence, and onto a voyage into rock mythology. Mark was one of the first to be affected and energised by their deeply aesthetic vision.

We talked about music and books and I became interested in the writers that my friends sought comfort in. I read their works and found for the first time I was living these books. As I read, I was in them, doing their everyday things, drinking in their bars, walking their hometown downtown streets. And I asked myself, Why am I doing it their way? Why aren't I doing these things myself with my rucksack and my money in my time?

I used to feel quite alone, but now I have realised wherever my friends are we're all under the same sky, and we were linked by our pens and our bluehearts and blue ideals under the immense oh so immense blue sky. So no longer did I yearn for Rusty B., Nicky Wire and Richey Zero because they were with me every minute of the day.

Mark's writing echoes the sentiments familiar to many thousands of the band's fans. A dedication felt by so many, often misunderstood and derided by onlookers. Could Mark Hambridge be described as the Manic Street Preachers' first proper fan?

Talking to Mark about his American trip makes two things clear. First, the enormous impact that Richey had on him personally; and second, the huge ambitions harboured by the Blackwood group, to embark upon a heroic odyssey worthy of the world's attention.

Of great interest to us in considering Richey's disappearance is the fact the Manic Street Preachers from the outset had a masterly grasp of how gripping narratives work, and the role of the striving individual at their heart.

In a music press article published just weeks before Richey disappeared, this objectivity, the band's insider knowledge of the working of heroic narratives, was made public and explicit, when reference was made to Joseph Campbell's *The Hero with a Thousand Faces*. A study in comparative mythology, its central premise is that a 'hero archetype' may be found throughout human history, literature, culture and society. In Campbell's own description, there exists a 'monomyth' whose structure is remarkably similar across countless incarnations:

A hero ventures forth from the world of common day into a region of supernatural wonder: fabulous forces are there encountered and a decisive victory is won: the hero comes back from this mysterious adventure with the power to bestow boons on his fellow man.

The Manic Street Preachers' story, but particularly Richey's, has a peculiar applicability to Campbell's outlined structure. That Richey was well versed in this work might help shed light on his later actions, not least for the fact that he and the band repeatedly emphasised their mission to forge a new and unprecedented 'rock myth'.

'We had this evangelical desire,' said Nicky Wire in 1996, 'to start the revolution and be absolutely fucking massive. It didn't just mean getting a record deal. It was all-conquering, psycho, egotistical.'

He would go on to admit that Richey's ambitions were at a higher level altogether. Mainstream music success was not enough for him; Nicky described him as 'aiming for the Pulitzer Prize'. The implication is that Richey's disappearance may itself be seen in the context of myth-building – inviting us to consider whether the scope of his ambition, and ability to do what others could not, might range far beyond what would normally seem feasible.

Without question, rock mythology and immortality held great fascination for Richey. In another school exercise book from his early adolescence, he wrote:

Thin or fat? Shrivelled by the sun, his face looked like tanned leather. Nobody believed that such a puny creature could have such reserves of strength. No one ever laughed at Kirk because they were scared of him and did not know what he would do because he was quite mysterious. Kirk was always a jump in front of everyone else because he always anticipated everyone's move and made sure that he had the best chance in any game they played. The qualities of a born leader are to be always out in front and whenever there is anything important to be done then the leader should do it best. A born leader should have a 'magnetic' personality and should be able to make everything he says seem believable, honest and sensible. A typical born leader is Robert

Nesta Marley. Kirk was rebellious and did whatever he felt like doing. If he got into trouble he was never caught.

The repeating theme in those early teenage stories, of revolt and exile, was even viewed in the context of music demigod immortality. Going with the hypothesis that this was a pattern of thought and feeling Richey carried over into his years with the band, a keen eye should be kept for discerning whether his actions support a pre-planned vanishing, a deliberately constructed mystery. Was, for instance, his semi-detached relationship with his allotted instrument an outer sign that he knew he would not be attached to it for long? Was it, moreover, evidence of his having placed his talent and focus outside of mundane guitar-picking, and that his sights were set on where the real rewards lay?

Richey Edwards played his first gig with the Manic Street Preachers at Swansea University in spring 1989. Dan Roland's membership of the Entertainment Society secured them a gig in the Mandela Student Union bar. Richey waited in the wings as the band played their first few songs before joining them on stage for the remaining three.

'I wasn't there for the gig, but I remember him preparing for it,' says Adrian. 'He had a white denim jacket and he wanted me to draw a military stencil on the back. So he bought some fabric paint and made me draw on the back of it when he was wearing it. When he took it off he said it wasn't "scuzzy" enough, and made me go over it again and again until it looked rough enough for his liking.'

A few months later, in September 1989, Rachel Edwards saw her brother play live for the first time at Cardiff's Radcliffe Square Club. 'Around that time Richard was buying stencil kits to decorate some of my mum's old blouses and encouraging the band to bring their clothes over so he could write on their shirts too. When I saw them play the Square, they came out with slogans all over them and did a really frantic, energetic set − but there were only about five of us in the audience, and about three of us paying attention.'

After playing a handful of South Wales gigs, including TJ's in Newport, Richey knew the next logical step for the Manics. 'We saw bands do all the pubs where we lived, do two hundred gigs a year, get really big local followings, and they're all under the illusion that somebody from Sony Music will be driving through the middle of South Wales and go, "Hey, what a good band! Let's sign here!"'

By contrast, within months of his graduation, and due to his relentless PR offensive, the Manics were performing in London, courtesy of Richey's pen pal Kevin Pearce.

'Kevin was at the heart of the fanzine circle,' recalls Alistair Fitchett. 'I remember him writing to me about a single he'd been sent, "Suicide Alley" – he said it wasn't that great, but it was the letter that Richey sent him that had made him want to hear more. He said it was the kind of letter you carry around in your pocket for days because it was so enthusiastic, so passionate and inspiring and was saying all the right things. He could see with someone like Richey, who appeared so clued into the rock and roll game, that something big was going to happen for them.'

On 2 September 1989, the Manic Street Preachers played to 17 people at the Horse and Groom, an old Victorian pub in the East End. Dressed in their DIY spray-painted shirts (ENGLAND NEEDS REVOLUTION NOW / CLASSIFIED MACHINE / SUICIDE BEAT) they performed nine tracks, including 'Suicide Alley' and 'Anti-Love' – to a lukewarm reception.

Bob Stanley of *Melody Maker* was there and remembers the audience's stifled laughter. 'I was asked along by Kevin Pearce because he'd read me one of Richey's letters and I thought there was something special in it, so it was worth going to check them out. We were laughing but only because it was so unexpected. The presentation was total Clash but they had an energy and conviction that was missing with so many other bands at the time.'

More pleased with securing a London gig than dejected by their reception, the band were delighted when they scored their first live review in *Melody Maker* courtesy of Stanley, and Kevin Pearce invited them back to play a further two gigs at the venue.

By now Mark Hambridge was the band's designated driver, allowing Richey to knock back some Dutch courage before taking the stage. Mark shows us a pile of water-damaged photos from the first Horse and Groom gig. The faces of the other three Manics have been corroded, but Richey's remains intact.

'We used to hire a van from a nearby garage and spend the day driving down to the gig and the night driving back,' says Mark. 'There was another gig I drove them to in the early days in London, and Richey got drunk. We stopped at a service station on the way back, and Richey went AWOL, and we couldn't find him. We were all looking around the service station, only to go outside and find him in the van, drunkenly doing circles of the empty car park. We were shouting for him to stop, and he only did when he bumped into a bin and dented the side of the van.

'We got back at 6am after that gig, and in the sober light of day, we all panicked because we had to return this rental van and get the deposit back. James and I took it on ourselves to fix it. I held the door open and James punched it to get the dent out. Luckily it worked, and the rental place didn't notice.'

Mark reveals the atmosphere in the van was always lively, with the band talking politics, music, sport and film, as well as usual laddish joking and mickey-taking. 'I remember the boys calling Rich "Norfolk" (No-fuck) because he'd told them he'd never slept with a girl. He didn't mind, though, it was just that kind of banter you have when you're a group of boys together. They were really happy, innocent times.'

During the band's early forays to London, they crossed paths with writer and film director Alan G. Parker. At the time working for the alternative punk magazine *Spiral Scratch*, he saw them at The Bull & Gate in Kentish Town, and became an instant convert.

'After the gigs, they'd hang around to talk to journalists,' says Alan. 'A lot of people were laughing at them, because they thought they were a Clash rip-off, but I remember telling everybody "I really *have* just seen the next Clash!"

'When you got talking to them, it was cemented because they had this integrity, and although they were very "boys next door", there was another dimension to them that made them so compelling. You knew there was so much more going on underneath. I remember chatting with Richey about conspiracy theories, and how he didn't believe Lennon got shot by a "mad fan". He'd talk about the CIA's covert involvement and was really clued in on what others would call conspiracy theories. He knew culture and he knew counterculture, and then some.

'They told me they were going to sell 25 million records and split up by burning themselves alive on *Top of the Pops*. Well, it was Rich and Nick's motto at least, but I remember telling James later on and he didn't have a clue about it, he was like "What?! They're *actually* serious?!"

'Nick and Rich wanted to be really big and throw it all away, because which band would actually do that? They were out to prove a point about music, the human psyche and the world at large. To get to a massive stage and throw it back in the media's faces. They were talking an A game, in terms of originality. They wanted to be immortal.'

'The only monument that counts is the one already imagined as ruin.'
Andreas Huyssen, US academic

In 1998 Sean told the BBC's *Close Up* documentary, 'Richey was, for want of a better word, our minister of propaganda. He'd studied modern political history so in a way he was our think tank.'

Rachel Edwards agrees. 'I do think Richard was the heart and soul of the band in those early days. As soon as he graduated in 1989 – he started making things happen for them. I imagine he could have joined any band and got them signed to a major label. You had lots of bands around here at the time like Funeral in Berlin, and others that faded into obscurity, but Richard gave the Manic Street Preachers his formula, and they reciprocated by letting him join the band, despite his lack of musical ability.'

'They knew how outrageous they had to be to get attention,' remembers Bob Stanley. 'They said they were all teenagers and Sean was still

16 and doing his GCSES when we first met. They knew how to play the game and how to get a reaction from everyone around them.

'Richey was definitely inspiring because he looked like a pop star, spoke like a pop star and had that extra "meta" layer where you knew he was fully in charge. He made such an impact on me that I went on to form Saint Etienne despite not being able to play an instrument. That was the point with the Manics – their whole deconstruction of the world of rock and roll.'

In their first televised interview in 1991, Richey defiantly stated: 'Youth is just the ultimate product. We just want to mix, like, sex and politics. We're the most original band in the last 15 years just because we don't want to do anything that's been done before. What we aspire to isn't what other bands aspire to.'

But exactly what would it take for the Manic Street Preachers to 'do what had never been done before' and to go where no other band had dared venture? And, pertinent to Richey's disappearance, was his commitment to propelling himself into immortal status greater than his peers?

'I didn't really know him well, but it seemed like he really meant everything he said in terms of going out in a blaze of glory,' says Bob Stanley. 'More so than the other band members, he had this need to prove he was authentic in his words, and he could walk it like he talked it. You just knew as a new band something big was going to happen for them.'

Chapter 6

Imitation Demigod

Over the ensuing years, the Manic Street Preachers were to jump through all the hoops of the music business: the radio interviews, autograph signings, TV appearances and awards ceremonies. Their adolescent dreams were realised – international tours, critical acclaim, bigger sales and plaudits than any Welsh artists of recent memory.

Leading up to this, Richey must have written to half of the London music industry. Rachel Edwards hands us a stack of correspondence from 1989 to 1991, comprising her brother's impassioned petitioning on the band's behalf. The letters captured Richey's naked ambition, with the guarantee of blood, old-school rock tragedy, and the alluring promise that industry types could 'do what they wanted' with the young band. Intrigued by these promises, one man emerged to help them secure their major career breakthrough.

Philip Hall had created his PR company, Hall or Nothing, in 1986, winning awards for his campaigns for the Pogues and the Stone Roses. It was a family business that involved Philip's wife, Terri, and his younger brothers, Martin and Michael. Hall was more intrigued by Richey's written manifesto than the music it accompanied. He drove down to South Wales with Martin to watch them rehearse and then secured them a gig at the Rock Garden in London. This show earned them an offer of a record deal from a hip independent label, Heavenly Records.

Philip Hall also made the Manic Street Preachers an offer. He wanted to be their PR man – and he also wanted to manage them. Having accepted both propositions, for the next few weeks the band drove between London and South Wales for meetings and for studio sessions financed by Heavenly.

'I remember them in the early days parking their van outside our office,' says former Hall or Nothing press officer Caffy St Luce. 'They were always so polite and unimposing. They'd rarely come into the office and we'd go out there with cups of tea and coffee for them. Sometimes they'd even sleep overnight in the van if needed.'

However, it soon became clear that if their thirst for world domination was to be realised, they would need to move to London. In January 1991, all four Manic Street Preachers moved in with the newly-married Philip and Terri in their house in Shepherd's Bush. James and Sean shared one double bed, Richey and Nicky another. The Halls re-mortgaged their house to finance their efforts and began to apply their ferocious hustling skills to furthering the Manics' cause.

It was certainly a seductive and persuasive cause. In 1991, music papers like the *NME* and *Melody Maker* were still packed with guitar bands revelling in English parochialism. It was all about the apolitical 'shoegaze' scene and the idea of bands passing political or social comment seemed passé. It was no longer possible to be a rock rebel.

To break that apathetic mould, new tactics were required. Yet initially the Manics' outspoken interviews and barbed sloganeering grated on London's musical tastemakers. Was their rhetorical brashness, their cocky sloganeering, genuine? Or was it just a knowing piss-take? If the Welsh upstarts really were more than empty blowhard bluster, where was the proof?

Richey Edwards famously upped the ante spectacularly at Norwich Arts Centre on 15 May 1991. After a rather lacklustre gig, then *NME* journalist Steve Lamacq, who was on the road with the band, told Richey: 'I just don't think a lot of people will think you're for real.'

Richey reacted by taking a razor blade and gouging '4 REAL' deep into his own arm. 'He was dripping blood all over the floor,' a shocked

Lamacq was to report. 'I went out and found the manager and told him to get backstage pretty damn quick.'

Richey was bandaged up, but spotting *NME* photographer Ed Sirrs, he rolled down the dressing and invited him to photograph his gaping wounds. Sirrs and the *NME* had their money shot – and Richey was taken to hospital to receive 17 stitches. As the damage was self-inflicted, Richey, ever thoughtful, was adamant all the other casualties should be seen before him.

As we discuss this infamous incident with Rachel, she places a maroon leather washbag on her mother's living-room floor. Inside are blister packs of Prozac tablets; unopened packets of Durex, dated 1989; military face paint; Soviet-era military badges; French Paradox pills; mascara and foundation ... and a small pack of double-edged razor blades.

Richey Edwards's life trajectory arguably hinged on this brutal self-assault. Whatever their critics thought of them, it stopped people calling the Manic Street Preachers poseurs or charlatans and placed them on a plateau distinct from their peers.

Richey's alarming self-mutilation nudged the most astute critics into understanding the subtler sensibilities that he, and the band, had on offer. They had to ask, what kind of person lay behind this act? From Sid Vicious to Iggy Pop, self-mutilation as a form of showmanship was nothing new in the world of rock, but this latest public act captured the attention of a new generation of music fans. And many were left wondering how far did Richey's suffering extend? Was he 4 REAL in his suffering or was it part of the rock 'n' roll package?

An *NME* editor, future *Loaded* founder James Brown, contacted known Manics fanatic Alan G. Parker, begging for the pair to take a trip to the Valleys, to sample first-hand the bleak caricature of a place which dominated the band's fabulist back story.

'James Brown wanted to go to Blackwood,' says Parker. 'We journeyed up on the train, just to see. Yes, they captured our imagination to that extent. Blackwood? They could have come from space!'

The Manics' genre was not so much punk as 'meta-rock'; they seemed to relish playing the music business the way Richey probably should have been playing his guitar. Acutely postmodern, Richey and the band were aware of how the music business worked and weren't afraid to impart this knowledge at any given opportunity. Circumventing the apparent randomness or arcane formulas bestowing success or failure, they treated the affair as a game, whose rules could be known and which could be won. Nicky Wire had wasted piles of cash trying to beat the system on the slot machines during his time at university. Rather than waste endless months getting equally frustrated by provincial obscurity, it was as though Richey had swivelled the apparatus around, and invited the boys to laugh at the simplicity of the inner workings of this new and bigger game.

Yet if the band were to realise their grand vision, a cottage-industry indie label such as Heavenly Records could only take them so far. Having gigged continuously throughout 1990 and the first half of 1991, it was only after Richey's bloodletting incident that the major record companies came calling. Before long they had signed to CBS/Sony Records. They were later to explain that there were two basic reasons for this choice. One was CBS's previous involvement with their heroes, The Clash. The other was the enthusiasm of the pursuing A&R man, Rob Stringer.

As CEO of Sony Music Entertainment, Stringer is now one of the most powerful figures in the global music industry. In 1991, he had gone from being a graduate trainee in the marketing department of CBS Records to an A&R man, and was about to enjoy his first major success.

'[Manic Street Preachers] were the first band I signed at CBS,' Stringer has said. 'I went to see them at Moles in Bath. And I loved them. When I met them as people I loved them even more. It was something I believed in passionately from the start.'

A close and lasting relationship was formed between Stringer, Philip Hall and the band. When Stringer received a rapid promotion and become head of Epic Records the following year, he took the Manics with him.

Famously, the Manics then immediately and provocatively declared their intention to make one double album that would sell 20 million copies, change the face of rock and roll and split up. With hindsight, it has been suggested that Stringer indulged their vision too readily, giving them the go-ahead to release a 73-minute double album featuring 18 tracks.

'I didn't even try and talk them down to a single record, because that was the manifesto,' Stringer was later to explain. 'And if you were a Clash fan, and if you loved *London Calling* and *Sandinista!*, you understood. The truth is, as they'll tell you now, we barely had enough material for a double. We stretched it a bit. I love them, I love them as colleagues and partners and friends, but that first album ... we look back and laugh about it still.'

Manic Street Preachers entered Black Barn Studios near Woking, Surrey, in July 1991. Their declared mission was to record their one-and-only album to win over first America and then the planet. Notoriously, Richey played not a single note on the record that was to become *Generation Terrorists*. Nor, in fact, did Nicky Wire. Musically it was mostly all down to James Dean Bradfield, whose creative abilities surfaced in full, astounding his bandmates.

It has been widely reported that, making the album, Richey's total lack of guitar-playing ability bred in him a new crisis of conscience and confidence. Yet should his presentations to the other Manics be read at face value? Legend has it that musicians sell their souls to 'the man' for success. So did Richey's consciously continued non-playing in fact advertise his determination to keep his soul intact; to play the game on his own terms?

The band's would-be portentous, aesthetically definitive first album, *Generation Terrorists*, certainly had major expectations to fulfil. To the amazement of many, it largely came through with the goods. What was remarkable was the apparent ease and concision with which the Manics got to the heart of things. It was a sensitively wrought, insightful and compelling portrait of the nation's political and social predicament.

Consider its second track: 'Natwest-Barclays-Midland-Lloyds'. In October 1986, Margaret Thatcher's Conservative government had carried out its 'Big Bang' deregulation of financial services. Where previous rules separated retail from investment banking, suddenly those rules were gone. London became the world's predominant financial centre, surpassing even New York.

In this song, the Manics recognised the human consequences of society's shift to usury-on-steroids. Such deep structural transformation barely registered with most musicians, but the Manics provided a brilliant, laser-point dissection of how contemporary society was organised.

'Another Invented Disease' dared to suggest that the AIDS epidemic was a deliberate attack, a suggestion also made by conspiracy researcher Milton William Cooper and Louis Farrakhan's Nation of Islam. Yet rather than Richey endorsing such conspiracy theories, his allusions were more likely shrewdly embedded provocations.

Musically, *Generation Terrorists* flagrantly pinned much of its strategy for success on co-opting the Guns N' Roses sound. The band confidently expected to win over hordes of sleaze/glam-metal fans across the world. They were more than aware of bands like L.A. Guns, Mötley Crüe, Poison and Ratt via their considerable T-shirt sales in the Valleys of South Wales, and saw their fans as sitting-duck targets.

It was a calculated route-one strategy, but would it work? If they dragged these unsuspecting punters in with the music, the album's content would certainly make them think. Listeners were left to make sense of pithy quotes from artists, philosophers, novelists and poets, including Karl Marx, Friedrich Nietzsche, Public Enemy's Chuck D, Confucius and William Burroughs.

It all set out the parameters of the band's playing field and threw down a challenge to the London music scene. London may be big in a British context, said the Manics, but it is provincial on the world stage, as is its current guitar music. The message, *Don't judge us on your paltry terms, we intend to step over your heads*, was delivered with disarming bravura.

For the album's front sleeve, there was a basic photo of Richey's chest and upper arm. Its iconic, Warhol-ian simplicity hinted at future classic status.

As purportedly the Manic Street Preachers' only album, *Generation Terrorists* was released with a bang. Alan G. Parker recalls that during the London launch party, 'Philip Hall was running around the crowd, telling everyone when to shout FUCK OFF during the chorus of "Stay Beautiful". Sony spent a lot of money that night, on 4 REAL make-up compacts; Richey gave me loads to take home. And, of course, all the newspapers were there, the music writers from the mainstream press. The band had gone beyond basic *NME* reach, which is exactly what they wanted.'

The Manics' audacious amalgam of 'lowly' pop music with more 'serious' concerns such as philosophy, economics, poetry, literature and academia created an ironic distance between the band and their art. For those able to decode it, *Generation Terrorists* was not just a great rock record, but a meta work of art, analysing and subverting the genre even as it joined its canon.

Advertising, celebrity, consumerism, cheap mass culture – the Manics were willingly allowing themselves to become subsumed by their environment; by the conditions of postmodernity. U2 arguably did a similar thing with their Zoo TV tour but offered only a passive, non-critical embrace. The Manics were on the hunt for a position from which to take pot-shots.

Richey demanded his bandmates read Greil Marcus's *Lipstick Traces*, an exploration of shared threads linking 1970s punk to 1960s radical intellectual groups such as the Situationist International. The Situationists developed a range of strategies to criticise all-consuming capitalism. One was '*détournement*', in which familiar artefacts from the consumer environment were transformed, turning their original message inside-out – billboard posters were subverted to reveal hidden truths. Richey's vision for *Generation Terrorists* was a '*détournement*' of the standard American rock form into an incendiary report on the modern human condition.

In 1992, not everyone recognised the timeless portent in *Generation Terrorists*. Yet as we wrote this book, over a quarter of a century later, strangers contacted us online, imploring us to delve into the 'hidden history' of the Manics' early material. Perhaps a new generation, raised on internet conspiracy theories, is now able to read more into *Generation Terrorists* than its original fans.

They pointed us towards the album sleeve. The back cover carried a photograph of the European flag set aflame – is it totally fanciful to imagine the ever-prescient Richey prophetically anticipating Brexit and the collapse of the entire EU project? There are interesting symbols on the front cover, too. Richey's tattoo, a rose, and hanging against his chest, a cross. Did these universal signifiers contain more than they did at first sight?

Conspiracy theorists see the manipulating hands of the Illuminati-Rosicrucians-Freemasons in every corner of society. Given that Rosicrucianism's symbol is the Rosy Cross, was Richey, typically responsible for choosing cover art, firing a cryptic broadside at a so-called New World Order?

By the early nineties, rock groups posed no threat to the order of things. Multinational corporations would gladly repackage and sell absolutely any rebellious forms back to us. Here was where Nicky Wire and, particularly, Richey felt their auto-didacticism and academic nous could play to their advantage. Knowing how the modern world was composed, they knew which buttons to press.

Many online conspiracy researchers feel that a penchant for conspiracy-oriented content runs through the Manics' history. Early single 'Motown Junk' introduced the band's worldview, involving rock mythology, cultural iconoclasm and dark allusions to political conspiracy.

At a superficial glance, the line about laughing when John Lennon died seemed one of the dumbest lyrical sentiments ever. It was, however, a reference to the interpretation of the Beatle's death in Fenton Bresler's book *Who Killed John Lennon?* (1989). Bresler rejected the theory that Mark David Chapman acted alone. The Manics were not scoring cartoon-punk points by gloating over Lennon's death, but referencing this assassination hypothesis. Bresler could be forgiven his laugh; he was convinced Lennon's death was the work of the CIA.

Nicky Wire has spoken of two coexisting Manics histories – the known, public one; and another, submerged, only glimpsed or hinted at. For the Manic Street Preachers, but particularly Richey, conspiracy theories, and the CIA specifically, were a source of great fascination.

Alan G. Parker is the co-author of the 2003 book *John Lennon & the FBI Files*. Becoming friends with Richey through 1991–2, he saw up-close his fixation with stardom and rock legends, and his mission to insert his own name among them. Richey was intrigued that Parker had stayed with Sid Vicious's mother, Anne Beverley, while researching for his 1991 book *Sid's Way: The Life & Death of Sid Vicious*. 'Richey was into the mythology, the myth that Sid became. And I'd tell him, "Yes, it's great in parts but don't lose yourself in it. Rock and roll has always been a silly place to live."'

Yet the will to lose himself in the mythology, in rock immortality, was the mainspring of Richey's mission. His years of bedroom meditation, soaking up life-affirming music and culture and dreaming himself into its maw, were a gestation period. Now the vision was to metamorphose.

To what degree was Richey familiar with conspiracy material? The most notorious early nineties musician subsumed in that world was Public Enemy's Professor Griff, who was cast as the group's Minister of Information.

As a voice against the New World Order and the Illuminati, Griff has been a prominent contributor to rising debate about the influence of secret societies in the music industry. For most people such theories are preposterous, but some hold them to be established fact, including, apparently, artists who are now household names.

There is a deep and long-lasting narrative describing the tragic fate of countless musicians at the hands of the all-powerful. Richey's name never appears on the list of artists supposedly sacrificed by an evil corporate elite, but this only makes his story's applicability to such theories more intriguing.

Conspiracy peddlers talk of 'blood sacrifice': to pass beyond a certain threshold, an offering must be made, and someone usually must die.

Richey's favourite band, Joy Division, saw this same mythic trope woven into their own history, having supposedly signed their first contract in their own blood.

When Richey notoriously spilled his own blood for the *NME*, was he consciously acting out his role in a Faustian deal for wealth and fame? Just six days after the blood-strewn '4 REAL' incident, the Manic Street Preachers signed a record deal with Sony. A photo showed them lined up behind a desk, offering ironic grins and handshakes to their new bosses, Richey's arm still in bandages.

Released in February 1992, *Generation Terrorists* reached number 13 in the UK. Sony Records took unilateral measures to ensure it sold better in the States, removing or remixing some tracks, rearranging the running order and changing the sleeve as they aimed the Manic Street Preachers fair and square at the US college radio circuit that had propelled The Clash and Guns N' Roses to superstardom. The band were not consulted on any of these changes.

Two months later, the band finally reached the land upon which their widescreen dreams were projected. Their meagre six North American dates included New York's Limelight Club, The I-Beam in San Francisco and LA's Whisky a Go Go. They were not huge venues but lent a flattering, fleeting fingertip brush with fame.

However, for *Generation Terrorists* to attain the desired multi-platinum sales levels, timing and the cultural climate would be crucial. The band's boast of having a collective finger nearest the historic pulse needed to be true.

While they were in the US, news reports were dominated by sudden massive urban upheaval in California. The April/May LA riots were triggered by the trial of LAPD officers for a brutal assault on an African-American man, Rodney King. The trial exonerated the officers but sparked urban warfare as (mainly) black protestors began rioting, looting and shooting. It was all broadcast live to a world audience newly conjoined by satellite television.

Flush with legends of the turbulent sixties, of Guy Debord and the Situationist International, of the UK's own urban riots immortalised in the very naming of The Clash, surely the Manics were tailor-made for this moment? Their LA debut should have been the perfect soundtrack for the chaos engulfing parts of the city. And yet, despite a decent response to their shows on Sunset Strip, the band was despondent.

The *NME* accompanied Richey on a lazy daytime shopping trip down Melrose Avenue, boycotting the trappings of sleaze rock and buying a jacket, a postcard ('I Shop Therefore I Am'). However, it was clear that, despite the ongoing societal meltdown, the Manics and their album were of little consequence. Local radio stations played the Manics' track 'Slash 'n' Burn', but Richey was not deluded – the band were not in contact with the social upheaval.

'In terms of something explosive,' he remarked, 'I don't think it will happen. People just aren't interested any more. They're too selfish.' Only a couple of months out of the starting blocks, an air of anti-climax already engulfed *Generation Terrorists*.

As the Manic Street Preachers toured the album around Europe, Richey took every chance to disabuse the record-buying public of their wrong-headed fantasies about the touring lifestyle. After a while it was, he insisted, a routine as bad as any other; 'Wake-up, travel, sound check, gig, wake-up, travel, sound check, gig'.

Rory Lyons, the band's tour manager from 1991 to 1994, documented this repetitive regimen in a batch of paper files containing itinerary details from each Manics tour. Rachel Edwards shows them to us, and as we flick through, several pages pique our interest.

Lyons has decorated blank pages with funny clippings from tabloid newspapers. One cartoon is a Gary Larson 'Far Side' strip, but Rory has Tippexed out the original speech bubble and replaced it with an in-joke. A bespectacled man hangs out of a house window, with a megaphone: 'Hey! Rat race! My name is Rory Lyons and tomorrow I'm moving to an island in the South Pacific where I'm going to sit on a beach, sip coconut milk, and watch the sun go down! Kiss my butt goodbye, human cesspool! Ha ha ha ha ha ha ha!'

Beneath details for a date in Trier in Germany, Rory writes: 'No support. Today, your other tour manager is 34. All washed-up in Brazil.'

On another page, covering a stay in Munich, he scrawls: 'Get the promoter to take you to the Hofbrau Haus. It's where that man started planning that thing we're not allowed to mention.'

Lyons's words were salutary. It was on the road that Richey seemingly began further to develop his growing sense of personal alienation and became estranged from the rest of the band. His core truth seemed to be that even the beginning of his desperately craved musical career could not cure his profound feeling of isolation.

'Get in the van, and it's like four people with CD Walkmans, Sega games, just sitting like that,' he was to comment. 'It's an existential nightmare! Our lives haven't changed at all.'

There were early, occasional dalliances with groupies, but this was not really Richey's way. Cast adrift on the road, he began to pine for one particular person who was playing an increasingly large role in his life and psyche.

Richey was always eager to spell out in countless publications his preferred type – thin, blonde and androgynous, much like Kate Moss in her early nineties adverts for Calvin Klein. Yet Jo, the London girl he was seeing, was a dark-haired, curvy 17-year-old of mixed-race heritage.

The extensive correspondence that was to pass between the pair, and that we have been shown while researching this book, suggests a close and heartfelt relationship. In later years, Jo was to share with Rachel Edwards photocopies of a precious batch of letters from Richey. A constant theme was that Richey longed to be with Jo rather than languishing alone in some hotel room in the middle of nowhere.

'You are the first person to make me feel safe, even if I never express myself very well. Just being in your bedroom makes me feel more secure than a thousand concerts or TV shows ...'

Richey, letter to Jo, 1993

Chapter 7

New Improved Formula

*'A lot of people in Japan took all the "one LP and then quit" business
very seriously,' Richey smiles. 'They had us down as this Hara Kiri
Mishima kind of character who believes in making your own
moment of greatness and then Suicide Central here we come!'*
'Going 4 Gold', *Metal Hammer*, July 1993

The very concept of a fleeting rock moment, of the band that rises high
to explode on a vast scale, creating its own self-conscious legend, was
core to the Manic Street Preachers. And so, following what were to
prove to be disappointing sales of *Generation Terrorists*, they were forced
into a very public climb-down.

Apparently, they really would now become just another band in the
racks. For Richey, it was an unthinkable compromise, humiliating and
excruciating. For the following year, he bit his lip as the Manics examined where they had fallen short, and gathered their resources for
another hubristic grab at corporate glory, this time with their aptly
titled second album, *Gold Against the Soul*.

During their early notoriety, and before the decision had been made
to record a debut double album, they had considered releasing a quick-
fire standard two-sided long-player, described by Nicky Wire as 'an
album of Motown Junks'. The conscious shift-change, from the punk

stylings of these early singles to the slick MTV rock of *Generation Terrorists*, had blatantly sought to widen their appeal.

Yet little did the Manics realise that a fresh form of 'punk' was about to break into mainstream America. In retrospect, the release date of *Generation Terrorists* and its densely packed nature were poorly judged and badly timed. But nothing they could have done would have countered the rise of a generation-defining new album and genre set to captivate music fans across the world.

Generation Terrorists was destined by fate to be completely eclipsed by Nirvana's *Nevermind*, released just four months earlier, and the arrival of 'grunge'. Seattle birthed something the Manics had openly craved for years – a new movement, informed by punk and metal, that was generation-defining and seminal. It all conspired to make the Manics' plans appear deeply flawed.

During Richey's university years, Guns N' Roses' energy, attitude and swagger had transfixed the indie-obsessed boys from Blackwood. But 1988's 'most dangerous band in the world' were, by 1992, looking slightly passé. While Nirvana front man Kurt Cobain was famously revelling in taking the piss out of Axl Rose, the Manics were lumbered with flogging a carbon copy of the Guns N' Roses sound around the venues of North America. Their genius war plan had misfired.

'The first album was meant to be a full-stop,' Richey told *Kerrang!* 'It was also supposed to be a 20-million [selling] full-stop!'

The Manics' original plan to call it a day after hitting superstardom with their debut would have been a quixotic statement. But the album's low sales meant there would be very little interest even if the four did disappear back into obscurity as planned. In a 1993 interview with 1.FM radio, James commented: 'It couldn't help but miss the target, so to speak, because we set ourselves a higher target. So, some people think we have eaten a lot of humble pie since.'

For the time being, the Manics ploughed on, as though embarking on the kind of decades-long career Richey had decried so many times. Nicky Wire said, 'We are real fans of pop music and rock music throughout history, so we will always go out of our way to make something which we think is really commercial. To please ourselves, not to please other people.'

Generation Terrorists went gold in the UK, but sold only 32,000 copies in America. Their second album appeared far more intent on infiltrating the mainstream. *Gold Against the Soul* took great pains to convince, and to appear less conspicuously clever to, the average music buyer. It appeared not so visibly constructed, and less postmodern.

It possibly felt the need for less Richey Edwards. It seemed to be moving away from his deft handling of rock music as a studied art form, and away from the objective sensibility that had made *Generation Terrorists* such a profound lyrical and stylistic statement. In place of cultural studies, textual gamesmanship and foreground, the band's streamlined second offering was that of Album Orientated Rock.

Richey's guitar playing did make it onto the record – some tentative strokes for the opening number, 'Sleepflower' – to fend off those constant jibes that he was 'not a musician'. But the reality was that Richey's role was markedly diminished; a fact openly acknowledged in interviews at the time.

'There's no way I'd be allowed to be in any other band in the world,' he told *Select* magazine. 'But James would never come into my bedroom and say, "I think you should play your guitar a bit better!"'

'It's about being intelligent about what we do,' Bradfield explained. 'And not letting our egos get in the way. A band should be a positive division of labour; people should do what they're best at. I'm not going to let Richey try a solo just because I think it'll do his self-esteem a load of good.'

Continued belief and investment in them by management and record company gave the Manics some reassurance. But it also meant they were about to toe the line and construct a more polished, consumer friendly end-product. This included recording at a top-end, super-expensive studio.

Located at Hook End Manor in Checkenden, Oxfordshire, Hook End Studios was described by Marillion's Steve Hogarth as 'England's most luxurious recording studio'. Built in 1580, and having served as a monastery in Tudor times, the property had recently come into the hands of rock's nouveau riche. Ownership passed from Ten Years After front man Alvin Lee, who had originally built the studio, to Pink Floyd's David Gilmour, and part of Pink Floyd's 1983 album *The Final Cut* was recorded here. Hook End Manor was rumoured to be haunted, and Gilmour and his wife Ginger moved out after a series of so-called supernatural events.

When the Manics arrived in January 1993, they knew Pink Floyd's giant inflatable pig was stored in a nearby outhouse, and that the Manor's previous recordings included The Cure's *Disintegration* and Morrissey's *Bona Drag* and *Kill Uncle* albums. The band's label had presumably forked out for the best resources to try to persuade the bruised Manic Street Preachers to play the game the proper way.

The decision to record at Hook End Manor, and the choices made during that period, would weigh heavily on the band's conscience. Richey endured the new regime through gritted teeth, nonetheless making plain his feelings both in the choice of title for the album and through his writing.

Lyrically, the new album would be one of the tamest of the Manics' career. The few chosen targets for venomous insights betray Richey and Nicky's nagging obsessions. 'Drug Drug Druggy' was aimed squarely at the growing trend for illicit drugs as a badge of rebellion and retro authenticity for nineties youth. The media had recently been awash with tales of Kurt Cobain's heroin addiction and reports that Courtney Love had allegedly been using while pregnant. Possibly still reeling from having their thunder stolen a year before, one line appeared to offer a very Richey-flavoured, razor-sharp dig at grunge's celebrity couple.

Revelling in their signature untimeliness, the Manics spelt out how they felt drugs are a weapon used by the global oligarchy to control the masses. Standing pretty much alone in the face of an era of Ecstasy-fuelled faux-utopian hedonism, the Manic Street Preachers' contrariness offered a rare glimpse of something approaching unpalatable truth.

Drugs arose again in 'Nostalgic Pushead', a clinically descriptive vilification of the kinds of music industry figures the band found in London. Middle-aged owners of the music scene relived their past vicariously through the young, sang the Manics. Some lines referencing Soho Square, Paul Smith and Gaultier appeared to fall just short of naming actual individuals.

James commented, 'It's a bit of a recurrent theme, of loss of innocence, just the nature of being in a band. We are used to a new bourgeoisie now, certain people that we know, in "our" industry, which sicken us.'

The word 'slavery' is repeated 24 times. Any personal sly digs would not have gone down well at Sony/CBS Records housed on the aforementioned Soho Square. On one of Richey's personal tour itineraries from this period, next to a list of Sony's A&R men, we discover he has written across one page in large letters, 'Love: none! Care: none! C.B.S. = Cold Blank Stare.'

At Richey's instigation, each new Manics album came accompanied with a new visual aesthetic. Among his archived materials, we find that each of the first three albums has its own designated A4 folder, filled with scribbled notes. There are also numerous sketches for cover art concepts, all decorated with circular coffee-mug stains, burn-holes from cigarettes and more than a few splashes of blood.

The *Generation Terrorists* file had contained endless pages bursting with existential hellish boredom, ambition and anger, politics and passion. For *Gold Against the Soul* there was far less textual content. But what really stood out was the sheer volume of visual material, including cut-outs from magazines, newspapers and posters.

Sadie Frost, Ethan Hawke, Brian Jones, pages from the graphic novel *The Crow*, Emma Balfour, The Clash, Tom Jones, Christine Keeler, John Hurt, Red Hot Chili Peppers, Oldman playing Oswald in *JFK*, The Black Crowes, Nick Kent, Mia Farrow, Brad Pitt, Kate Moss, Linda Evangelista, James Dean, Elvis, Mickey Rourke, Ian Curtis and Brian Epstein feature among the pages and pages of cut-out images.

CHAPTER 7

Creating collages was one of Richey's favourite pastimes, but now the images were deliberately pasted and interwoven alongside his latest crop of lyrics and ideas. It arguably suggests he anticipated presenting the Manic Street Preachers as occupying the same cultural terrain as the most universal media icons of the age.

Those recipients of Richey's earlier, enlivening and politically motivated letters could have been excused for wondering whether he and the band had effectively sold out, and so soon.

'Is anyone out there angry?' asked the *NME*'s John Harris in a piece titled 'From Sneer to Maturity'.

Do you feel cheated by the fact that a band who once said their music would make 15-year-olds want to burn down banks are now dealing in existential introspection ...? You shouldn't be ... They were built on the flurry of myth-making that occurred during their first burst of interviews; when they created an alluring legend: ... the Manic Street Preachers were four working-class desperados who'd never left their home town ... Rock and roll was the only alternative to working in the local Pot Noodle factory, so they would steer their way to a major label contract, release one album and split up, returning to South Wales as self-created missing persons. What a story!

But Richey was still immersed in that story and the myth he had woven around himself as the main protagonist. In accusing the Manics of once having planned to become 'missing persons', John Harris was referring only to their insane, masochist game-plan to down tools after only one album. But had thoughts of suddenly and dramatically departing the scene in fact grown, and become more acute, in the mind of one of the band members? Weighed down with a deep desire to enter the pantheon of rock star immortality, Richey may not have let the idea die.

'Rebel. Rocker. Idol. Vanished.'
Tagline for *Eddie and the Cruisers*

113

The idea of the rock star vanishing in order to achieve immortal status wasn't an entirely original one. Twelve years before Richey's disappearance, the 1983 film *Eddie and the Cruisers* had already told the story of a 1960s rock and roll band and its lead singer, lyrical genius Eddie Wilson, who vanishes after a dispute with his record label over the band's second album.

Twenty years after his disappearance, television reporter Maggie Foley (played by Ellen Barkin) interviews the surviving band members to gain more insight into Eddie's mysterious disappearance. Believing she has uncovered the keystone to the entire puzzle, she resurrects the story by examining his references to the French poet Arthur Rimbaud. Maggie believes that by naming the album *A Season in Hell*, after Rimbaud's seminal work, Eddie was deliberately planting clues that he, like the poet, would also disappear, and survive in exile.

Rimbaud revolutionised poetry, and his legend would impact the rock and roll world, his life and works heavily influencing countless artists of a literary mindset, with Bob Dylan, Van Morrison and Patti Smith all namedropping the mythic poet who disappeared.

Although *Eddie and the Cruisers* doesn't make for easy viewing thanks to its clumsy script and the appalling lip-synching music performances, the film does try to capture the mechanics of rock mythology, and what it takes to gain immortal status in such a sphere. Both P.F. Kluge's 1980 novel upon which the film was based, and the portrayal of Eddie Wilson by actor Michael Paré, very blatantly drew much of their inspiration from an earlier and real-life concoction of the Rimbaud myth – that of the life and 'death' of the Doors front man, Jim Morrison.

Rumours of Morrison faking his own death and completing a successful vanishing act from Paris in 1971 have become part of his posthumous legend and helped immortalise him to rock god status, due in part to the 1980 Morrison biography *No One Here Gets Out Alive* by Jerry Hopkins and Danny Sugerman.

'Talking to a musical and literary aficionado like Richey, you knew he was well aware of the Morrison myth,' says Alan G. Parker. 'Not only had Richey read all the books, but most people on the rock scene were aware of the mystery surrounding Morrison's death and how there's been no official testament of anyone ever actually seeing his body. Not even Morrison's own family.'

'We have read all the books. But I think all the best bands have. I think
they've always been really aware of what's gone on in the past.'
Richey Edwards, *The Beat*, ITV, 1993

Throughout Richey's teenage years and up until the end of his time with the band, he referenced Rimbaud continuously, and would have been acutely conscious of elements of the poet's disappearance spilling over into rock and roll terrain. Despite Hopkins and Sugerman suggesting that Morrison had faked his own death, no rock star had yet officially been bestowed the status of 'missing in action'. Richey's mission statement was 'to do what no band had done before', and what better way to achieve that, maybe, than to leave fans and critics alike with a perpetual conundrum.

Neither alive or dead, neither existing or not existing, the idea of a man and his life as a question mark hanging in thin air becomes the perfect rock and roll fairytale all too worthy of legendary status.

With *Generation Terrorists* having fallen way short of the band's boastful plans, Richey had seemingly gone along with being reined in artistically, hoping at least to achieve proper mainstream success with *Gold Against the Soul*. And yet his perennial narrative, that an abrupt ending and accompanying inevitable immortality were just around the corner, continued unabated.

'We're under no illusions with this album,' he said. 'At some point people will stop listening. And when they do we'll know it's time to stop. It might well just happen with this album.'

Photos from mid-1993 show Richey holding a copy of a paperback book, peering over it suggestively to the camera, as though signalling its significance. Some light magnification reveals it to be Oscar Wilde's *The Picture of Dorian Gray*, the novel in which the title character fears losing his intense physical attractiveness as youth fades. To retain his good looks, he sells his soul, in a pact closely resembling the Faust legend.

Richey knew the power of Faustian mythology in Western culture, selling one's soul to the devil in exchange for new powers. Passed down through Marlowe and Goethe, it also famously plays a part in the mythology of blues music, and rock after that. When Richey flags up favourite novels like *Dorian Gray* or Bulgakov's *The Master and Margarita* based on the Faust legend, does he deploy them to help us decipher his difficult relations with the industry, as well as his final decision in early 1995?

Even the title *Gold Against the Soul* spoke to the Faust legend, which entered Blues mythology in the notorious story of singer Robert Johnson and his pact with the devil at a Mississippi crossroads. In the Johnson legend, he sells his soul for success; a trope since done to death by generations of musicians. While Richey's fellow band members were apparently more willing to accept the rules of the game, and to play it the industry's way, it soon became clear that Richey's spiritual stand-off with the devil in corporate dress would come to a head. 'Failing fills us with dread,' Richey confessed to *Select*. 'This album is the best thing we can do. If it fails, we deserve it, we'll be totally humiliated.'

Gold Against the Soul was released on 14 June 1993. However, after several subsequent months of touring and intensive publicity, it had fallen even flatter than its predecessor. And if Richey was experiencing humiliation, the last months of 1993 would conspire to test the strength of his personality to its very limits.

One contributing factor to his blackening mood came when Nicky Wire got married to Rachel Bartlett. Wire had played his part in the band's early rock 'n' roll indulgences and debaucheries, but he now called time on all that, setting the tone for much of his life in the years to come – domestic, routinised and conservative.

Richey knew his earlier closeness with Wire would never be recovered. The onus was now on him to catch up with his three bandmates and get a relationship of his own. His then 18-year-old sometime companion Jo was the likeliest candidate for that role. Yet a conversation she had with Rachel Edwards later revealed Richey's lingering attachment to Wire and the impact of the inevitable new distance between them. 'Jo said, "I can't explain why, but I think Richard was in love with Nick,"' remembers Rachel. 'Apparently, Richard was in a terrible state at the wedding, walking around the tables, picking up drinks and crying uncontrollably. I don't know if it's because he felt he was losing his closest friend, or if he felt in competition with Nick because he wasn't able to have that kind of close relationship with a partner.'

Terri Hall, wife of manager Philip, saw Richey openly boasting that he would not be left behind in the love stakes. Commenting on BBC2's *Close-Up* documentary, she said, 'Richey didn't know how to live and how to be happy. I remember him saying he was gonna be married by the end of the year. It was like, well, have you got a girlfriend, Richey? And he felt that, because me and Philip were happy, or his parents were happy, then – happiness, let's get married! I mean, there was no girlfriend.'

The fact that Terri Hall was at the time unaware of Richey's quasi-relationship with Jo spoke volumes. His failure to commit, due to his own sense of inadequacy, jealousy and a pessimistic view of monogamy, meant he kept Jo on the periphery throughout 1993.

Jo wrote to Rachel Edwards in the months after Richey vanished: 'He was terribly jealous of the others. Nick being married, Sean's girlfriend and James being a bit of a lad. He understood ideology, concepts, theory, philosophy completely, but when it came to his own feelings, his own thoughts, expressions, he couldn't cope.

'Emotionally immature isn't quite right because there was no logic to his feelings. He was convinced I was seeing every man I spoke to, even though he knew it was rubbish, but he could still manage to convince himself that the ridiculous was in fact the truth. I mean he could do it easily. I mean, you can tell yourself it's just self-pity, self-indulgence. I think he did genuinely feel worthless, just useless and no amount of persuasion could change his mind.'

Jo's letter echoes the sentiments which Richey had admitted to in his correspondence with Claire Forward during his university years: insecurity, envy and, most of all, inward resentment for feeling that way.

'Deep down he was really traditional,' recalls Claire, 'and I think if his insecurities exacerbated with age as they can with many people, I can imagine he would have felt trapped in a really lonely place. He used to be so shy and embarrassed talking about how he felt with me. It's hard to explain those kinds of feelings to people without them thinking you're possessive or controlling, which is why he must have felt so insecure and worthless, and needed that almost constant reassurance. It seemed Rich longed for a relationship but it could never live up to the expectations in his head.'

Shortly afterwards, one of Richey's closest school friends, Richard Fry, underwent a life-changing experience and came out as gay. He made the first efforts in some time to reach out to his old confidant.

'We'd been out of contact for four years, so I wrote Richey a letter. I don't even know if he received it as I didn't hear anything back, but Graham's attitude towards me changed ever since I put that letter through the bungalow door.'

Fry believes Graham Edwards found his news difficult to deal with. 'I was gay, and Graham was old-fashioned. After I came out in that letter, whenever I bumped into him in Blackwood, I didn't get a very good reception. Graham was always great with me before that, and I used to love going over to Richey's house. But Graham's not to blame in any way, shape or form; that's just the era he was brought up in. Graham was a man's man and I don't know how difficult that was for Richey when he was growing up.'

'I'm too much like my Mother. Too sensitive. Not enough like my Father.'
Richey notes, 1994

Fry last set eyes on his old friend a couple of months later, when he spotted Richey outside Virgin Records on Cardiff's Queen Street, signing autographs. 'I didn't speak to him; I was afraid of what reception I would get. At first I didn't recognise him because he had lost so much weight. That was the last time I ever saw him, and you always think – if this, and if that. It's the biggest regret I will ever have.'

Those surrounding him spotted how Richey's nerves were frazzled by the year's events. He was booked into a health farm that summer, accompanied by Martin Hall, who had become more involved in managing the band due to the increasingly poor health of his brother Philip. Among Richey's archive are photographs of the pair at the spa, including one as they sit in individual steam capsules. Enclosed up to their necks, we see only their half smiles, relaxed yet seemingly reluctant to be snapped.

Within a matter of months Martin and the band would be devastated by the tragic and untimely death of Philip. He was 34 years old. Philip Hall had guided the Manic Street Preachers to the kind of success their teenage selves should never have realistically expected. Through the last two years of his time with them, he had done it all while battling lung cancer; which was a testament to his commitment to them and the other artists he stewarded, but which placed significant weight on the Manics' conscience to repay his efforts with increasing sales.

The band's tours in the summer and autumn of 1993 promoted *Gold Against the Soul* across the UK and Ireland, Europe and Japan. On 7 December, they played what would be their last live show of the year, in Lisbon, and it was here that they heard that Philip had passed away.

In their tributes to him, the band acknowledged their manager's crucial role in their miraculous journey from provincial obscurity to a degree of mainstream success. On a professional level, Philip had been pivotal and indispensable – yet he was also their friend and mentor.

Philip's illness had already had a tangible emotional effect upon the band long before his death. At their 1992 Christmas concert in London, Nicky Wire had caused shock and outrage by wishing that recent rumours about R.E.M. front man Michael Stipe were true, and that he would die of AIDS. Wire's outburst betrayed his sense of injustice that one deadly disease garnered so much more public sympathy than the other.

'Philip was a very special person to us,' Richey told MTV. 'We spent maybe a year and a half writing letters, phoning journalists, any address or phone number we got, and there was never any response. Philip drove down to see us practise in a crappy little schoolroom in South Wales, and looked after us.'

Nicky Wire later pinpointed Hall's death as the start of a disastrous crisis year for the band, 'No one in my immediate family had ever died, so it was the first funeral I'd ever been to. He wasn't just a manager.'

Over Christmas 1993, Wire recognised the effects of recent events on Richey's fragile psyche. 'I felt he was the oldest and yet the youngest of us all. He'd only experience things by forcing himself into situations. He was quite immature in terms of what he'd experienced in life, never been in a relationship, things like that. So perhaps then I realised that he was beginning to feel emptier. No matter what I said, there was nothing I could do to make him feel better.'

Richey's family only learned much later that he had spent time at a health farm, and experienced difficulties throughout 1993. 'The first time he went to a health farm was the summer of that year when *Gold Against the Soul* was released,' says Rachel. 'The second time in December after Philip died. We thought he was away doing band-related things, so when we found out a year later he wasn't, it came as a surprise to us. I don't know if he felt he couldn't talk to us about going there because he didn't want to upset my mam and dad, or because he may have felt like he was failing with his career in music, and didn't want to admit it to anyone outside of the band's circle.'

Looking back on 1993, the band agreed something had been lost with *Gold Against the Soul*. It was, they admitted, an album made to please the record company. James Dean Bradfield said, 'I think we became bland. "La Tristesse Durera" sounded like a video storyboard. *Gold Against the Soul* was too song-y, there was no linear directive.'

If they feared they had sold out, it was arguably confirmed in September, when they played two shows supporting Bon Jovi at Milton Keynes Bowl. Richey would later comment, 'What definitely came out of [supporting] Bon Jovi was that our next album will be a complete artistic statement. I love *Gold Against the Soul*, but the next one will truly represent us. Whether that means fifty minutes of misery or complete and utter punk, we don't yet know.'

As 1994 dawned, it found the Manic Street Preachers hell-bent on steering clear of the compromises involved in trying to repay others' investments in them. January kicked off with some gigs around the UK, and the band's desire to ramp things up musically and lyrically was complimented by a new sartorial aesthetic. 'We went out of our way, going to every military surplus store in the country, just picking up little bits, so we could assemble our stage personas,' Sean later explained. 'We just picked up on bits of ideas we saw with The Clash and *Sandinista!* and tried to be really obvious about it.'

Donning actual uniforms felt to the Manics like an inspired return to their earlier all-white wardrobe splashed with spray-stencilled slogans. Nicky Wire would later remark, 'To have the security blanket of wearing those clothes and feeling really comfortable again in them – the inspiration of Echo & the Bunnymen and *Apocalypse Now*, that era – it was a massive release. We went to the *NME* Awards, and it was the height of Brit Pop; Damon was snogging Justine. And we were all in the corner, dressed like military outcasts. We just felt brilliant, we felt this is where we should be, looking really odd in the corner, but feeling utterly united.'

Publicly, it was a show of band solidarity, in what Sean Moore looks back upon as the 'Manic Street army/people's army' phase. And Richey's role in forging the new era was critical. James Dean Bradfield recalls, 'Richey had got his black sailor suit, and I remember going into an Army & Navy shop and seeing a white one. His looked really cool, so [I thought] I'll have the white one. And I think it pissed him off a bit.'

Of all the band members, Richey clearly harboured the greatest impatience with recent wrong turns. He led the way out of what seemed a careerist impasse and, as ever, forged ahead, setting the new style and content for the band's next (and defining) chapter.

'He has nothing left for his life but his prejudices.'
Oscar Wilde, *The Picture of Dorian Grey*
– quoted in Richey's notebook, 1994

On 5 April, Kurt Cobain committed suicide. The Nirvana front man's death was to have an indelible impact on the Manics, and on Richey in particular. A decade later, Nicky Wire looked back on the precise moment the news came through, and the inevitable links that he, and everyone else, was making between Nirvana and the Manics.

'Obviously we were huge fans as well. We were aware of every move within Nirvana that year, the constant breakdowns and the fuck-ups and everything. I remember we were in Britannia Row, which was where Joy Division recorded *Closer*, when we heard that Kurt Cobain had killed himself. We were mixing 'The Intense Humming of Evil', or some other really bleak track. It actually felt like a lot of connections were falling into place.'

In 1993 Richey had developed a new-found appreciation for 'grunge'. Previously meriting barely a mention by him, suddenly artists like Pearl Jam and Alice in Chains became firm favourites. He even described the latter as the modern answer to Joy Division. The Seattle bands became part of the Manic Street Preachers lexicon.

In a February 1994 interview, however, Richey's jealous resentment of the rise of Nirvana at the Manics' expense had surfaced. 'I wish Nirvana had split up after *Nevermind*. I wish Kurt had never had the child; it's like he's some sort of representative for American family values. There's not much difference between listening to Kurt now and listening to the wino down the street.'

If he was insinuating people ought to question Cobain's 'for-realness', the latter's suicide, just weeks later, bounced the ball back into Richey's court. The very fact that the Manics had given so much time and space to singing about, fantasising over and publicly praising the topic of suicide meant they felt obliged to react.

Richey may have intuited a public expectation that he should play catch-up with Cobain's death. Such phenomenal irrational pressure could not have arrived at a more dangerous time for his fragile mental state. Several sources have confirmed that early 1994 saw a marked increase in his drug taking, accompanied by a new development – a penchant for advising others to follow suit.

A former member of the Manic Street Preachers road crew who spoke to us anonymously for this book tried at first to whitewash the whole issue of drug taking within the band. 'There were never any drugs with *any* of them; at no point, never,' he told us. We reminded him that Richey's drug abuse had already been made public, the band admitting in 1994 that 'even Richey is spliffed out these days'. The crew member then confessed that Richey had been smoking the occasional joint during that year, to curb his alcohol intake and help him sleep. He then admitted having himself introduced Richey to cannabis in an effort to reduce his dependence on alcohol.

Yet smoking joints is ubiquitous in the music business, and does not equate with the disturbing talk of 'drug abuse' that whirled around Richey that year. Was he partaking in stronger substances? How would the rest of the band have felt, considering their very public condemnation of drug taking?

Two years after Richey's disappearance Nicky Wire told the *NME*, 'I find people who take drugs incredibly tedious. People don't seem to realise that their brains are being crushed day-by-day by it. They think they're really intelligent when you're talking to them and you're thinking, "Why don't you just shut up, you boring fucker! I don't want any of your fucking marijuana."

'It's just bad experiences [I've had] of being around people on drugs. I don't mind legalising them as long as no fucking cunt comes up to me and starts talking about being on drugs and how great it is and how it expands your mind when all it does is kill your little brain cells bit by bit.' Could these sentiments have reflected Wire's own experiences with Richey?

In March 1994, Richey moved out of his parents' bungalow in Blackwood to the burgeoning former dockside area of Cardiff. Once the second busiest port in the world, thanks to the coalmines of South

Wales, it had recently undergone a massive regeneration project which saw it transformed into 'Cardiff Bay' – with desirable new housing, cafés and hotels pushing out its previous inhabitants.

While driving past show homes on Schooner Way, Richey made an impulsive decision. 'I saw my flat one day, and I bought it the next, just like that,' he told *Melody Maker* in December 1994. 'I hadn't thought about it before. I was just passing by, and Nick said, "Oh, let's go and have a look at these," and I thought this is all right. I asked her how much it was, she told me, so I said, "I'll buy it."'

Rachel recalls how her brother put down a £10,000 deposit in cash. 'He told me that the estate agent looked at him wide-eyed, as if wondering, "Who the hell *is* this guy?" It was definitely an impulse buy, and something I think he felt he had to do at his age, rather than wanted to. He'd end up checking into the Marriott hotel down the street from him in Cardiff so he wouldn't feel so alone.'

Richey soon began to make new contacts on the streets of Cardiff. He was now living in Butetown, adjacent to the city's 'red-light district', and could step outside his apartment block and immediately find himself right in the capital's centre for violent crime, prostitution and drugs.

Rachel also tells us that after moving to the city, Richey began to frequent the newly opened Hippo Club, a nightclub situated just behind Cardiff Central Station, and a mere two minutes' walk from Richey's apartment. The Hippo was a dance club that drew in punters from across Wales, and had become notorious as allegedly *the* place to score a variety of drugs.

Richey would soon experience first-hand the potential dangers of moving in new and unfamiliar circles. The same roadie who sought to disperse any talk of illicit substances says that Richey told him about a very frightening incident. Not long after he had moved to his new apartment, Richey ventured out in the Docks area to hook up with some new contacts, intending to buy marijuana. He was unable to get away from his dealers, who put him in the back seat of their locked car – sandwiched between two men – and proceeded to drive around Cardiff with him for several hours.

At first glance, this could be no more than some Cardiff hard men going out and parading their local rock star around the area, perhaps to show off. Yet considering he disappeared mere months later, could the incident have sinister implications? The roadie says that Richey was frightened by the occurrence and had hinted heavily at something quite serious going on behind the scenes, yet had refused to say any more.

Could Richey have fallen foul of local drug dealers and, if so, could this be of possible significance to the disappearance? If nothing else it gives an insight into his state of mind during that year, with drugs and the threat of violence perhaps exacerbating his feelings of vulnerability and paranoia.

Richey's falling deeper into habitual drug taking seemed to clash hypocritically with 'Drug Drug Druggy', and the accusations made in the lyrics of the Manics' second album against the amorality of a sleaze-ridden music industry. The third album, *The Holy Bible*, was in the process of being written, and all signs suggested its dark subject matter would eclipse their earlier productions.

One of the few politically inflected barbs on *Gold Against the Soul* was a line in the title track about Thai labour. By early 1994, the band were in the middle of a surprising burst of popularity in Thailand. The *NME*'s Barbara Ellen flew out to cover the Manics as they played two nights in Bangkok.

The trip was the closest the Manic Street Preachers ever came to Beatlemania. However, it is also infamous as the moment Richey's personal crisis surfaced very publicly. With the band having set out their moral stall with lyrics lambasting the abuse of Thailand's working poor, the trip could be seen as a test of their integrity. Could they resist savouring the temptations offered to tourists by the fleshpots of the Patpong red-light district?

Richey's words and actions in Bangkok informed Barbara Ellen's notorious *NME* cover story ('Bangkok Sucker Blues', 28 May 1994). The Thai trip signalled a rupture between Richey and the other Manics; the first indicator perhaps of that later permanent split. In Ellen's account, every member of the Manics touring party (except Nicky Wire) enjoyed some of what Bangkok had to offer, including visits to sex bars. They were all intent on enjoying themselves. It has since passed into the orthodox retelling of Manics history that Richey went one step further, and was the only person who paid to go with a prostitute.

Two decades on, we spoke with people from inside the band's circle to gather further facts that may have been missing from the standard history. Some people recalled that Richey was becoming distanced from the band during the Thai trip. On the outgoing and return flight, while the rest of the party were socialising, he was tucked away at the back of the plane, estranged and alone.

Barbara Ellen arrived a day or two into the trip and had not been there on the day that Richey was alleged to have visited a prostitute. So, how had she learned of his transgression? Easy, Richey had told her himself, as they were about to board the plane home.

She wrote: 'Richey slides into the seat next to me, and with an awesome articulacy – considering he's drinking as heavily as everyone else – starts talking about what he sees as the misguided liberal snobbery aimed at Thailand. "All developing economies abuse their young. When Britain was a developing economy we sent our children up chimneys and down coalmines and out into the street to steal. This is just abuse on a wider scale."'

The whole debacle was an opportunity to share with *NME* readers something of the sordid truth of life in the music industry; and the way it enables well-off, middle-aged men to feed off the young. Taking the story to Bangkok was to witness the exploitative music industry in a fitting habitat.

Having so often described himself as asexual, Richey was apparently detached from what Bangkok had to offer, 'Very lame, it's a male fantasy island for an older generation. Just an opportunity for middle-aged businessmen to buy women and feel like studs again'.

The other members of the band were similarly un-enthralled, reported Ellen. 'James rests back in his seat, eyebrows arched, chuckling every now and then at the torrent of lad's talk spewing from the Cummins/ Stringer corner [*NME* photographer Kevin Cummins].' Her article would go on to describe record-label boss Rob Stringer as 'the living embodiment of capitalist evil', after he threatened her with libel lawyers several times during the trip. 'He was paranoid about his corporate identity,' James told *Kerrang!* later that year. 'He didn't want to get caught up in any of the seediness.'

Was Richey's confession a legitimate one, or was it a device to implicate others in the touring party? It could well have been both, but the effect created an uncomfortable distance between Richey and the band, and quite possibly between himself and those at the record company.

The trip to Bangkok had a huge impact on the band. Interviewed in 2014, Nicky Wire admitted, 'Then all that goodwill kind of collapsed when we went to Thailand, I think. You've only got to read [Barbara Ellen's] *NME* piece really, it's the best document of a band on the edge.' James concurred, stating, 'There was something about that whole tour that unleashed a symptom that felt incurable to me. I think in Thailand, there was a bit of a bad feeling among the band.'

After their final night playing to three thousand fans at Bangkok's Mah Boonkrong Hall on 23 April, *NME* photographer Kevin Cummins was witness to an incident that would not only demonstrate Richey's vulnerability but create one of the most startling and iconic images of him.

Cummins recalls: 'A fan sent some miniature ceremonial swords backstage before the gig with a note attached, asking Richey to slash himself onstage. He thought that was tacky. Towards the end of the show, James sang "Raindrops Keep Falling on My Head" solo and I went backstage to get some pictures of the rest of the band looking exhausted. I saw Richey looking at himself in the bathroom mirror [with his] chest slashed. I was shocked. I asked him why he did it and he said, "He asked me to. I didn't want to let him down."

'Some people ask me how I could have taken those photos. They were surface cuts, nothing more. A bit showmanship-esque to a degree. There are some things as a photographer I'd never have taken pictures of, Richey cutting 4 REAL into his arm for example. I would have taken him straight to hospital. I'm not a war photographer, I'm a myth-maker, and I believe he had some control of what he was doing at the time. But, sometimes in a band people get lost, and I think Richey was a little lost in the way he navigated the adult world.'

'Everyone wants me to chop up my arm on stage. It's just like they're waiting for a car crash to happen. What a shit thing to be remembered for.'
Richey, letter to Jo from Bangkok, 1994

Richey's letters to Jo were chaotic, angst-ridden adolescent rants, reflecting inner turmoil. This was a contrast with Nicky Wire, who acknowledges that the once inextricably close friends had drifted apart. 'I was in quite a happy place, at the time. I had got married, just bought this little house. I had been living with my in-laws up until then. So, I had no problems at all with Richey writing probably 75 per cent of the lyrics. The references he was coming up with as well; I don't pretend to even know half of them. He was reading five books a week. I was still stuck on [Yorkshire cricketer] Fred Trueman's autobiography or something. I just wasn't on my game so much.'

Wire's relaxed, debonair mood contrasted dramatically with Richey's encroaching life-or-death crisis, as shown by the latter's comments to MTV: 'The last album was called "mature", which is something that I find difficult to live with. But I guess it was. I mean, the older you get, the more life becomes miserable. Definitely. All the people you grow up with die. Your parents die, your grandparents die, your dog dies; your energy diminishes. You just end up a barren wasteland, trying to find something new; which never really occurs.'

Further compounding Richey's bleak post-Bangkok mood, an urgent phone call from Graham Edwards informed him that his close univer-sity friend had committed suicide. Suffering with the pain of unrequited love, Nigel Bethune was in London when he took his own life.

'Nick told me that Richard was in absolute awe of Nigel doing what he did,' says Rachel. 'He was upset about it but also carried a deep admiration for the fact someone he knew could do something so powerful. Nick said it was almost like Richard was jealous that Nigel had the guts to do something like that.'

'All my life I have had the utmost admiration for suicides.
I have always considered them superior to me in every way.'
Thomas Bernhard, *Gathering Evidence*, 1985

Nigel's suicide contributed to Richey's dark and devastating 1994. The impact is confirmed in letters that Rachel received from Nigel's sister after Richey's disappearance. With Nigel and Richey both gone from their lives, Emma Bethune and Rachel got together for an emotional meeting in London. Rachel brought along photos of the two boys, previously unseen by Nigel's family, some of which are reproduced in this book. It also emerged that, on hearing of his friend's death, Richey wrote a heartfelt letter to the Bethune family, his devastation all too clear.

Nigel's suicide, after a perceived rejection, entrenched Richey's own deeply ingrained trepidation about the lethal instability of love. With his one-time ally in the 'Anti-Love' pact, Nicky Wire, now firmly bedded down in domestic bliss, Richey may have felt pressure to prove he was capable of something serious and lasting. Nigel's death had Richey focus on the closest thing he had to a proper partnership. But the forecast for any possible future with his on-off girlfriend Jo was unpromising.

'Trust me [are] two of the most frightening words
brought together. Like hands up or look out.'
Richey's archive, 1994

A member of the Manics' road crew recalled Richey continuously warning him off talking to Jo. 'He had massive trust issues when it came to the people he was meant to be close with. He pleaded with me not to try and shag her. She was too important to him.'

In a letter that Richey sent to Jo from Thailand, he responded to Jo's attempts to allay some of his paranoid fears that were throttling their relationship. '"Say what you mean." I know you always say that to me. Tell me. Listen. I am not hiding a dark secret. I just can't cope with even simple things. You are the first person I've met who I believe (not think – BELIEVE – important difference here) I can trust implicitly. But I find it hard, so hard to reconcile that with what goes on in my head. I respect you, I love you, I love every millimetre of your flesh, your beauty. Your beauty. I cannot understand why you would talk to me / stay with me / be faithful to me. I don't know anything.'

After the death of Philip Hall, the events in Bangkok and Nigel's suicide, Richey's fraught emotions reached peak sensitivity, heightening his sense that he might never overcome his jealousies and form a lasting relationship. One badly timed insult to his fragile state was all it might take to push him past the brink.

Two months after his return from Bangkok, Richey was back home in his Cardiff apartment when Jo phoned him from Italy, where she was holidaying. She told Rachel later, 'Speaking to him, he didn't seem all there. He sounded like he was in another dimension.'

As with his previous girlfriend, Claire Forward, Richey's intense jealousy was sparked by the slightest hint of something going on between the object of his affection and other men. With Jo so far from home, nothing could help Richey's deteriorating state of mind. Her efforts to phone him over the following weeks met with no answer – either he was refusing to pick up, or something was seriously wrong.

'Then I spoke to Graham,' says Jo. 'He sounded so cagey; he just said Richard was unwell and his nerves were "shot to pieces". Right that second, I knew it was serious, something awful. I thought he was probably dying.'

Chapter 8

Negative Capability

'I no longer see people. I see only blood and guts wrapped in soft skin.
The kind of men who marry girls who can't speak their language.
Why can't I think of nothing, instead of all these stupid things.'
Richey's archive, Priory notes, 1994

Inspecting Richey's 1994 address book, most of the entries are of friends, family and music business contacts, plus some female acquaintances. Pasted across the opening two pages are images cut from an unknown graphic novel.

A man in white shorts is slumped over a wash basin in a squalid bedsit apartment. A group of his friends burst open the door and find the room spattered with blood. 'Marty?' A girl picks up a piece of paper. 'Look, he left a note. Listen to this. "There's Nothing Left!" On the next image, another friend enters a bathroom, where they find a message has been scrawled in huge red letters across a mirror: 'It's Not Funny Anymore'.

Above these comic-book images, someone has scrawled down an instruction: 'Don't bother with the X's.' It is not Richey's handwriting but that of Lizzy Gould, former secretary at Hall or Nothing Management. She used the address book in 1995 to ring his contacts in the hope of finding some clues. Names marked with an X – of which there are plenty – are those already spoken to, who came up with nothing.

It is uncertain whether Richey pasted the pictures into his address book before or after his mental collapse. But they are another example of his propensity for viewing even the most harrowing moments in his life in terms of their narrative potency. Unlike earlier obviously private address books, this last one has aspects that seem to anticipate it one day having an audience. The illustrated scenes depict a possible analogous representation of a most fateful episode in Richey's life – his suicide attempt in the summer of 1994.

Until now, many have doubted whether Richey had ever actually tried to end his life, but when Rachel hands us a copy of a thin, worn paperback book, inside the front cover is Richey's brief and matter-of-fact farewell note. Addressed to nobody in particular, it reads: 'No music to be played. Only immediate family to come (includes band & Jo & Dan). Maybe a poem – Tulips by Sylvia Plath. I LOVE YOU. I'M SORRY I JUST NEEDED TO FEEL SOMETHING MORE.'

The slim volume in which Richey penned these parting words was a 1984 Penguin edition of Sir Peter Shaffer's 1973 play, *Equus*. It tells the story of a psychiatrist who attempts to treat a conflicted adolescent boy with a pathological and religious fascination with horses. Dr Martin Dysart sets out to cure the teenager, but questions whether the treatment might have the effect of crushing the child's passion and individuality in later life. The play's main themes deal with modern society and its expectations of normality, together with repression's role in the cause of madness.

'He'll be delivered from madness. What then? He'll feel himself
acceptable! What then? Do you think feelings like his can be simply
re-attached, like plasters? Stuck on to other objects we select? Look
at him! My desire might be to make this boy an ardent husband –
a caring citizen – a worshipper of abstract and unifying God.
My achievement, however, is more likely to make a ghost!'
Dr Martin Dysart in *Equus*, Sir Peter Shaffer

On the afternoon of the 18 July, Richey phoned his mother and confessed that he'd done something he might regret. His parents immediately sped down from Blackwood to his dockside flat in Cardiff Bay.

They discovered his apartment in total disarray. Empty drink bottles, rubbish strewn across the floor and graffiti daubed all over the plain white walls, most of it pertaining to the recently deceased Kurt Cobain (Graham later had to re-paint the walls white). Richey was lying in a bath filled with cold water, coloured by the blood seeping out of his forearms. On the edge of the bath rested a block of cannabis and an empty vodka bottle.

In terms of a musician's rock 'n' roll breakdown, this scene draws instant analogies with the cult film *Pink Floyd – The Wall*. The 1982 musical drama centres on Pink, a troubled rock star who suffers a breakdown in his hotel room during an episode of heightened mania. Having sunk into a depressed and dissociative state, Pink loses his mind as the film progresses, and his inevitable collapse results in the band's manager and paramedics breaking down the hotel door to revive him, just in time for his next performance. Richey had his own copy on VHS, the synopsis on the back reads:

The movie tells the story of rock singer 'Pink' who is sitting in his hotel room in Los Angeles, burnt out from the music business and only able to perform on stage with the help of drugs. Based on the 1979 double album *The Wall* by Pink Floyd, the film begins in Pink's youth where he is crushed by the love of his mother. Several years later, he is punished by the teachers in school because he is starting to write poems. He slowly begins to build a wall around himself to be protected from the world outside. The film shows all this in massive and epic pictures until the very end where he tears down the wall and breaks free.

Graham and Sherry took Richey immediately to Cardiff's A&E unit, at that time situated at the Royal Infirmary five minutes away. Because Richey was still under the influence of cannabis and vodka, the doctors could not assess him. Concerned about letting him go back to his flat alone, they allowed him to spend the night at his parents' in Blackwood providing he returned the following morning for assessment.

Rachel was then living and working in Cardiff and the next day she joined Richey and her parents in the infirmary waiting room. 'The first thing I thought was that he didn't look like himself,' she says. 'He was dishevelled and his hair was unkempt. It was long, matted and curled under at the back. He wasn't making much eye contact but I noticed the hair in between his eyebrows that he used to shave had grown. He had tears in his eyes but he wasn't crying. He just seemed totally impenetrable, like everything had become so deeply internalised that he didn't even try to speak.'

> *'If a goldfish has a five second memory and it takes the fish 60 seconds*
> *to suffocate out of water – does the poor goldfish think he/she*
> *has spent its entire life gasping for air? La tristesse durera –*
> *this sadness will last forever???'*
> Richey's archive, 1993

Richey was called in to see the consulting psychiatrist. Rachel doesn't know what was said in the room, but when the family were called in an hour later, they were told that Richey was suffering from severe depression, he needed serious medical attention, and he had agreed to be voluntarily hospitalised on the psychiatrist's recommendation. There was a space immediately available at Whitchurch Hospital, an NHS psychiatric institution in the suburbs of Cardiff.

For people across South Wales, the word 'Whitchurch' has long signified more than just a northern area of their capital city. It conjures up its infamous mental hospital and generations of rumour and gossip. For many, the threat of being 'sent to Whitchurch' was enough to rein in eccentricities or bad behaviour in children and adults alike.

In Edwardian red brick, dominated by the instantly familiar green copper-domed water tower, the hospital's Gothic structure was known to anyone in Cardiff – and conjured up all the worst suppositions of what went on inside. Straitjackets? Electric shock treatments? Padded cells? Welsh novelist Trezza Azzopardi wrote about the hospital in *The Hiding Place*, in which the young protagonist views the Whitchurch of the 1960s with terror, and many who faced confinement there feared never seeing the light of day again. By the 1990s, the hospital's daunting reputation had scarcely improved.

'The place was renowned in the Valleys when we were growing up,' says Rachel. 'It was quite foreboding, because you'd hear people saying "They'll end up in Whitchurch!" if someone was acting a bit strange or out of character. It was a bit like when people mentioned the Bedlam of old.'

Rachel and her parents drove Richey to the hospital on the outskirts of Cardiff. 'He cried on the way there,' remembers Rachel. 'He sat in the back seat just looking out of the window forlornly. We couldn't get any sense out of him.'

He was admitted to Whitchurch on 19 July, walking into the hospital with the support of his family. 'It was a crumbling red-brick building with a really haunted feel about it,' remembers Rachel. 'The corridors seemed to go on forever, they were long but claustrophobic. The décor was cracked, all peeling paint and echoing voices. Richard was shivering despite it being summer because it was such an old, cold place.'

Richey was soon checked into a mixed sex ward on W1A – a long room with 25 beds, and only a thin curtain separating each for privacy. He would later tell the music press about his time in Whitchurch. 'I think NHS hospitals are people banging off the walls in long corridors. Long, endless corridors. In communal wards, nobody sleeps. They can give you as many drugs as they want, but the noises in there are pretty horrendous. Then the next day, you wake up, have your drugs and sit in a big communal room, and you hardly see any fucker. And then you just, if you're like me, try to keep out of everybody's way. Know your place. Don't get in anybody's shadow.'

'It was horrible,' James told *Select* magazine. 'People have got this strangely romantic Cuckoo's Nest image. It's not even that disciplined, it's just a floatation tank for people who can't cope. They're in stasis, in limbo, kept stable with doses.'

Rachel recalls Richey's frustration at the time. 'Every visit I made he'd say the same thing: "All they do is come around on drug runs and tell me to loosen up." He said there was nobody there to talk to, and a few of the nurses even told him to go and see the new Flintstones film so he could "cheer up" and "have a laugh", which obviously didn't go down well with him.'

Marginally more constructive was one nurse's suggestion that Richey read a book, *Depression and How to Survive It* (1994) by comedian Spike Milligan and the popular television psychiatrist Anthony Clare. 'I went into town and bought that book on his asking,' says Rachel. 'I took it back to him and remember looking at the cuts on his wrists and saying, "You must be in so much pain," and he snapped back that it was nothing compared to the pain he was feeling on the inside.

'I think Richard identified with Milligan because they were both so sensitive to everything. In the book Milligan is described as skinless and a lot of things that wouldn't concern others would end up really worrying him. At the time, Richard was engulfed by worry and anxiety, and didn't seem to have the ability to cope with even the smallest of problems, let alone the bigger ones.'

During Richey's more lucid moments he continued with the artwork and upcoming promotional material for the Manics' next album, *The Holy Bible*. 'He was still working despite being in hospital,' recalls Rachel. 'He was making phone calls to the album designer and re-arranging lines ready for the printed lyric sheets. We kept telling him to take a break because he didn't need the stress, but he was a perfectionist when it came to his work. He just couldn't switch off or relax. It was like he fluctuated between two states – being flat and depressed or being anxious and depressed.'

James Dean Bradfield said in an interview to *Melody Maker* at the time of Richey's hospitalisation: 'Richey never had as many setbacks as a kid as me, he's more acutely intelligent than me, he's more beautiful than me and yet he has more problems. Problems that I'd just snip off with f***ing scissors in two seconds flat really get to Richey. A misprint on a lyric sheet, or whatever, would just upset him so much.'

'Last time I went to Cardiff I saw the drunks outside the market.
I heard lipstick girls saying "That's disgusting." I did not see the same
thing. I saw a victim of society, I see my responsibility, I accept the blame.
I spend hours asking myself why, why, why and then, then I spent
hours asking myself why those girls didn't care?'
Richey, letter to Claire Forward, 1988

'He was overly idealistic,' remembers pen pal Alistair Fitchett. 'Very much so, and I feel Richey perhaps could never have gotten to the stage where he could overcome this almost adolescent-like idealism when it came to the ways of the world.'

'So you'd rather know the truth and be mad?
No, I just want the truth to be different.'
Richey's archive, Priory notes, 1994

'I've never thought about this until recently, but ever since his adolescence Richard was always referencing *One Flew over the Cuckoo's Nest, Suddenly Last Summer, Betty Blue*, and films about mental patients and institutions,' remembers Rachel. 'Was his hospitalisation a self-fulfilling prophecy? Was it a statement he felt he had to make to go in tandem with the album?

'He admired people like Yukio Mishima, who put themselves in every possible situation they could, no matter how extreme, just to participate in as much of the unknown life as they could. I wonder if Richard felt he needed to experience those kinds of situations for himself.

'Even though he could identify with the sadness and desperation that drew him to those books, films and individuals, by 1994 his sense of self and his identity were so shattered that these could have influenced him further, in ways he wasn't even consciously aware of.'

While writing *The Holy Bible*, Richey read a biography of the French philosopher Michel Foucault. One of the chapters was called 'Archives of Pain', which became the title of one of the album's tracks. He would also tape a BBC documentary about the controversial author, wherein Foucault stated an artist's life and work should always be judged separately and the work must stand alone on merit, and be as far removed as possible from the life the artist lived.

'Whether or not Richard felt he should or even could separate the two, I honestly don't know,' says Rachel. 'But I do wonder what kind of pressure he felt to prove the very real depression and pain he was suffering to the outside world, especially to the music press that had him under a microscope after Kurt Cobain's death.'

A physical examination in Whitchurch recorded details of the self-inflicted lacerations from Richey's suicide attempt, described by the doctors as 'superficial wounds'. This verdict was surprising news for Rachel, and immediately invites the question: was it more of a cry for help?

'One doctor's opinion on superficial wounds could completely differ from the next doctor's opinion,' says Rachel. 'Because of the scale of Richard's self-harm in the past, and the depth of the cuts he'd made through the years – especially the 4 REAL incident – I don't know if the medical staff were judging them by those previous standards. But Richard knew his self-harm was escalating, and he admitted he no longer had any control over it. He definitely needed some kind of intervention.'

The routine in Whitchurch for patients like Richey consisted of the sleeping ward being emptied at 8am and the patients herded into one big communal room. They were allowed back to their beds at 10pm. Other than a table for tea and coffee, a television and the opportunity to interact socially with fellow inmates, there was little on offer that was conducive to helping with Richey's state of mind at the time. Breakfast, lunch and dinner punctuated the day, together with breaks for medication, and visitors twice daily. Patients could walk the grounds with staff, and some, depending on the severity of their illness, could enter the nearby village, to browse in the local shops.

A young psychiatric nurse who was working on the ward at the time, and who recognised Richey Manic, gave us his recollections. Understandably limited in what he could say, and necessarily anonymous here, he remembers Richey as an isolated and lonely figure, even by Whitchurch standards.

'He would sit alone and keep himself to himself most of the time,' he says. 'We had one patient on the ward who was prone to "acting out". He'd tip over coke machines and knock over the tea and coffee tables and could get quite violent within what were the very small surroundings of the communal area.

'I remember this happening twice, and both times Richey's eyes locked on mine and it was a stare like "What the HELL am I doing here?" He was one of the more fluid ones, who'd be able to bear witness to what was happening around him.'

Richey made one friend during his time on the ward. A female in her early twenties, who was 'quite mysterious. A dark-haired, dark-eyed girl – very quiet, very beguiling,' remembers the nurse. 'She was an artist and an academic, and if he'd go out for a smoke she'd go with him and they seemed to get on.'

This girl later moved to Israel. It may be telling that before the fateful trip to America that Richey never made in 1995, he told Rachel that he would much rather visit Israel.

In a 2009 interview, James related how Richey would speak of 'token gestures of insanity' during his hospitalisation, and how he was tempted to start 'hiding in bushes, barking orders, putting an éclair on his head, and talking to an imaginary giraffe' in order to be able to get the treatment he felt he needed.

Later that year, when speaking to the music press, Richey described Whitchurch as a place with little funding and scant resources. He also sought to clarify his emerging reputation as rock's next doomed poet, and turned the attention away from himself to highlight the plights that others using the facilities were facing.

'The Cardiff hospital was no good for me. After eight days in there, I didn't know what the fuck was going on. James will tell you, I couldn't even talk, I was just stuttering. I was taking medication – Librium and stuff. Though it calmed me down, because I could get to sleep at night.

'I mean … a lot of letters I've got have said, "Oh, it's natural, it always happens to poets." Which is fucking bullshit. When you're in the places I've been in, the first place especially, it's just any job, any occupation. Housewife, bricklayer, plumber, somebody who works for South Wales Electricity Board, whatever.

'It's very romantic to think, "I'm a tortured writer," but mental institutions are not full of people in bands. They're full of people with so-called normal jobs. Sixty-eight thousand beds have been closed down in the last couple of years, which I wouldn't have been aware of unless I was actually in one.'

Richey's erratic state of mind was evident in Whitchurch. During one of James's visits, he offered to leave the band. The two discussed what would be best for him and what would aid his recovery. They agreed Richey could contribute artwork and lyrics without the stress of being a performing member – much like how he had begun.

Richey waved James off at the hospital doorway. Yet, by the time James arrived back in Blackwood, Richey was on the phone in fits of tears saying he'd changed his mind, he wanted to stay a full member of the group in every aspect.

'I don't know if he was testing the waters in terms of if the band would carry on without him,' deliberates Rachel. 'He used to point out to Jo after he came out of hospital how Joy Division could just carry on without Ian Curtis, as if he was so easily forgettable and replaceable. He felt really useless, and I think he was testing others' opinions to see if they felt the same.'

Richey was to tell the *NME*, 'It's not enough for me to do the words. I kind of think I'd be cheating on them 'cos the touring part is the worst bit, the bit that no band really enjoys. It's the thing that makes it feel like a job because you know what you'll be doing in three months' time at two o' clock in the afternoon.'

Yet despite Richey's professed animosity towards life on the road, he clung to it. He would often say the band was all he had. At the time of his hospitalisation Richey wasn't in contact with Jo. His desire to build the perfect relationship, coupled with his insecurities and jealousies, meant the two broke off contact only days before his arrival at Whitchurch.

Band manager Martin Hall visited Richey at the hospital. After seeing him spaced out on meds, he made arrangements to move him somewhere he hoped would prove more beneficial. On 28 July, Richey moved to the world-famous Priory Hospital in Roehampton, south-west London.

An ornate Grade 2 listed white Gothic mansion just north of Richmond Park, the Priory could not be more different from the dark, provincial Whitchurch. Indeed, one tabloid described it as 'The Savoy spliced with Broadmoor'.

It is known as a place where celebrities confess their sins, purge themselves of the excesses of their lives and publicly press the restart button. Stars who have crossed its threshold include Kate Moss, Amy Winehouse, George Best and Robbie Williams. Richey's hero, Rolling Stone Brian Jones, had repeatedly checked in. When Richey entered the Priory in the summer of 1994, there were already several well-known faces in situ there.

'I exist to worship the past, dead poets and Brian Jones. Icons are my anchor. My only chain of reference. My one constant love. I could travel anywhere. I could have any habit I choose. But I don't. I just sit and stare/ alone. I entered a paper chase. It led to burnt books – and a dead end.'
Richey's archive, Priory notes, 1994

The Priory is often mistaken for an exclusive health spa but in reality it is a serious psychiatric clinic, top of the range and with the price tag to prove it. In 1994 a day's stay would cost £310. It treats a number of disorders, including anorexia, alcoholism, drug addiction, severe mood disorders, and a variety of other complex cases, of which Richey was one.

Presenting with symptoms of self-harm, low weight and non-dependent use of alcohol and substances, he was placed in the Galsworthy Lodge Addiction Treatment Unit, an annexe adjacent to the main building. There he began their strict six-week regimen.

On entering the building, patients are frisked for contraband items, with even mouthwash removed for its small alcoholic content. Automatically each inductee is obliged to undergo three days of cold turkey withdrawal from whatever substance they were abusing. Richey was able to forego that part of the process, having already been alcohol and drug free in Whitchurch for eight days. It was mandatory that he should sign up to the Alcoholics Anonymous Twelve Steps programme. He also had to take a 60mg dose of fluoxetine (Prozac) daily. This is the maximum recommended dosage, and is normally prescribed in the hope that it will improve the patient's mood sufficiently to motivate them to begin eating again.

Each week, a daily schedule was drawn up to occupy the patients' time from 8.30 in the morning until 9.30 at night. Along with group therapy and private counselling, the Priory offered more alternative occupational therapies including classes in yoga, drama and flower arranging. Unlike Whitchurch, the patients were given some semblance of personal privacy with an en suite room of their own, and the luxury of an onsite swimming pool and gym.

However, according to ex-patients, spending too much time alone or immersed in activities outside the suggested daily routine was generally frowned upon. Galsworthy Lodge residents were expected to work, eat and live together, and aid each other's recovery as part of a collective group process.

A couple of the names found in Richey's last address book were of people he befriended at the Priory. One was journalist Rosie Dunn. She now specialises in real-life crime stories and tales of survival, and has written books on the murdered Liverpool toddler James Bulger and, more recently, the publicly executed soldier Lee Rigby.

Rosie was an in-patient at the Priory and attended the same daily therapies as Richey. Then Crime Editor at the *Sun*, her work involved hanging out with some of Britain's biggest gangsters, and inevitably necessitated late nights and considerable heavy drinking, which led to her eventual alcoholism. Richey was admitted days after her arrival.

'He was just this skinny, tiny, fragile-looking little lad, with a white T-shirt and a man-bag across his chest,' she remembers. 'Drainpipe jeans and converse pumps. He was just so sweet-looking, with these huge Bambi brown eyes. He was like a little baby brother that I wanted to look after.

'I had absolutely no idea that he was part of this really huge cult band. I didn't know he was famous, I didn't know he was a rock star. When I asked him, "So, what do you do?" he said, "I'm a musician" and didn't elaborate further.'

With only a year between them, the two became firm friends and were to keep in touch up to Richey's disappearance.

'He loved what I did for a living,' says Rosie. 'He thought it was fantastic that I was a girl, who wrote about crime for the *Sun*. He was the famous one, but he always wanted to hear my stories. Many people are snobbish about red-top papers, but he didn't have a snobbish bone in his body.

'For someone so highly intelligent and literary, it wouldn't have surprised me if he had been somewhat uppity about the paper, but he loved that my writing could reach so many people. So to wind up in a hospital with a crime reporter with all this juicy gossip was heaven for him.'

All patients on the Galsworthy programme started the day by taking medication and reading motivational material to prepare them for the day ahead. At 10am, a group of ten to fifteen patients would meet for their group therapy session, and everyone would spend a few minutes reflecting on their current mood and thought process.

'Group therapy was always quite highly strung,' confirms Rosie. 'It was the time of day where you go in and you're supposed to get off your mind what's going on inside. The whole point of getting better is not to get angry or emotional and then to turn to a substance to make you feel better. It's about reaching out to fellow people who understand, and expressing yourself so that you don't feel the need to go and anaesthetise it.

'Sometimes there were fights. People would even throw chairs at each other. You've got a lot of creative, emotional people, who are coming off various substances, and they've all got a lot to say. In many respects, a lot of people were vulnerable and fragile, but a lot of them also had a core of steel running through them.

'Richey was always very outspoken in terms of what he felt needed to be said. He could get quite angry, there was a lot of fire in his belly, but I remember the first time I saw him shout at another person – I was like "Wow! Go Richey, go!" I didn't know he had it in him.'

During his time at the Priory, Richey took a personal dislike to a retired ex-army captain who he felt was macho and repressed. The two would often get into heated discussions. It came out in group therapy that Richey felt uncomfortable with the man because he reminded him of his father.

'He loved his dad dearly, there was no question about that, but he felt frustrated that he never expressed his feelings properly,' says Rosie. 'He told us about the time he heard his dad crying through the walls when his nan died, and how he just couldn't get to grips with the fact that men had to be so macho and weren't supposed to express their feelings. That was such a huge frustration for him, and I think it left him very confused in terms of how to react emotionally to certain situations.'

After the morning session, Richey and Rosie would often walk down to the old chapel in the main building. Sometimes they would be joined by a well-known singer, who was also undergoing the same treatment. The three would sit alone, and the singer would sing hymns and prayers to the empty space. 'Once the singer sang "Ave Maria",' remembers Rosie, 'and we sat there listening in awe. It was a spine-tingling, goosebumps all over moment for me and something I'll remember until the day I die.'

The singer wrote Richey a letter which starts: 'NEVER be ashamed of your Tenderness. Nor of what you had to do to cover it up. We all have man AND woman inside us. What's wrong in the world is that people have lost contact with the feminine.' They also enclosed books with the letter, saying 'My favourite poem in the whole world is "Emerging from Childhood". The first poem in the book. It's by a man called Khayapati – or something [Vidyapati] – it's to DIE for (Don't take that literally, ha ha!)'

One of the books the singer mailed Richey after leaving the Priory remains in his family's possession, and is a copy of *Sacred Sex: Erotic Writings from the Religions of the World* by Robert Bates (1993). Richey's copy has the corners of several pages turned down, drawing attention to poems related to disappearance. In the chapter titled 'Islam', verses about slipping into madness and wandering the world as a nomad are highlighted.

Both of them rebellious, sensitive, wounded, angry, androgynous, and brutally truthful – it should not be a surprise that Richey and the singer made friends at the Priory, and kept in touch afterwards, with the singer apparently retaining an interest long after his disappearance.

Could it be that this singer brought into Richey's world a very pertinent text at that susceptible time? Certainly, some of the material could be read as having the alchemical potential to take what he felt were his deepest problems, and transform them into the basis of divine wisdom in the universe.

All patients on the Galsworthy programme had to attend an evening AA meeting three times a week for the duration of their stay. A minibus transported them to the Priory's sister buildings in nearby Chelsea and Richmond, where groups of 15 to 20 patients met to speak about their alcohol dependency. They would also hear from fully rehabilitated ex-addicts who acted as group mentors.

It's well known that, for Richey, the hardest part of his treatment was the Alcoholics Anonymous Twelve Steps programme. It is frequently accused of having religious connotations, with confession and restitution at its commandment-like core. At the end of each meeting, members are expected to recite the AA 'serenity prayer', and vow to 'keep coming back' to help them recover. James Dean Bradfield described Twelve Steps as a 'quasi-religion', with Richey struggling to get past the second step: 'handing your power over to a God of your own understanding'.

When Richey had left the Priory, *NME* journalist Stuart Bailie told him that Happy Mondays singer Shaun Ryder used an image of his nan in step two to represent 'God'.

'Lots of people have said things like that,' replied Richey. 'But I could never pick things like that because they would die. How can you reconcile yourself to a living god like that? Some people take their cats or their dogs as their god, but I think that's nonsensical, because your god is not gonna die on you. The closest I can get to it is nature probably, but then nature is very cruel.

'Step one is fairly easy: to admit you are powerless over your addiction and your life has become unmanageable. Well, it's easy to *admit*, it's hard to accept in your own mind. Because I do feel my mind's quite strong. Obviously not as strong as it could be. It's just a question of working it all out, and I've got a lot of time on my hands, so I can think about it.'

Richey did think about it, and in the Priory kept an A4 folder that documented his wariness about the Twelve Steps process and other matters. Its many dense pages capture a mind hurtling towards a deep existential crisis, fast losing faith in all around him.

'The bottom line is doubt,' James Dean Bradfield would say in 2009. 'When you're a teenager it's all about nihilistic anger and then that anger turns to disgust, and the big hurdle is what does that disgust turn into? And for him, I think it just turned into doubt on every level: personally, politically, idealistically, whatever. This was the first time I became aware of perhaps how Richey failed to deal with things. He didn't have any perspective. His anger turned into disgust, turned into just doubt. And that left him flailing.'

CHAPTER 8

'And new philosophy calls all in doubt,
The element of fire is quite put out,
The sun is lost, and the earth, and no man's wit
Can well direct him where to look for it.'
John Donne, 'An Anatomie of the World'
– quoted in Richey's Priory notes, 1994

'It was an intellectual crisis. Not in a highfalutin sense, but in the sense of a total collapse of the mind in terms of not having faith in any kind of belief system,' says Rachel. 'Although he was reading a lot, and taking everything in around him, his thoughts were scattered. He'd lost faith in what knowledge, thoughts and sensations were real to him and nothing held any true essence for him any more.

'He was exploring everything and came to no conclusions. When you look at people he quoted like Camus, who used to argue that the only question worth asking in life was whether to kill yourself or not – it seemed like Richard too was seriously deliberating the futility of everything around him.'

'Then came human beings. They wanted to cling but
there was nothing to cling to.'
Albert Camus
– quoted in the music video for 'Love's Sweet Exile', 1991

In Jo's letters to Rachel she recalls Richey's fascination with suicide: 'He always talked about it. We would always argue about it, he would always justify it, we spent hours arguing over it. It's hard to explain but if I talked about getting old he'd just say, "Oh, I'll either live until I'm over seventy or I'll kill myself."

'It wasn't said dramatically or childishly, or like he was trying to provoke, but just matter of fact. I mean, you can tell yourself that it's just self-pity, self-indulgence. I think he genuinely felt worthless, just useless, and no amount of persuasion would change his mind. He said it was the only act of free will.'

In February 1994, Richey gave an interview to a Sheffield local radio station, which highlighted his deteriorating state of mind prior to his hospitalisation. It was later transcribed by the fanzine *Counter Language*, and has since gained a reputation among Manics fans as being the bleakest interview of Richey's career.

By then, he could no longer reconcile the outside world with his own interior worldview. The interview shows him discrediting moral values, disproving vast beliefs and punishing himself with his unflinching commitment to life's harsh truths. 'I think Richard had stripped back life to such a degree that everything seemed futile,' says Rachel. 'He was suspending his judgement on a lot of fundamental things, not just in terms of morals and ethics, but becoming sceptical in every conceivable sense.'

'All sensations are FAKE. Keep left finger under a cold tap, another right finger under a hot tap. Put both hands in a toilet bowl – left finger is hot, right finger is warm simultaneously. How can the water be hot AND cold? Object the same and senses lie. If non-complex objects lie, what of man?'
Richey's archive, Priory notes, 1994

Sceptical theory dates back to 360 BC and encompasses the belief that certain knowledge and fundamental truths are impossible for human beings to attain. One of the first noted sceptics was the Ancient Greek philosopher Pyrrho of Elis, who is cited with creating Pyrrhonism – the first formal approach to scepticism in Western philosophy.

Frustrated by the Dogmatists, a school of philosophers who claimed to possess certain irrefutable knowledge and truth, the Pyrrhonists main epistemological argument was that no belief, theory or view could ever be supported or justified rationally because there would always be doubt. Their answer to living life under this unquestionable doubt was to suspend all judgement and belief, neither affirming any thoughts, feelings or sensations as true, or denying them as false.

Inspired by Socrates' belief 'I know that I know nothing', Pyrrho believed that by suspending his judgement, and by asserting no definite or concrete mind-set to the world around him, he could escape the complexities of everyday life and achieve peace of mind. During Richey's time in the Priory, he wrote of his own moral dilemma with coming to terms with fundamental truths, pertaining to subject matters like good vs evil, natural law vs civil law, lust vs love and questioning their very foundations and stability within the human psyche.

Pyrrho and many sages since have claimed that when one realises the fragile nature of truth, and the fact that it can never fully be attained, all that is left to do is to achieve a form of enlightenment known as 'ataraxia' – a state of tranquillity that comes from the suspension of all beliefs.

'I can see that some of Richard's writing on *The Holy Bible* was teetering towards that kind of scepticism,' confirms Rachel. 'When you get lines talking about "Mensa", "Miller", "Mailer", "Plath", "Pinter", it may have been him developing that sage wisdom away from Western ideals and dispelling all notions of what was considered intellectual.

'There was also the line about believing in nothing, and to me that can be seen in a negative or positive light in terms of how he felt at the time. Could he have succumbed to that emptiness and felt quite isolated and alone in that nihilistic space, or could he have attained some semblance of peace as time progressed? Was that why he was getting into Ecclesiastes by the end and finding a way to reconcile himself with this all-consuming futility he felt?'

'You take an onion and peel it and peel it right to the heart and there's nothing there. There must be something, you believe there must be. You take another onion and start peeling it. Keep on peeling. At last, nothing. Do you understand the sadness of this monkey?'
The Saga of Dazai Osamu
– quoted in Richey's Priory notes, 1994

On 1 August 1994, a few days into Richey's stay at the Priory, 'Revol' was released as the second single from *The Holy Bible* and reached a disappointing number 22 on the UK singles chart. More pressing was the fact that Richey's hospitalisation was about to hit the headlines. Media reports claimed he was suffering with 'nervous exhaustion' – the usual celebrity cover-all for anything from drink and drugs to depression and anxiety.

To fund Richey's considerable medical bills, James, Nicky and Sean continued with most of the band's scheduled performances. Playing their first gig as a three-piece on 30 July in Scotland's T in the Park festival, James gave the music press an insight into Richey's state of mind: 'It wasn't a breakdown. It was much worse than that. If you have a breakdown it sounds like the kind of thing you give someone a couple of Valiums for and then they're OK again. Richey went bonkers, something just flipped in his head. It was dramatic.'

Despite *The Holy Bible*'s disturbing lyrics – including several of an unmistakably autobiographical nature, and examined at length in the following chapter – the other band members failed to draw any real inferences that things might have been about to come to a head. Asked how they could not link Richey's lyrics with his state of mind, they said that their songs were not usually about themselves, and that if Richey was sending out distress signals among the new songs, they had failed to make the connection.

Onlookers could view the band's previous canon – which included titles such as 'Suicide Alley', 'Spectators of Suicide' and their cover of 'Suicide is Painless' – and wonder whether *The Holy Bible* was merely carrying on in much the same vein. Years later Nicky Wire would confess to Radio 4's *Mastertapes* that he didn't take Richey or his problems at face value. 'I probably blanked it out,' he admitted. 'We told ourselves he was writing about these dark things in a journalistic kind of way, writing from the point of view of an anorexic, and so much of our stuff was loaded in that way ...'

The band played as a three-piece throughout the remainder of August, appearing at festivals in Germany and the Netherlands, and ending the month on the main stage at the Reading Festival. Richey's notes from the Priory show that he was deliberating joining them there but decided against it at the last minute, for reasons unknown. He stayed in the hospital. 'He's having these intellectual battles in there right now,' Nicky Wire said at the time. 'He knows what they're doing, all these questionnaires: "You can't trick me!" He's on some sort of prescribed drugs and shit-loads of therapy and he's even doing fucking drama classes. There are obviously things that Richey will not do; I can't see him putting up with that "I am a cushion" stuff somehow.'

Adding to his discomfiture, Richey and the others on the Galsworthy programme had to gather twice weekly for individuals to share their own life story. Each session centred on one member of the group who would document their memories as far back as they could, in the hope that they would reaffirm their past values and connect with one another on a deeper level.

'I was there when Richey did his life story,' remembers Rosie Dunn. 'He felt uncomfortable about it, so he asked me if I'd read out some of the lyrics to his songs instead. One of them was "4st 7lb", so in my opinion, an eating disorder did form a part of his mindset when he was in hospital.'

This session was attended by a patron of the Priory, guitar legend Eric Clapton. Clapton had spent time as a patient in Roehampton recovering from drug and alcohol addiction in the 1980s, and came in to support the occasional group workshop. Clapton's former fiancée Alice Ormsby-Gore (daughter of Lord Harlech – Britain's ambassador to the US during the Kennedy administration) was also in residence during Richey's stay, being treated for heroin addiction, and the two formed a friendship. In his autobiography Clapton mentions that Alice had 'disappeared' while in France months before, resurfacing some time later ready to accept Clapton's offer of treatment at the rehabilitation centre.

'After I'd read Richey's lyrics to the group, Eric came up to us and congratulated him on the album,' recalls Rosie. 'He said it was absolutely brilliant and that the lyrics were "just amazing". He recognised Richey's talent with words and was really gushing over him like he was one of the biggest superstars on the planet. Although he was brilliant in there, a nice man and very supportive, Richey didn't seem enamoured by the fact Eric was a rock god. He liked him and got on with him, but Richey always had this normality about him, and he wasn't star struck by Eric, unlike a lot of people in the group.'

Later on, Clapton popped his head around Richey's bedroom door and asked if he should bring his guitar so the two could jam next time he visited. Richey would later tell James, 'Just what I need. I'm going to be confronted by God, and God's going to realise that I can't play the guitar!' (God being a nickname bestowed upon Clapton by fans of virtuoso guitar playing.)

In a 2004 interview in *The Word* magazine, the remaining band members wondered whether Richey had embellished or even invented the story. They hoped it was true for its obvious comic effect. Yet why would they have doubted Richey's story in the first place?

> *'I sometimes exaggerate when expressing an opinion or something*
> *I experienced, but it's more to frame my own experience or points*
> *of view, and I would never deny if or when I am exaggerating.*
> *Exaggeration promotes understanding.'*
> Patient, Borderline Personality Disorder Central website

Richey had been at the Priory for two weeks when he was diagnosed with Borderline Personality Disorder. This was still a relatively unknown condition within NHS hospitals. When Richey left Whitchurch it was with the understanding that he was suffering with severe depressive disorder and a secondary diagnosis of non-dependant use of alcohol and substances.

The term borderline was originally coined because it was thought that the afflicted were on the 'border' between psychosis and neurosis. It is an umbrella term used by mental health professionals. The sufferer presents severe personality disorganisation, with instability in self-image, mood and behaviour, plus disturbance in patterns of thinking and perception. They can indulge in destructive and impulsive behaviour, form intense but unstable relationships and, and are prone to 'meltdowns' when their fragile defence structure crumbles.

Central to borderline personality disorder is the sparse sense of identity coming from intense feelings of emptiness and loneliness. When patients describe themselves, they often paint a confused and contradictory self-portrait. They fear abandonment, yet actively push others away to avoid the pain of their imagined rejection. Sometimes, to overcome their indistinct and negative self-image, the borderline will make like an actor, and place themselves in good or entertaining roles to fill the void in their identity.

Many adapt like chameleons to their environment, and assume some traits that are present in those that they admire so as to gain a more tangible sense of self. Throughout Richey's archive, from university onwards, he would write out – sometimes repeatedly – quotes from favourite books, films and albums in order to memorise them off by heart. Like many borderlines, he often felt that others could define his thoughts and the contradictory opinions that inhabited his mind more succinctly than he could himself.

The lure of hedonistic experiences, whether through drugs, self-harm or other means, is often known to give a semblance of identity and feeling back to the borderline patient. During intense periods the sufferer can turn to drugs, alcohol or meaningless sexual encounters as coping mechanisms. It is thought that when their struggle to find an identity becomes intolerable, the solution is either to lose any sense of self altogether, or to receive a semblance of identity through pain and numbness.

Their emotional instability means frequent mood swings from an empty, depressive state to one of anxiety, irritability or anger. They can feel suicidal with despair, only to feel positive an hour or so later. In the 2005 documentary *No Manifesto*, Nicky would comment: 'Some people like chaos in their lives, and we don't. When we had Richey, Richey was chaos. A more disciplined chaos than a lot of people, but still chaos. I mean it in intellectual, nasty, brutish, tender, loving, emotional extremes all in one day syndrome.'

'Being a borderline feels like eternal hell. Nothing less. Pain, anger, confusion, never knowing how I'm gonna feel from one minute to the next.

Hurting because I hurt those whom I love. Feeling misunderstood. Nothing gives me pleasure. Wanting to die but not being able to kill myself because I'd feel too much guilt for those I'd hurt, and then feeling angry about that, so I cut myself or take an overdose to make all the feelings go away.'
Patient, Borderline Personality Disorder Central website

One of Richey's favourite books, Jeffrey Eugenides's *The Virgin Suicides*, is based on five sisters with borderline tendencies, who are impulsive, reckless and sexually promiscuous. The book ends with their suicides, and the narrators, their ex-lovers, are left only with a sea of stories and theories and the possessions of the girls they loved. They feel they never knew them as well as they thought, nor will they ever know the motives behind their suicides.

After Richey's disappearance, Nicky Wire admitted that it felt like he and the band may not have been as close to Richey as they had once believed. 'I mean, I thought I knew Richey, but maybe I didn't.' Later on he would postulate, 'There was the possibility Richey just didn't like us any more.'

For the borderline, identity disturbances, such as confusion about their friendships, career choices, sexuality and values, happen almost daily, along with the deep-seated notion that one is flawed, defective and bad at the core. They often go to extremes in their daily thinking, feeling and behaviour, and under considerable stress the borderline can detach from reality completely and suffer from various dissociative states. These can include depersonalisation and derealisation – a sense that the self and the world are not real – and, more rarely, fugue-like states where sufferers completely shut down, forget their identity and assume a new sense of self.

When considering Richey's own family history and the life and death of his great aunt Bessie, is it possible that there was some familial predisposition to Richey's behaviour? Bessie John had once been living among friends and family, engaged to be married, and holding down a steady job. However, she would go on to shut out all those she had previously shared her life with, and pursue a solitary existence until the end of her days.

Rosie Dunn says Richey was unperturbed by this diagnosis. 'We both thought Borderline was a really lazy diagnosis. He knew the doctors wanted to slap a label on him as fast as they could. He asked me, "What does a personality disorder *actually* mean? You're not functioning like the average man on the street?"

'He knew it wasn't right to feel the way he did, but he also thought it was absurd how others could just ignore all the problems in the world, and certain inevitabilities that came with life and getting older. He never reconciled how those who felt really deeply were labelled as having some sort of deficiency, nor how other seemingly "normal" people could deny another level of complexity to themselves and carry on walking around selectively blind to what they did and didn't see.

'It wasn't like he was snubbing the idea of help, because he tried to engage with the physicians there. But because he was so clever, there was not one person in there that was going to unravel his mind. You can tell a psychiatrist anything they want to hear if you're clever enough. I don't think being hospitalised bothered him at all; it was probably an interesting chapter in his life. There was none of this "I don't want to be here" or "this sucks" like a lot of other patients. He took what was on offer, but he was a very questioning, intelligent – and most of all extremely complex person. By the end I don't think he felt there was a way to normalise his foundations and to separate his problems away from what made him Richey at the core.'

'The Normal is the good smile in a child's eyes: – alright. It is also the dead stare in a million adults. It both sustains and kills – like a god. It is the Ordinary made beautiful: it is also the Average made lethal. The Normal is the indispensable, murderous God of Health, and I am his priest.'
Dr Martin Dysart in *Equus*, Sir Peter Shaffer

On one occasion when Rachel visited the Priory, Richey told her of yet another diagnosis he had been given. 'He told me he'd been talking to the hospital's counsellor, who believed that the death of our nan, seven years earlier, had left him suffering from unresolved grief,' Rachel says. 'I can see how this conclusion was drawn, because Richard did idealise his childhood a lot.'

Years later, Rachel spoke to the counsellor in question. He said he didn't believe Richey suffered from Borderline Personality Disorder, and although unresolved grief played a part in his adult difficulties, it was not the sole issue. He declined to elaborate any further.

Did Richey receive the appropriate treatment at all? Medical notes show he was exasperated at being put in the Alcoholics Anonymous group. He believed that the AA see drinking in binary terms – you are an alcoholic or you are not. He told staff at the Priory that he could make it through most days without alcohol or substances. Many close to him have since commented that he wasn't as alcohol dependent as his reputation suggested.

'He could and did give up alcohol very easily,' recalls Rachel. 'He didn't drink every day or mask daily reality with it. He would use it sometimes to get on stage and occasionally to sleep. He felt that he had more pressing problems that demanded more attention beyond the drinking and he never reconciled why the Priory thought the Twelve Steps should be the main course of treatment for him.

'I feel with Richard's level of questioning, especially of the 12-step process, it became a case of doctors throwing up their hands in despair. I don't think anyone knew what to do with him by the end. I had a mental health professional tell me that they'd rather treat a hundred patients with depression than one with Borderline Personality Disorder because they're far too clever for their own good.'

'But simple people don't understand complicated ones and thrust the latter back on themselves, more ruthlessly than any others, I thought. The biggest mistake is to think that one can be rescued by so-called simple people. A person goes to them in an extremely needy condition and begs desperately to be rescued and they thrust this person even more deeply into his own despair.'
Thomas Bernhard, *The Loser*

CHAPTER 8

Towards the end of Richey's stay at the Priory, his weight dropped further, despite an initial gain at the beginning of his treatment. In his last few weeks there, he would sit in the cafeteria with Rachel and their father, picking at his food, only to immediately excuse himself to use the bathroom afterwards.

'It made me wonder if he was being sick in there, because at the time he had been put on a special diet to gain weight,' says Rachel. 'Towards the end of the year, Richard's teeth were starting to corrode, and I know that's something that can happen if you're bulimic, or if you abuse drugs.'

Living nearby, James Dean Bradfield was another frequent visitor. During one visit, Richey told him, 'You know if you took just one of these tablets a day you could really open up your creative senses!' To which James replied, 'No, Richey, I don't really think so.'

James continued to visit the Priory, taking his guitar and a Nirvana chord book, to help 'the poet who couldn't play guitar' finally master the instrument. Richey was experiencing a deepening anxiety about being publicly 'caught out' and he would discuss this worry frequently with Jo, on leaving the Priory.

Given the explicit message-driven content of *The Holy Bible*, did Richey feel he was failing as the band's wordsmith and chief strategist, when the album's singles kept charting so low? Did he believe that by becoming a proficient guitarist, he could assuage some of the guilt he was feeling?

'When he was in the Priory, he may have been searching for a definition of himself, and what he could and couldn't be,' says Rachel. 'Being a part of the creative division and unable to play an instrument, he might have thought that his place in the band was in jeopardy.

'His sense of himself as a good lyricist may have been hard for him to see at the time, but with a proper skill, like learning the guitar, it would be something more tangible for him to prove his worth within the band. He told the psychiatrists that all he wanted was to find one thing he could do that would give him confidence. He knew he could give up the bottle, but he told them he needed something to feel confident and passionate about when he came out of there.'

'Passion, you see, can be destroyed by a doctor. It cannot be created.'
Dr Martin Dysart in *Equus*, Sir Peter Shaffer

Implicit in the treatment programme was the hope that patients would be able to reconnect with their lives prior to becoming ill. Richey, as well as acquiring new guitar skills, also attempted to rekindle past passions.

'He would talk a lot about the interests that he had as a child. We were both into animals and animal rights in a big way,' explains Rosie Dunn. 'Some weekends we were allowed to bus into central London and once Richey went to London Zoo. He came back really upset because all these beautiful beasts were caged.

'If you listen to his later lyrics, you can see "Small Black Flowers That Grow in the Sky" as a metaphor for how trapped he, himself, was feeling. He used to have interests, that I would call his "obsessions" at the time – he'd talk continuously, and go on and on about the concept of a Perfect Circle, the Fourth Dimension and *Apocalypse Now*. I can't say I fully understood them at the time, because he was a level beyond when it came to that kind of talk. One thing I thought was strange, was how much he used to talk about liking the old television show, *The Fall and Rise of Reginald Perrin.'*

A 1970s BBC sitcom based on the David Nobbs book *The Death of Reginald Perrin*, the series told the story of Reginald Iolanthe Perrin, a middle-aged executive in the throes of a mid-life crisis. To escape his dreary existence, he faked his death, leaving his clothes on a Dover beach. Such a pseudocide is consequently often colloquially known in Britain as 'doing a Reggie Perrin'.

'Richey kept mentioning it to me, like he wanted it to hit home somehow,' says Rosie. 'But I didn't really think about it until after he'd disappeared. I don't know if he would have done a Reggie Perrin, or if he just found [the idea] appealing? Maybe it's just what he wanted other people to think, regardless of what actually happened to him.

'Richey could be very provocative and would make all sorts of bold statements, some things he really meant, and other things you knew he didn't – often he was just looking to get a reaction. He could be really shocking at times, and there were many unfathomable layers behind his behaviour, which you couldn't quite unravel.'

Rosie says, as do many others we have interviewed for this book, that Richey could never be read simply and taken at face value.

'One day he didn't turn up for group therapy, and when I went to look for him he was in the hospital wing, having cuts on his arms stitched and bandaged by the nurses. I'll never forget him smiling at me after he'd done it. I was saying, "You silly bastard!" I kept asking him for days, "Why?" And he'd tell me there was no way anyone could have talked him out of it, because the only way to alleviate the emotional pain was to administer physical pain as a distraction.

'He told me he was going crazy and had to empty his emotional dustbin. But it also seemed like a statement, and it was almost like he was proud of what he'd done and was testing my reaction to the fact he'd cut himself so badly – I mean right down to the muscle! What stood out was the way he seemed to find it so amusing that I was so disturbed about it. I felt like I'd failed him because I thought we were close.

'I never got the impression he tried to slit his wrists to die, [it was] just a release. There were times when we were fed up, and down, but our talking would bring us out from that. We had a laugh. Never once did I think this is a man who wants to die, and slit his wrists properly.

'What's hardest for people to reconcile is that he wasn't all doom and gloom. He was honestly the funniest person I've ever met. His sense of humour was so silly, and really imaginative. I had a horrible boss in work at the time, and Richey and I used to think about scenarios where he'd transform into a fly, and how we'd swat him. It was that "out there" and zany sort of humour that not many would associate him with.'

On 8 September, after six weeks in residence, Richey's treatment at the Priory officially ended. Staff recommended he stay longer, believing he could benefit from further support. Richey thought the programme was doing him no good. He declined their offer.

Still eligible for the Priory's aftercare plan, Richey was expected to attend follow-up appointments at the hospital, go to AA meetings, and maintain contact with others on the programme. Crucially, on-release individuals were encouraged to make a conscious effort to change the habits which had led to their hospitalisation. However, less than a fortnight later Richey had joined the Manic Street Preachers in France for the first leg of their European tour.

'When you come out of the Priory, it's a brand new world and reality. A sober world, a scary world,' remembers Rosie Dunn. 'Drinking was a by-product of my job, and I imagine it was the same when Richey was on the road. The fact he went on tour with the band, and to play on stage sober only two weeks out of the programme must have been really daunting for him.

'You're meant to do things gradually, but he made himself so vulnerable. It's not just about putting down the drink; it's about your whole lifestyle. He went straight back on the road and straight back to his old way of life.'

Chapter 9

The Holy Bible – the Powers of Horror

*'Greetings from a dead man. Don't get off the boat. I will not be sacrificed
to barbarians. Imitate February, then. This is February. I take a purge.'*
Richey's archive, autumn 1994

On 30 August 1994 – nine days before Richey's discharge from the
Priory – *The Holy Bible* was released. The band had been talking about
the album since its inception, promising an uncompromising, raw,
unflinching record. As they told *Melody Maker* at the start of the year,
'On the next album, there will be nothing left out. Whether we get
crucified or not.'

Considered the band's Guernica, *The Holy Bible* is the album by
which the Manic Street Preachers are still to this day defined, and
a testament to Richey's raging war against the world, history and
himself. *NME* called it a 'vile record'. Halfway through the album,
it samples J.G. Ballard talking about his 1973 novel, *Crash*, a fiction
that explores the perverse world of car-crash fetishism. 'I wanted
to rub the human face in its own vomit and force it to look in the
mirror.'

*'But there are more words than sacrifice and responsibility. Try Fucking.
Try Prostitution. Try Suicide. Try Sodomy. Try Charity Work. Try*

Murder. Try Infection. Try History. Yes, Try History. It leaves you
worse than nothing. Anyone who reads History and still has
self-respect has not read History properly. FACT.'
Richey, letter to Jo, 1993

Despite failing to chart in mainland Europe or North America, *The Holy Bible* reached number 6 in the UK and remained in the top 40 for 11 weeks. Its content blatantly and unashamedly confronted modern morals and ethics. It threw up questions about everything from sex workers to desire, Nazi death camps to British imperialism, anorexia to mass consumption.

Before this album, the Manic Street Preachers had largely immersed themselves in pop aesthetics based on their favourite films, music, poetry, theory, clothing, artworks, slogans, and a general interest in style as a positive refuge from the mundanity of everyday living. In 1994, however, their focus was on a new, joyless austerity.

When writing *The Holy Bible*, Richey was inspired by the ideas of the philosopher Michel Foucault and the novelist Octave Mirbeau; and as a result the album was an ethical protest against inhumanity and barbarism, littered with lists of serial killers, public servants and political leaders, in whose crimes, Richey suggested, we are all complicit.

The album's imagery was deliberately confrontational and aimed to shock. The front cover was the painting *Strategy (South Face/Front Face/North Face)* by 23-year-old artist Jenny Saville. A triptych image, it depicts an unhealthily obese woman, seemingly staring down upon society. Her demeanour appears to be portraying pity, disgust and judgement, alongside compassion, self-consciousness and sadness. Here was the whole un-pretty truth that we as human beings should consider when confronting life's harsh realities.

Similarly, *The Holy Bible* represented the Manic Street Preachers' transformation into an appalling and gruelling spectacle; the life-affirming redemption of previous years was gone, and the record represented encroaching disaster.

While penning the previous two albums, Richey and Nicky would usually write together, or split the lyrical output 50/50. This time around Richey took 85 per cent of the writing credit. In light of his disappearance, the obvious temptation is to dig into and dissect his lyrics; to find hidden context and new layers of meaning.

Over the years, the band encouraged this sort of approach from their audience. They were influenced by the cultural critic Greil Marcus, taking the name of his seminal work *Lipstick Traces* as the title of their 2003 B-sides album. The theory running throughout Marcus's book was that threads can be found subconsciously and consciously throughout history – in culture and the arts – and can possess much greater significance if thought of in terms of cross-referencing and historical lineage.

'There's a secret history out there,' Nicky Wire told BBC Wales in 2017. 'That things lead you on a path to a different reality, that was our fight really. That there was such a glorious world of music, culture and connections if you know where to look for them.'

In his 1979 picture book *Masquerade*, British author Kit Williams set out 'to do what nobody had ever done before' and create a new genre: armchair treasure hunts. His work concealed visual clues to the location of a jewelled ornamental golden hare, which he'd hidden somewhere in the British Isles. Readers had to decipher the images and solve the clues to find the prized hare. Williams created a tapestry full of meaning and coded messages, requiring readers to study the artwork carefully rather than idly flipping through the book.

Could Richey have had the same in mind, when laying out an album that still to this day baffles critics, fans and his bandmates alike?

'We thought we could resist record-company pressures. All we wanted to do was go under the corporate wing, but you do get affected, and we lost the plot a bit before. Now, we're back to speaking in tongues.'
James Dean Bradfield, *Select*, 1994

The previous summer's *Gold Against the Soul* had been mercilessly panned by the music press. One *Q* magazine reviewer described it as 'superficially competent, of course, but scratch below the surface and you'll find few signs of life, just a vaguely expressed, bemused and bored dissatisfaction.' The band even appeared in one music publication depicted in cartoon form, dressed as bakers shovelling pages of the album's lyrics into a giant furnace, while shouting to each other that the lyrics and concepts on the record were 'only half baked'.

The Manics were (and still are) famed for quoting back their own reviews to nonplussed journalists. It's no great stretch to imagine Richey could have been feeling a great responsibility to step up and create the all-encapsulating album the band had been promising since day one.

'I think he put a lot of work into condensing things he'd learned as far back as college, and making the band's third album a statement that couldn't be faulted in any way,' says Rachel. 'He was putting himself under a lot of pressure to create this ultimate masterpiece.'

Interviewed for *Raw* magazine in 1994, James would talk about the stress Richey had been feeling: 'Don't forget you're talking about a guy here who wanted to call the album *The Holy Bible*, because everything has to be perfection.'

Nicky Wire confessed that *The Holy Bible* was a welcome shift from the 'hollowness' of *Gold Against the Soul*: 'This is an album for *us*, where *Gold* was pretty much an album for MTV, the album company, the radio.'

In 1994, the band decided to regain creative control, by producing an album that would remain largely untouched by their record label. Richey had an increased role. As he explained it, 'The record company originally asked us if we wanted to go to Barbados to make the album and we said, "Fuck off! No way!"'

Feeling stifled by their experiences in high-budget locations, the band felt the need to break away in a show of authenticity. James said they chose their Cardiff recording studio for a specific reason, 'We gotta get away, it's gotta be boot camp, it's gotta be nasty, like Michael-Caine-in-*Mona Lisa* naasty! And it was a touch of method, recording it in the red-light area in Wales.'

As soon as the recording began, James was enthused by the return to their roots, 'I felt there was tension and there was pressure, but it just felt good straight away. I felt alive with something again, whereas before that I was just fearing things – the end of the band ...'

Years later the Manics revealed that before and after the release of *The Holy Bible*, they had been on the brink of having their contract terminated by Sony. Speaking in 2014, Nicky Wire said, 'Rob Stringer recently told us that we were quite close to being dropped; he was the one who kept us. One of the chiefs said, "They'll never have the X factor." But Rob insisted on keeping us. Even through something as dense and grim as "Archives of Pain" he could tell that there was something important as well as commercial.'

The music on *The Holy Bible*, driven largely by James and Sean, was an attempt to enter avant-garde territory. They had been listening to the likes of Joy Division, The Pop Group, Public Image Limited and Wire – innovators in post-punk's 'make-it-new' ultra-modernism.

In his notes for *The Holy Bible*, Richey penned instructions for composing the end to 'Of Walking Abortion': 'Maybe end like Rage Against the Machine, "Killing in the Name Of"?'

Despite years of on-off guitar practice, Richey was still unable to attain a level of proficiency. Aware of his lack of musical prowess, Richey's final year with the band was overshadowed by a crisis of confidence which would go on to further aggravate his psychological problems, and gnaw away at his sense of worth as a member of the band.

An appraisal of Richey's lyrics and archive from *The Holy Bible* period suggests that the album was assembled as a deliberate incendiary device. He raised the stakes, often in arcane ways, beyond his bandmates' comprehension, with an apparent design to take the Manic Street Preachers right up to the precipice of potential career suicide, in a kamikaze mission.

In this final artistic statement to the world, we looked for clues that might provide insight into his state of mind, a glimpse of his real or imagined future, and signs of any pre-planned exit strategy.

'Ultimately, we wanted to be the perfect band that could make a record that sold globally, millions – and there'd be no need to make another record. All we've ever been interested in doing is making a record which encapsulates a mood and a time and then it can be a full stop – bye bye.'
Richey Edwards, *NME* Brat Awards, February 1994

Contained in Richey's *Holy Bible* folder are copies of poetry he wrote in late adolescence. Having spent so long in the music industry he so disparaged, was he now seeking to draw inspiration from his earlier work, to try to reconnect once more with his authentic sense of self?

There were mutterings about Richey wanting to 'do a Salinger' as far back as *Generation Terrorists*, and there are certainly clues in *The Holy Bible's* lyrics hinting that his later disappearance may have been pre-meditated. They deserve close examination.

'Faster'

'Most people in this business are totally insensitive. Most are downright evil. I personally don't know anyone who is in a band that I respect. And no one at the record companies really care about the bands.'
Richey Edwards, last ever interview, *Music Life*, 1995

'Faster', the first single from *The Holy Bible*, was released on 6 June 1994. It begins with a sample from the film adaptation of George Orwell's novel *1984*: 'I hate purity. Hate goodness. I don't want virtue to exist anywhere. I want everyone corrupt.' John Hurt utters these words as Winston Smith, *1984's* protagonist, a low-ranking citizen within the super-state of Oceania. Written as an everyman character, Smith represents the struggle of the individual under the boot of a totalitarian party and its oppressive regime.

He has realised that to overthrow the autocratic system in a country filled with orthodox and complacent citizens, there must be individuals who are impure and wicked in the eyes of the state. Only the 'corrupt'

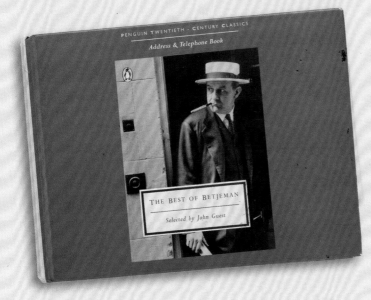

Richey's final, John Betjeman-detailed address book, 1995. It contains only a very few names compared to address books from previous years.

"Kinnock, Scargill, Hart and Thatcher,
Should be flying the peoples banner.
Black South Africans have no rights,
My fascist duck has done alfright."
    I recited the second line of my poem that had taken me just two days to write quietly to myself. When my father asked me what I was doing I showed my poem to him. He laughed and asked what was a fascist duck and I explained that although it had an obscure meaning it contained a message of deep significance.
    I realised that everyone thought my poems were childish and insignificant but I was determined to prove them wrong. I decided to take my poems to Cray Charles, the well known Liverpuddlian poet, and ask him for his opinion.
    ? Later that evening when my parents were in bed I placed my favourite five poems in my bag. The poems

Richey's English homework, 1981. A year after Bobby Sands died from his hunger strike, Richey wrote this short story titled 'The Intruder' in which the protagonist set out to become a poet who would highlight political injustices. In Blackwood, Richey's peers viewed his passionate stance on current affairs as eccentric.

were "My Fascist Duck," "Alcoholic Industrialists," "The
Pinstripe Borderline," "Roland Hill reformed the Post Office"
and "Repatriation."

Quietly I opened my bedroom window and stealthy I
crept out. I made sure to avoid the freshly dug
patch of soil in my garden as I was sure that my
footprints would easily be seen the next morning. I ran
to the edge of the street and then I relaxed hoping
that the most difficult part of my journey was already
over.   Why the secrecy?

It was (around) six o'clock when I reached Newport
Train Station. I could tell it was six o'clock because
the traffic was slowly beginning to edge (its) way towards
the town centre. I paid my £13 train fare and sat
down in the heavily vandalised chair. I had already
spent half of my money and I realised that I would
have to find Cray Charles very quickly. I knew that
he was touring with the cult pop group "Einsturdenne
Neubauten" and had the address of their gig which
was to be held in three days time.

The train journey seemed to last for hours although
I knew that the journey would take hours. When I
arrived in Paddington Station in London I asked a lady
who seemed to be quite pleasant and unassuming to direct
me towards the "Marquee" which was where Cray Charles
would be performing. She refused to answer and it was
then that I realised how suspicious (very) Londoners were.
Although I had no intention of harming her she seemed
convinced that I was going to assault her. I walked
away feeling sorry that the world was such a frightened
place.

I had no idea where the "Marquee" was and
tried for hours to find it. Eventually I found a

Richard Edwards 5TB

Tourist Information Centre and asked the woman behind the desk where I could find (this) hidden refuge for poets. She retorted in a sharp cutting voice that she did not know and it was not her job to tell me. She directed me towards another woman who kindly told me where I could find the "Marquee" Another aspect of London life had (cropped up) : a woman who was supposed to help tourists would not be bothered if it was not her job to do so.

I reached the "Marquee" later that evening and discovered that it cost £2 just to enter the building. I paid my money and found Cray Charles on the second level of the building. He invited me to recite one of my poems and I obliged.

"The following lines are from "Roland Hill reformed the Post Office"" I told Cray.

" Political Opponents,
  Using Roland Hills components,
  Little bugs impossible to find.
  Poised. "

I finished reciting my poem but Cray did not seem to be impressed. In fact he burst out laughing and when he had calmed down I asked him what was so funny. He said that it was my poem that had made him laugh. I told him that he would regret his decision and one day thousands of people would look upon my poems as superb pieces of English Literature.

I stormed out of the room and found myself crying. I knew that I would get the recognition that I thought deserved and began devising a plan that I hoped would get my poems publicity.

After three days of sleeping in streets full of refuse

and rats I waited for the evening to come.

At 8 o'clock that evening I paid another £2 and entered the "Marquee". There was a large, well-built man guarding the ~~door~~ stairs that led to the stars' dressing rooms. All I had was £9 on my ~~minder~~ person and I offered this to the "minder." He accepted and did not ~~seem~~ to want to cause any trouble mainly because he felt that I would not cause Cray ~~and~~ any problems. After all, I was only about five and a half feet high.

I entered ~~the~~ Cray's ~~bedroom~~ dressing room and demanded that he read one of my poems at the concert that evening. He laughed and ~~seemed~~ to think that I, like my poems, were of little significance. I pulled out a knife which I had found in the streets and ~~threatened to kill Cray.~~ <u>ridiculous!</u> I clearly saw the panic on his face and he appeared to be very concerned about his welfare.

I waited with my knife held tightly in my sweaty palm until Cray was called for by the Manager of the "Marquee." I thrust "My Fascist Duck" into Cray's hands and told him that I would be watching to make sure that he read ~~I~~ my poem.

We left his dressing room with Cray telling the Manager that I was his nephew and would be allowed to stay behind stage. Two hours later I heard the subtle tones of Cray's voice reciting the opening lines from "My Fascist Duck":
 "They've called me a ~~communist~~ dictator,
 They've called me a fascist king,
 They've called me the devil incarnate,
 But I know I'm Jesus in skin."
At the end of the poem the crowd cheered and because

Richard Edwards 5TB

Cray realised that they loved the poem he announced that he had wrote the poem.

It was too much for me to take and I thrust the knife into my side. I cried out in pain and someone rushed to my side.

I awoke the next morning surrounded by police-man and reporters. I told them the whole story; and they seemed to believe me. My poems were to be printed in the Sunday Times I discovered and two weeks later when I was lying in bed my father brought me that very paper. Their review of my poems made me extremely happy and the lines " a masterpiece of English Literature" proved to my parents that my poems really were superb.

(23) Well written but not much of a story really

Below: Richey's student desk in Swansea University with the lyrics to the Manic Street Preachers' 'Suicide Alley', 1989.

I WANT TO KISS A GIRL.

HR emotional.

Parnell – political genius?? or lucky opportunist, inconsistent. What he stood for vague – due to his inability or brought about by complex situation. Indeed all HR movement vague. Parnell, once Libs accepted HR, content to sit back, concentrate on England / Slut O'Shea, glad to be out of Ireland OR a realistic politician knew events would now take place in Westminster.

I AM UNBELIEVABLY HORRIBLE AND SPOTTY AND NO ONE LOVES ME

Richey's college file doodlings, 1985. Mark Hambridge recalls, 'I don't think it was until university he started to entertain the notion seriously about becoming a rock star. He'd try encouraging others to take the stage and I think that was because of that shyness he had, and because he was so self-conscious when it came to his skin.'

I NEVER KISSED A
GIRL BEFORE,
TO SHY TO GO OUTSIDE
MY DOOR

⌐ THE UNDER ~~LOVERS~~ ⌐

| WHAT DO I GET |

I JUST WANT A LOVER
LIKE ANY OTHER BUT
WHAT DO I GET? . . .
. WHAT DO I GET? NO LOVE!
WHAT DO I GET? NO SLEEP
              AT NIGHTS!
WHAT DO I GET? NO GIRL
              AT ALL, AT
              ALL, AT A
I DON'T GET SCREWE

Richey's college file doodlings, 1985. '*People are just little sodding deadbeats who need beer/sex to give them an excuse for being the scum of the earth. Could it be that I'm going to be a great thinker …*'

A water-damaged photograph of Richey performing in 1989 at the Horse and Groom, where the Manic Street Preachers played to seventeen people. The faces of the other three Manics have been corroded, but Richey's remains intact.

LIVE

MANIC STREET PREACHERS
HORSE AND GROOM, LONDON

UPTIGHT, everything's alright. Fresh from their "Suicide Alley" debut single, this is the first London date of Manic Street Preachers. Bluntly, they are a four piece from South Wales with a '77 fixation and more than a few cutting melodies — I'd hesitate to call them angry young *men* because I don't believe the drummer was even born in 1977. They also have a natty line in shirts, all spray painted with slogans like "suicide beat", "classified machine", "England needs revolution now", reminiscent of primetime Age Of Chance but I'm sure they'd mash my face if I suggested it. They look so *intense* as they hurtle through the barbed-wire jagged "New Art Riot" (so much snarling and synchronised kicks in the air, detractors could claim them as a triumph of attitude over content), I feel like shouting "lighten up!" But they do anyway: after the first song the singer — with regulation sharp haircut — shyly stammers "Th-thanks, that's the most applause we've ever had." And I'm won over. As for the rest of the audience, some are almost hysterical but then that could just be nostalgia.

Right now, Manic Street Preachers are too reverential, they've got to loosen up and translate their undoubted ferocious potential from their shirts to their guitars. As it stands they already have the attitude, tunesmanship and hungry youth to show laff punch merchants like The Family Cat and Mega City 4 where to get off. Given enough rope they could become champions.
BOB STANLEY

The Manic Street Preachers' first live review, *Melody Maker*, 1989.

Richey's band file, set-list and gig photograph, 1989.

MANIC
PR

THE IDeOLOgY of SPEEDATTACK

-numbers 1 to 10-
new art riot
strip it down
dead yankee drawl
anti-love
soul contamination
destroy the dancefloor
sorrow sixteen
faceless sense of void
suicide alley
i get low

The politics of prote

a night of HATENOISE at London's

Fresh from their
is is the first Londo
luntly, they are
a '77 fixation
odies—I'd
g men because I
even born in 197
rts, all spray
le beat", "classifie
ition now",
Chance but I'm
ested it. They lo
ne barbed-wire
orting and
ctors could claim
ontent), I feel
ney do anyway:
r—with regulation
ners 'Th-thanks, that's
d.' And I'm wa
ce, some are
uld just be

Retrogressive, exciting and
inspired. You'll probably hate it.

hen fresh faced
udy T-shirts ma
roll which they
would shame t
overnent.
their undoubted ferocious potential fro
to their guitars. As it stands they alread
attitude, tunesmanship and hungry you
laff punch merchants like The Family Ca
City 4 where to get off. Given enough r
could become champions.

White Rock Rebelboy Single
The Week! Check the letter
nd
d

ossible (eg '80s p
he long running
imsical pop essa
musical

rnism!)
zes w

STREET EACHERS

990 STARTS HERE

UseLESS vALUeS USEleSS EgO — deAd lifE kill All YR HAPpineS

SUICIDE BEAT

cut your hair infront of businessmen. we are the scum that remind You of MISERY. GO TO HATE......

e & Groom, Great Portland St NOV 17th ESURIENT

Political economy looks on, furiously disapproving, jealous, adult, conservative – desirous of hindsight blessing. In Tiananmen Square, old men let students be murdered in their thousands. Teens whose only crime is being bored flood the city, scribble messages of blunt hate in their own blood on makeshift Democracy Walls. They become the people. Levis, Wham! and Coca Cola – the almost-approved material pop-carriers of 'spiritual polution' (translated: desire) – had arrived. Subjects became hooligans. Materialism isn't yet a trap – it's a fuel. Teens, as they wander the city streets with weird words scrawled on their trousers, are furnaces of as yet unchannelled desire. The situationists never forgot the sense of arrogant power that radical subjectivity brings, the sense that they can't be bought. Teens, without histories of their own, are not empowered by anyone else's. All old codgers' stories to them are the same old codgers' stories.

Above: One of Richard Fry's photos of teenage Richey with the family car. He wanted to document his life before he became famous so people could see his origins.

Left: Richey at a Steve Strange gig, Blackwood, 1985.

Below: Richey and Graham Edwards in Richey's Blackwood bedroom, 1992.

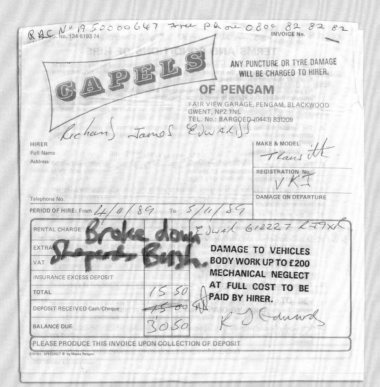

Richey's van hire certificate, 1989. 'We used to hire a van from a nearby garage and spend the day driving down to the gig and the night driving back,' recalls Mark.

Left: Richey during the early years in the band.

Richey's collage of his university friends in Swansea, 1989.

can oppose the party and its prevailing status quo to kick-start the revolution. By rebelling against a state that practises omnipresent surveillance of its citizens and persecutes individualism and independent thinking, Winston advocates that everyone becomes virtue-less and corrupt – for only then can they become the saviours of the state, and in turn themselves.

The lyrics of 'Faster' bewildered Richey's bandmates. In August 1994, Nicky Wire told *Melody Maker*: 'Frankly, a lot of it is all Richey again, and I was always completely confused by it. But when he wrote it he told me it was about self-abuse.'

However, in June of that year, Richey had told *Raw* magazine the actual meaning behind the song. 'It's about the sort of people who take their frustrations out on other people, particularly those who can't defend themselves.' He talked about dining with a record company executive in a plush London restaurant. 'Oh God, it was pathetic. He caused a really big scene with the waiters, just because his fucking wine wasn't chilled enough or something. It put me right off my food.' These were unequivocally intimate, first-person lyrics inspired by direct personal experiences.

'There's a poem by Tennessee Williams called "Lament For Moths", one of the first poems we ever read, which is about how the moths, the sensitive people, will always be stamped on and crushed by the mammoths – that really hit us, the sudden realisation that we were the moths of the world.'
Nicky Wire, *Melody Maker*, July 1994

Certainly relations between the band and their label at the time were not straightforward. A former Manics roadie told us of one encounter. 'At the start of 1994, Rob Stringer came out of a meeting on the tour bus with the band. When I asked what was going down, he said "the usual power struggle" and laughed it off.

'It happened again that autumn. This time Rob left the meeting ashen-faced, without the joviality he had the first time around. It seemed a lot more serious. He told me it was another "power struggle", but the way it was implied was that this time, it was between Richey and the [rest of the] band.'

'I think in early 1994, Richard, Nick, James and Sean stood fully aligned with their creative vision,' says Rachel. 'That "Us versus the world" mentality. I believe that deteriorated towards the end of Richard's time with the band.'

Fighting the label, then pitched against the other band members, Richey may have found catharsis by documenting his own personal narrative and hurling it back at the record label in defiance and vindication. The lyrics of 'Faster' also appear to contain a pre-emptive strike against his bandmates.

The opening couplets juxtapose two aggrandised and opposing statements – 'architect' vs 'butcher' and 'pioneer' vs 'primitve' – against the backdrop of a savage, unrelenting and jagged guitar intro. In the first line of each couplet, Richey establishes himself, only for the second line to counter this with an accusation that seeks to paint him in a contradictory light.

In calling himself an 'architect', was Richey claiming credit for engineering the band's initial success? Yet with his radical lyrics, and their use on *The Holy Bible*, he could now be accused of 'butchering' the band by alienating the public and their record label.

Political and socially aware lyrics in pop were out of favour, so Sony may have considered Richey's provocations a retrograde step. Did the line about 'cold made warm' refer to the record company reneging on promises of supporting the band? Or was it a criticism of Nicky Wire defaulting on the Manics' original anti-love pact and getting married? It's possible that by this point Richey was feeling set adrift, having lost his former 'Glamour Twin' to domestic bliss and now standing alone in his faithfulness to the band's early manifesto.

Richey fluctuated between hopefulness and hopelessness in most aspects of his life, and in the line referencing the 'idiot drug-hive, the virgin' could have been feeling the necessity to counter some of the band's allusions to his lack of sexual experience and suggestions that he was a far heavier drug abuser than was generally known.

He also incorporated a conversation with Gillian Porter, a PR at Hall or Nothing. After he had opened up to her about his problems, she abruptly countered, 'Self-disgust is self-obsession, honey.' Publicly and defiantly Richey repeated her remark and retaliated on record, 'and I do as I please.'

The chorus, which references 'Mensa', 'Plath' and 'Pinter', defiantly indicated that he would allow nobody to dumb him down intellectually. Other lines can be interpreted as the band's movement away from their working-class roots. His record label paymasters had not reckoned with Richey bringing up controversial, hard-line 'deep politics' and setting them before the music-listening public. As he repeatedly said, the band's whole purpose was to talk about things nobody else would talk about; the Manic Street Preachers were all about changing people's lives through empowering them with knowledge.

One of the most seminal and oft-quoted lyrics on the album, about believing in nothing, may have been Richey maintaining that he still had a sense of personal identity within a version of 'nothing' that belonged to him, and to him alone. He would not reduce himself to an easily defined artist who could be used by Sony to pigeonhole the band as a more saleable commodity.

'As soon they take the cheque that buys their identity, they become as processed and meaningless as the item they are promoting.'
George Monbiot, *Guardian*, 2017

Paraphrasing the Japanese proverb 'The nail that sticks out gets hammered down' in the next verse, Richey suggested that he was making a target of himself. Lyrics about sleep and shadows signified he was unwilling to sleepwalk through life, oblivious to the world's chaos and corruption.

The talk of 'false mirrors' could be Richey promoting the Marxist theory of false consciousness. His favourite political commentators, the Situationists, based one of their main ideologies around this argument.

Guy Debord claimed that the government, media and ruling elite erect 'false mirrors' which reflect back an unrealistic image that transforms the way people view and live their lives.

When ending the verse with a couplet about honesty, was he suggesting the people around him had complied with an Orwellian programme and performed like diligent, unquestioning robots?

The song's finale comprises a stark mantra: 'man kills everything'.' The 'man' in question is probably 'the man' – a derogatory slang expression for corporate or authority figures. Was 'Faster' effectively 'sticking it to the man', i.e. a record label that attempted to restrict any radical strivings towards individuality or references to unsavoury or incendiary topics?

If viewed in this light, 'Faster' could embody Richey's own resistance. Although he admits that it would be 'so damn easy to cave in', the very fact that the song and others on the album made it past the censors – due in part to deliberate lyrical ambiguity – meant that Richey had succeeded in bringing a personal critique of his predicament into the public domain.

'I do think Richard underestimated the music industry,' considers Adrian Wyatt. 'He was highly intelligent but slightly naïve in thinking he could have any creative control in terms of how he and the band would be presented to and perceived by the public.

'He miscalculated that big companies don't care about the truth or how pure your motives are, or how quickly they and the press can turn on you. By the end, I believe, he'd got to the point where he wanted to take back as much control as he could, in terms of his image and output.'

'I think because *The Holy Bible* wasn't the commercial success Richard and the band had hoped for, they were forced to rethink their creative priorities with regards to what came next,' says Rachel. 'I think James, Nick and Sean reassessed their initial position and went on to stand shoulder to shoulder with Sony.'

In early 1995, just before he vanished, Richey told an old university friend he believed that without his initial input, the band would never have caught the eye of a major record label. One of the last works of art that he completed before he disappeared was a collage. It gathered photographs of various musicians, models, religious and cult figures, nestling together in a typical piece of Richey artwork. However, emblazoned in the bottom right corner of the frame were these bold, yellow highlighted words: THE MORON SPASTIC PREACHERS.

'The Manics were such a wonderful dream but I fear I have utterly woken up. Now I am resting all my hopes on another band to resurrect that dream. But they'll probably turn shite too and forget what they were all about to begin with, grow beer guts and swathe themselves in the flag of the nation they started out despising. They're like a once great friend who has joined the Conservative party and keeps phoning you up to rub it in by extolling the virtues of the free market. Ah me, dumb flag scum anyone? I guess that's Mr. Wire now.'
Phil Rose, *REPEAT*, Manic Street Preachers fanzine, 2002

'Revol'

'There were at least two sides to Brian's personality. One Brian was intro-verted, shy, sensitive, deep-thinking. The other was a preening peacock, gregarious, artistic, desperately needing assurance from his peers. He pushed every friendship to the limit and way beyond.'
Bill Wyman on Brian Jones in *Stone Alone*, 1990

Following the release of *The Holy Bible*, Richey's bandmates were at a loss to explain the meaning of 'Revol'. It continues to baffle them to this day. After Richey's disappearance, Nicky Wire commented 'Revol?' I just didn't know what the fuck he was on about. All the weight of reference to Eastern Europe or Nazi culture and figureheads. Even Richey said afterwards that he didn't know what it was about. It's lover spelt backwards, or so he kind of tried to explain it. A decline in rela-tionships ... I don't know.'

The song's lyrical conceit is founded on the 1960s cliché that the 'personal is the political', making the connection between subjective experience and broader social structures. 'Revol' playfully utilised this idea to allude to what appear to be references to Richey's life in the Manic Street Preachers, and his desire to escape it.

'Revol' could in parts be read as essentially a lyric about Richey's plans to leave the group. The lyrics contain threads that refer to falling out of love, separation and exile. Did he use political analogies to trace his time with the band, and then, in the final verse, tell them how he is planning to disappear?

The song essentially tells of a one-time love/lover scenario that has been reversed: Richey falling out of love with being in the band, with the band members, or both? With the benefit of hindsight, the lyrics appear to contain coded references expressing a desire to disappear.

Specifically, in the second verse Richey names historical political figures whom Richey has sought to link together by virtue of common and definitive associations, including Che Guevara, Pol Pot and Farrakhan.

Guevara, a South American revolutionary, vanished into exile two years before he was killed by the CIA in Bolivia in October 1967, a matter of weeks before Richey was born. Guevara became a revolutionary hero, and his romantic image adorned the bedroom walls of generations of students and activists worldwide. A man of principled action and political intrigue, his iconic status was more typical of that bestowed upon a departed, beloved rock star. Before Guevara's departure, he wrote a farewell letter wherein he severed all ties with his former Argentine comrades to devote himself to worldwide revolution, and changed his appearance drastically by shaving his head, as did Richey, prior to his own disappearance.

Pol Pot was the founder of a Maoist guerrilla group known as the Khmer Rouge who became the leader of Cambodia before withdrawing from public view in the early 1980s. He went on to live in isolation in Thai border country until his death in 1998. When 'Revol' was composed in 1994, Pol Pot was still very much a figure of mystery, existing in the shadows of self-imposed exile.

When Richey Edwards writes a lyric like 'Withdrawn traces', and then goes on, several months later, to withdraw all traces of himself, how can you not question the significance of the reference?

Louis Farrakhan was the controversial leader of the Nation of Islam. A separatist black nationalist, he advocated partition from the United States, to be funded by reparations compensating for the country's history of use and abuse of its black populace. Again, this can be seen as having an association with Richey. Seeking to divorce African-Americans from the rest of the US, Farrakhan demands alimony. With the previous couplets referencing disappearance, exile and separation, the mention of alimony further suggests that Richey may have been considering going his own way.

The chorus includes four lines of German and Italian words – *Lebensraum, Kulturkampf, Raus raus, Fila fila* – and also heavily suggests a desire to separate and escape. Delivered as barked instructions, they consolidate the album's recurring theme of domination and totalitarianism.

'Lebensraum' (living space) was brought into the political lexicon by Imperial Germany, outlining its planned territorial gains after victory in the First World War. The word is more synonymous, however, with the territorial expansion aims of Hitler. But why should such references be deployed to form the central pillar in a song about failed relationships, and falling out of love?

The Collins dictionary entry for *'Kulturkampf'* reads: 'any serious conflict over values, beliefs, etc. between sizable factions within a nation, community, or other group'. Had Richey suffered a 'serious conflict' with people surrounding the Manics, or with the band members themselves?

'Raus' and *'Fila'* can be interpreted as orders, with connotations of the commands delivered to prisoners of war in Nazi Germany and fascist Italy. Commanding somebody to *'Raus! Raus!'* (Out! Out!) in context of *Lebensraum* and *Kulturkampf* suggests a person or persons

being removed or purged, in effect a pogrom. But which side was Richey himself taking in this, if any? *Fila* is Italian for file; connoting forming a queue. Is Richey advocating that he, or others, proactively absent themselves from a restricting situation? Or was he the recipient of these orders, feeling pressure that ousts him from his current life in the music industry? Was Richey looking to find living space outside of the band?

Ultimately the lyrics are probably best understood by disregarding any notion of a broader 'political message' and by accepting the cliché that personal is political. It may also hold some significance that Richey posed in front of a mirror inscribed with the words of Solomon Northup (author of *Twelve Years a Slave*) when promoting the album. Northup vanished without a trace in the nineteenth century. His disappearance has never been solved.

Decades on, James Dean Bradfield's relationship with 'Revol' seems to have swung full circle. What he once dismissed as 'dog shit' now earns his respect. In 2014, he told the *NME*: 'I think I fell back in love with "Revol" because it's one of those songs that actually becomes a tiny bit more relevant as time passes. You can't live in the age of Berlusconi and not actually find a tiny bit of relevance in "Revol".' However, such 'damning with faint praise' may highlight Bradfield's desire to play down the far more contentious aspects of the song, which perhaps Richey originally sought to expose, and which have assumed a far deeper relevance in the years which have followed Richey's disappearance.

'I think I've said to you before about what he said if he left the band.
They wouldn't care, they'd carry on. He just said it straight –
he wouldn't be missed.'
Jo, letter to Rachel Edwards, 1996

During 1994, Richey's bandmates had to dispel the notion that some of the album's sentiments could be interpreted as politically conservative, even fascist. The music press also noticed that Richey was taking an interest in the Quran and Sharia law, while his notes outlining plans for the 'Faster' single suggested that its front cover depict a gold Star of David against a black background with the word 'Jude' emblazoned beneath. Operating in an industry famously populated with Jewish movers and shakers, it appeared that Richey was being deliberately provocative.

How much had Richey's contrary, bloody-minded 'political incorrectness' begun to generate in-camp difficulties? What was at stake, in his mind, was the freedom for artists to speak on any manner of topics, without censorship. During the band's notorious trip to Bangkok, Richey had told Barbara Ellen how much he hated both 'political correctness' and censorship. 'Shutting down the BNP could lead to so much [that is bad],' he said. 'If you give any government the power to silence a political power [BNP], however dodgy, they will end up abusing that power.'

Is it reasonable to suggest that certain lyrics on *The Holy Bible* were deliberately and provocatively politically incorrect? Further evidence of Richey's apparent obsession with the perceived evils of political correctness could be found on the songs 'Yes' and 'P.C.P.'

'P.C.P.' and 'The Intense Humming of Evil'

'Schindler's List – The most dangerous film ever made – that man was a bastard, pure and simple. He exploited Jews.'
Richey Edwards, 'Blood, Sweat and Tears', *The Face*, June 1994

Contributing to the overall sense of mischievous provocation, 'P.C.P.' went to the heart of the nature of power in the Western democratic world, where liberalism dominated the social-political landscape.

Traditionally, rock music culture could be said to celebrate the freedoms of the liberal West; to explore all opportunities for individual self-expression. Yet 'P.C.P.' implied that liberal freedom is shallow freedom. We are not permitted to speak truth to power.

'You're obliged to pretend respect for people and institutions you think absurd. You live attached in a cowardly fashion to moral and social conventions you despise, condemn, and know lack all foundation. It is that permanent contradiction between your ideas and desires and all the dead formalities and vain pretences of your civilisation which makes you sad, troubled and unbalanced. In that intolerable conflict you lose all joy of life and all feeling of personality, because at every moment they suppress and restrain and check the free play of your powers. That's the poisoned and mortal wound of the civilised world.'

Octave Mirbeau, *The Torture Gardens*
– quoted on the album sleeve of *The Holy Bible*

Presented with what 'P.C.P.' called 'systemised atrocity', liberalism's greater concern with the use of inoffensive language only fosters impotence in the face of unaccountable power. Richey's reference to 'stiff upper lip' conjured memories of the morality that the British Empire foisted upon the world. The implication is that imperialism continues to exist, but we are not allowed to discuss its new forms; obligated to remain silent because 'we are free'.

'P.C.P.' located its sympathies with Europe. Having studied modern political history, Richey confidently diagnosed what he considers to be the modern malaise; Europe cannot express strenuous objection to American culture and American agenda, cannot tell the truth and forgets the past as a point of principle. Discourse is straitjacketed.

For the casual observer, the band's interest in the Holocaust, and other Jewish-related issues, may have added up to nothing more than a thoroughly politically correct revulsion at the horrors of twentieth-century history. After all, the band were known to have visited concentration camps on their European tour earlier in 1994, inspiring the *Holy Bible* songs 'Mausoleum' and 'The Intense Humming of Evil'.

There was evidence of James being anxious about the content of *The Holy Bible* and how it might affect their reception in the US. Asked if he ever objected to the lyrics he was obliged to sing, he responded, 'I didn't think the first draft of "The Intense Humming of Evil" was judgemental enough. It's a song about the Holocaust and you cannot be ambivalent about a subject like that. Not even we are stupid enough to be contentious about that.'

James's misgivings about some of the lyrics had apparently demanded modifications from Richey. Among Richey's *Holy Bible* papers are drafts of 'The Intense Humming of Evil', including one headed 'James's copy'. Two lines are crossed out, and replaced, but not in the manner typical of most of Richey's corrections. The final couplet has been very heavily scribbled out, almost blacked out, suggesting their urgent removal by James himself? The redacted lines were replaced in the final draft with a couplet about Churchill's duplicity.

On closer inspection, and some deft work with Adobe Photoshop, it is possible for us to read some of the lost content, which suggests that the first several missing words may have involved something positive in relation to Nazi Germany:

(...........................) ... Deutschland
How we long to be ruled and loved.

Richey's bandmates may well have been justified in wanting to weed out overly provocative lines. Elsewhere in the *Holy Bible* lyric drafts, Richey drew a diagram, possibly an idea for cover art. In a childlike scrawl he sketched four flowers, their long stems meeting at the centre, to form a cross. Adjacent to these was a swastika, and written alongside, in block capitals, B-E-A-U-T-I-F-U-L.

Richey clearly wanted to be an agitator here. He appeared to know exactly where the boundary of political correctness lay and knowingly dipped a toe over its border, as if demonstrating ambivalence where decent opinion demands steadfastness.

While some may speculate that Richey was using 'The Intense Humming of Evil' to make an inconclusive statement on the suffering brought about by religious persecution, he was contrarily more likely to be viewing the issue through the lens of class inequality rather than taking a religious standpoint. His university studies had made him overtly aware of the level of mutual hypocrisy between the opposing factions during the Second World War. In interviews before the release of *The Holy Bible*, Richey spoke of his disgust for the film *Schindler's List*, while his earlier academic studies subscribed to the erroneous notion that many rich Jewish factions profited from the war by funding both sides while the poverty-stricken Jewish population were exterminated in their millions.

Utilising the re-written couplet which had apparently proved so troublesome, Richey ends the song by highlighting the level of duplicity which was prevalent in the behaviours of both Hitler and Churchill.

Next, targeting another revered institution, Richey set about exposing the British Empire as driven by profiteering and greed. British involvement in India resulted in savage exploitation and the extermination of millions of Indians, many at death camps. He argued against the injustice of certain atrocities being conveniently ignored, while other acts of genocide can be referenced when it suits an agenda.

Richey's lyrics for *The Holy Bible* are often seen as confusing or just plain confused; their supposedly random mix of references and moral indignations can be seen as hinting that he may not have been fully compos mentis during the writing. However, a counter-argument holds that Richey knew *exactly* what he was doing and that, armed with knowledge of the boundaries of liberalism, he knew precisely how to dare reviewers to accuse him of being something he was not.

In 1993, Richey had listed his 'Top Ten Men of the Year' in *Melody Maker*. It included Dr Hassan El Turabi, a Sudanese politician whose impact saw a rise in the execution and torture of political opponents. This is how Richey explained his selection: 'I quite like what he's doing. Islamic fundamentalism scares the West, and makes us examine our own moral ambiguity. There was a programme on him the other night where a western journalist was condemning him, but he said: "We only amputate one per cent of the thieves we catch. One per cent may be a lot where you come from, but to me, one per cent doesn't sound like many at all." I know it's very easy to congratulate that from a distance ... but I AM from a distance.'

It is not as though this reference was a one-off. In a fanzine interview from the same period, Richey stated that meeting Dr Turabi would have been a fitting end to the year for him. It's difficult to come up with an explanation for this bizarre devotion. He was to admit that he 'had a very childlike rage', a fact supported by close friends who note that he could be difficult and subtly provocative. His apparently contradictory statements and lyrical sentiments find some unity in being interpreted in this way; that is, as a form of protest or personal lashing out, rather than as a philosophical agenda.

'I'd be sat next to him when he played devil's advocate in college,' remembers Adrian Wyatt. 'He'd love winding people up, and I recognised that sort of playful antagonism in his lyrics. He was out to challenge opinions in whatever way he could.'

The genius of *The Holy Bible* stemmed in part from its vast range of references, but also from its sprawling disjunctions, scattershot outrages and sheer cryptic messiness. Listeners may have had difficulty in sewing the disparate elements together, but they knew those words were authentic, a genuine snapshot of Richey's mind.

Speaking to *Melody Maker* in January 1994, Richey commented, 'When we write lyrics, sometimes we'll come up with something that we think is really good, and works really well with James's melody. And I hate having the thought in the back of my head, that we can't possibly print this in a lyric sheet, because people will misunderstand it.

'Look at *American Psycho* by Bret Easton Ellis. It was completely misunderstood by the media. And they probably knew why they were doing it, but they just chose to ignore it. When I read it, I didn't find it cheap at all. I found it frightening, and very moralistic.'

Adroitly positioning his lyrics directly in the firing line of mainstream reaction, Richey expected that some of *The Holy Bible*'s subject matter would challenge dogmatic thinking – and not just in relation to political correctness. The Manic Street Preachers were about to attempt their own devastating critique of something closer to home – the music business in London.

'Yes'

'There's new songs about snuff movies, and if you write about that you've got to go into some kind of graphic detail ...'
Nicky Wire, *Melody Maker*, January 1994

World history and current affairs were the main target of the album's anger, but *The Holy Bible* began with a more immediate target. 'Yes' reflects on Richey's experiences in the music business, and the verdict is damning. As he wrote in the Manics' *Holy Bible* tour programme: 'Prostitution of The Self', the majority of one's time is spent doing something you hate to get something you don't need. Everyone has a price to buy themselves out of freedom. 'Say Yes to Everything.'

The band had planned on releasing 'Yes' as a final single from the album, and had got as far as having the artwork mocked up. Its cover read: *'MSP – The Band that likes to say YES. 100% hypocritical guarantee'*. This was a play on a then familiar TV ad – 'TSB, the bank that likes to say Yes' – and the re-use was telling. Richey was disenchanted with prostituting himself for mainstream success. 'Yes' was a scathing put-down of the obvious hypocrisy in adopting a radical leftist surface layer while having willingly signed one's life over to its opposite.

In 1994, Nicky's own explanation for 'Yes' was in sync with Richey's: 'It looks at the way that society views prostitutes as probably the lowest form of life. But we feel that we've prostituted ourselves over the last three or four years, and we think it's the same in every walk of life.'

Further explaining the song, Nicky reminded fans of the indulgences available to recording artists. 'There's a line in there: "Tie his hair in bunches, fuck him, call him Rita if you want." You do get to a position when you're in a band where you can virtually do anything you want, in any kind of sick, low form. It's not something we've particularly indulged in, but it is a nasty by-product of being in a group.'

The band made clear their revulsion at the depraved entertainments sometimes dangled before them. Richey certainly did. 'The thing that pisses me off about all these charity appearances by pop stars is that the minute they come off stage, they're counting their record sales, pissing off to Brown's and snorting cocaine out of some six-year-old boy's backside.'

Whatever his prior experiences with groupies, by 1994 Richey was prepared to cross a hugely taboo boundary. One of *The Holy Bible*'s most controversial features saw Richey daring to draw public attention to the levels of corruption and hypocrisy entrenched in certain sectors of life in the British capital, particularly the entertainment industry's abuse of vulnerable children.

As this book was being researched, Operation Yewtree was forcing Britain to confront damning revelations about certain sectors of society. Representatives of the establishment, including politicians, members of the judiciary, the clergy and the entertainment industry, were being exposed for the systemic abuse of children over the previous decades. Their involvement was well known within certain circles but had been kept hidden from the broader population up until this point. Within the entertainment industry, police were investigating allegations of historic abuse against Jimmy Savile, Max Clifford, Rolf Harris, Gary Glitter and others.

Details from one horrific report from this time appear to have an astounding parallel with lyrics on *The Holy Bible*. In 1991, French police charged five people in Paris with possession of extreme child pornography, including a 'snuff' video of an eight-year-old British boy being murdered.

Clearly having been assembled using a significant budget and professional filming equipment, what became known as 'The London Tape' allegedly had a particular notoriety and popularity in those depraved circles. Among the description of its contents, certain details have an uncanny overlap with Richey's own description of a child snuff movie.

Throughout his time in the band, Richey was in the habit of speaking out against the levels of immorality and corruption that he discovered were inimical to life in London. As far back as 1992 in an interview with *Smash Hits* magazine, he alluded to 'pervy judges' in an apparently off-the-cuff comment. Sordid lifestyles existed in Wales too, of course, but not on the scale of debauchery tolerated in the English capital. In 'Yes' Richey castigates a society where money offered the opportunity to buy anything up to and including paedophilic snuff films.

The 'London Tape' snuff film reportedly contained footage of the British child having his penis removed with a scalpel, his killer then raping the remaining cavity. We could dismiss this similarity as mere coincidence were it not for the fact that the detail correlates so exactly. It is possible that Richey Edwards may simply have imagined a scene, whose detail just happened to describe the most harrowing scene from what was the most notorious of child snuff films.

However, bearing in mind his propensity to use his lyrics to report first-hand conversation verbatim, including home truths others might prefer never to hear, another possible explanation arises. Could it be that the song dared to share shocking information that Richey had actually been privy to, and with which he could taunt or scare whoever had shared such details with him? After all, 'Yes' was a song about prostitution, which took direct aim at the music business.

> *Interviewer: 'I find that, again, extraordinary – the chorus*
> *[of 'Yes']. ... Where's it coming from?!*
> Dutch Radio, November 1994

A characteristic that made the Manic Street Preachers stand out was their evangelising for a greater sense of humanity. Central to their narrative was the idea of their struggle against a social-cultural environment hell-bent on dehumanising and disempowering us all. The band contrasted so vividly with others of their era, whose whole style and approach articulated a voice that was barely human any more; crushed and animalised to the brink of insanity. For the Manic Street Preachers, the Sex Pistols represented a defiant display of greater humanity rather than lesser. They were, in Richey's words, 'One of the most intense and sensitive groups there's ever been, which always gets overlooked, I think.'

As reports of paedophile cover-ups began to fill the news, the media also carried the story that, at the peak of the Sex Pistols' fame, John Lydon had dared to speak out about a certain highly regarded BBC television personality. 'I'd like to kill Jimmy Savile. I think he's a hypocrite,' said Lydon in a recently discovered but unaired BBC Radio interview in 1978. 'I bet he's into all kinds of seediness, that we all know about but are not allowed to talk about. I know some rumours! I bet none of this will be allowed out, but nothing I have said is libel.'

Leaks of such information never led to serious investigation, let alone prosecutions, and the truth was deliberately covered up for many years. Speaking out decades later, at a time when the mainstream media was finally forced to confront the fact that so many of its household names had been sexual predators, Lydon revealed that his career had been affected as parts of the media establishment closed ranks. 'I'm very, very bitter that the likes of Savile and the rest of them were allowed to continue. I did my bit, I said what I had to. But they didn't air that. I found myself banned from BBC radio for quite a while, for my contentious behaviour.'

Whereas John Lydon's outspokenness in this particular interview may have been censored in the form of an unofficial ban from the BBC, Richey's later equivalent was less easily suppressed, arriving in the form of a lyric on the opening track of an album at the top of the charts. Undoubtedly, he would have taken great pride in accompanying Lydon in speaking out on these issues, but would Richey's more pointed outrage lead to trouble for him?

Was there someone in the wings, terrified that he could relay their words verbatim, and now wondering what he might say next?

In the autumn of 1993, the BBC broadcast the documentary *Michel Foucault, Beyond Good and Evil*. It described the French philosopher as 'a lone figure exploring the dark labyrinths of human experience; madness, criminality, perversion. He is the great explorer of the perverse.

He takes the victims of history, the mad, the bad, the sinful and the criminal, and doesn't romanticise them. He shows them as a mirror image of society.'

Within the horrors of *The Holy Bible*, Richey sought not only to hold up a mirror to society, but to stir up a moral consciousness in listeners through harsh and insightful truths. The album offered no positive outlook for change, nor was there anything that truly sought to effect solutions to the raw dilemmas it posed.

Before its release, the band said: 'The world is such a violent place. What we experience from the everyday world, what we read and what we see makes you realise that there's worse and worse things happening all the time. Perhaps it might reach such a low point of existence that something good may come of it.'

In defining this 'low point of existence' Richey was targeting his audience and imploring them to re-align their moral compass by facing up to the most uncomfortable of truths. He asked where humanity could go from here, and left the solution for his listeners to decipher.

In this sense, was *The Holy Bible* therefore the revolutionary album which the band had been promising since its inception; an invitation to their audience to rebel and reclaim the right to decide their own destiny? After this album, comprising more questions than answers, it is fitting that Richey's own personal fate leaves us with similar ambiguous and unanswered questions.

'Writing to each other all those years ago,' says Alistair Fitchett, 'we'd mostly talk about the ideas behind the lyrics and poetry of people we admired. What was their message, what did they really mean? Especially when it came to Rimbaud, whose work carried extra resonance because he gave up his craft at his peak, gave up his life, and disappeared to live overseas.

'Richey would have been aware of the image he'd have after *The Holy Bible* was released and, from the beginning, I believe he had a plan. Career-wise, he was always very clear about what the future looked like, and gave his ideas away inadvertently or overtly through interviews and lyrics.

'He seemed to have things mapped out so much more than anyone I've ever come across. He would know what the effects of every action would be. He'd have choreographed every idea, every scenario in his head and people's reactions to them.'

While writing *The Holy Bible* in 1993, Richey told the music press that 'If you have a record which encapsulates the mood of a generation, you should split up.' Following rave reviews, which described the record as a 'pinnacle of an album', was this the excuse he needed to make that break? Rachel Edwards believes so.

'I think Richard was laying out a ground work for something when writing the album. He'd definitely made some kind of decision to change his existing life with the band after what he called the "humiliation" of *Gold Against the Soul*. I think when he was writing it, he saw it as his final testament on record. It's a bit like Joy Division's last album *Closer*, and how in hindsight, fans have read it as *Close-r*. As if Ian Curtis intended it to be a full stop.

'With a mind like Richard's that was always changing, whether he was planning suicide or a disappearance, I think he'd covered those eventualities in the lyrics, and knew whatever he decided to do next, it would add extra credence to the words he wrote on *The Holy Bible*.'

'If this is our last album then it's a brilliant album to finish on.'
James Dean Bradfield, 1994

Chapter 10

Doors Closing Slowly

Straight from psychiatric care and back to the daily grind, Richey joined the Manic Street Preachers at Blue Stone Studios, West Wales, in September 1994 to rehearse for an upcoming tour of France. It would begin with them supporting the Northern Irish trio Therapy? and mark the start of the band's scheduled 54-date European tour.

A month after his release from the Priory, the front cover of October's *NME* featured Richey in Blue Stone, bleary eyed and hugging a statue. His body frail, and his arms covered in self-inflicted cuts and cigarette burns; the strapline read: 'THE SCARRED REVIVAL – RICHEY MANIC back from the brink.'

'It was a lot to take on so soon after leaving hospital,' says Rachel. 'I don't know if he gave himself enough time to get better. He never really stepped out of the spotlight, or away from the public "Richey Manic" he may have felt the need to live up to.'

In 1996, Nicky Wire looked back at the strains affecting Richey after his hospitalisation. 'We had to put him to bed one night 'cos he just burst out crying in the car. It did feel that we were taking it so far with the record, and some of the lyrics were so self-fulfilling for Richey. Like "Die in the Summertime". I'm sure he felt that "People are gonna say I'm a fake if I don't do something about it".'

Back on the road, with drink, drugs and over-indulgence all around Richey, it left those close to him wondering how conducive this was to enabling him to become well again.

'It was hard for him on all sorts of levels,' reflects Rosie Dunn. 'His mind, the type of DNA he had as a recovering alcoholic, and the line of work he was in. He told me he needed the lubrication of alcohol to perform on stage. To just be lounging around on the tour bus all day working himself up with anxiety for those nightly gigs can't have helped his mental state.

'Plus, the fact he couldn't sleep, and used alcohol as an anaesthetic. I think of all this extraordinary brainpower that he had, and how it must have been going around in his head on that last tour. Trying to make sense of this crazy world, without the respite of sleep – it must have driven him damn near insane.'

A *Melody Maker* article from the first leg of the French tour found Caitlin Moran describing Richey as back to some semblance of health, seemingly cheerful and stabilised: 'Richey looks well – very well – and, more than that, beautiful; and seems reasonably happy. Things are stabilising.' However, Richey's letters to Jo from that period suggested an altogether different state of mind.

I'm tired of opinion, to listening – Fuck it – Other people's judgements. No, no, no, no, no, that's simply not true. I worry about every triviality far too much. Stupid me. They're fools if they think I'm 100% well and healthy. You know how it is – a smile and an OK is all it takes to convince the world that everything's hunky dory. The sins of me – a shield, an invisible shield. Smiles don't mean a thing. A plastic smile always Wins. Goddamn Grin weighs me down. Others judgement. At least me and you try harder than most eh? Don't fear it. Make it your friend. It's nothing. We can't separate each other. We're the same – me and you – Us Against Them. There's gotta be some dignity somewhere.

During their 11-date support slot with Therapy?, *The Holy Bible* and its Richey-led material failed to impress French audiences. As James would explain to *Melody Maker* a month later, 'You develop an instinct for when a country doesn't get it. If there was any way we could have done this tour and bypassed France, we would have done.'

A further setback followed on the band's return to the UK when they released what was to be their last-ever single as a four-piece. 'She is Suffering' charted at a disappointing number 25. With a less urgent, slower-paced sound than other singles from *The Holy Bible*, and a video Nicky Wire described as 'shite beyond belief', critics were quick to concede that this was not the band's finest hour, with one journalist even joking that this was the first male rock song penned about menstruation.

In the accompanying *Holy Bible* tour programme, Richey explained the meaning of the song thus: '"She" is desire. In other Bibles and Holy Books no truth is possible until you empty yourself of desire. All commitment otherwise is fake/lies/economic convenience.'

Press articles following his stay at the Priory reported Buddhist literature among his reading material, and highlighted Richey's increasing interest in the religious and the spiritual. In 2009, Nicky spoke of his bandmate's growing fascination in attaining a simpler, more ascetic way of life. 'He was ridding himself at that time; he did seem to be ridding himself of any material complications. It was just books, or watching the TV or listening to music. There wasn't really anything else involved.'

That autumn Richey also began carrying a book of biblical quotes around with him, and took to writing the words LOVE on both his knuckles, with those around him noticing a marked change in his personality.

'He asked me for a copy of the Old Testament for Christmas, so that he could read the book of Ecclesiastes,' remembers Rachel. 'I think he was trying to channel this emptiness he felt inside into something, anything. Nick said that the Priory ripped out the man and left a shell; and that the cure was to totally change your personality. Richard seemed at the time to be confronting this emptiness he had, and filling it with whatever he could find from religious sources that gave comfort to others.

'But I think despite the changes he showed outwardly, deep down he still had the same cynicism he always had – so it must have felt like he was split in two. I imagine it was hard for him to connect with the others; he was on a different plain with his thought process at the time. His belief system was still very fragmented, and whatever he was feeling during his stay at the Priory came out with him, but this time he really was doing his best to change his frame of mind and address that scepticism.'

On 5 October, the band embarked on the first half of a 14-date British tour. One of the support acts was alternative Welsh metal-reggae outfit Dub War, and it didn't take long for their front man Benji Webbe to notice the stark difference from the Richey he'd met a year before his hospitalisation.

'He used to come to our gigs in Newport in 1993. But the Richey I saw in the past and the Richey we toured with were two totally different people. From the first day of the tour, he was as sketchy as fuck. If you approached him, he'd have no more than two words to say, and run off. After one concert, our bassist sat by him and Richey just blurted out, "You can't be here now," and so the bassist got up and walked away.

'Once I heard ear-splitting music coming from a pitch-black dressing room. I remember asking Ginge, our drummer, "Who's in there?" He told me, "Richey's on his own in there, listening to Sepultura." He was always on his own; I barely saw him with anyone, not even James, Nick or Sean.'

After eight days on tour with the band, and much to Benji's dismay, Dub War received a phone call from Hall or Nothing informing them they were no longer required for the latter half of the tour, and their contract was effectively terminated.

'We got the call saying we'd been kicked off the tour, because apparently one of us had said Richey was "swanning around" Blackwood showing off his cuts on his arms. That never came from the band, it came from our roadie. The *NME* had the choice whether to write that. Magazines know when members are ill, and all the rest of it. They chose to publish that, to bring Richey down, for whatever reason.

'The last time I saw him was in a hallway of the Manchester Academy before the gig. There was one of those doors, where you've got to key the numbers in. He kept trying and trying different combinations but he just couldn't get it. He was on his own, and he was just fucking well freaked out. Like a puppet with the key taken out of his back. There was no need for him to be freaked out, because he's got ten thousand fans all screaming his name every night, but he was just so shaky and scared. I remember looking at him and thinking he wasn't well at all. He just seemed like he didn't want to be there, didn't wanna play, didn't wanna be on tour.'

One pressure that was certainly not making life easier for Richey was the rumour, propagated by music journalists, that a 'Cult of Richey' had developed among his more obsessive fans. Letter pages of the *NME* and *Melody Maker* were filled with testimony, usually from young females, proving their discipleship with tales of self-mutilation, starvation and letters written in blood.

'She has a cult, and what the hell is a cult except a gang of
rebels without a cause. I have fans. There's a big difference.'
Joan Crawford on Bette Davis

'Some of the music press were adamant on turning him into some sort of a caricature,' remembers Rachel. 'It was only the very basic elements of his character being amplified – as if his cutting and diagnosis of depression were all there was to him. He was so much more than that, and I know he wanted to be appreciated for his poetry and sensitivity.

'Having this cult label was reductive for him, and did a lot of damage in terms of how people remember him. I've met many people through the years who've told me that when they've expressed admiration for Richard or his work, they've been labelled as having a depressive personality, or are some sort of self-harming nutcase. It's a shame that people can't show their appreciation of him without others making such assumptions.

'I know he was capable of playing up to the rock star myth at times, and I don't know how far he'd lost himself in that role, and how he viewed himself in terms of his own personal identity. I don't think those accusations helped, because it made me wonder if he felt like he had to perform all the time just to make an impact. That he had to act a certain way to gain attention and be loved? And worse still, some of the media just lapped up all his behaviour as if it had no personal consequences behind the scenes.'

'The less intelligent an animal is, the more it acts naturally. Man is born without the equipment to be free. Man is the only species that realises he will die. He is burdened with it and does anything to avoid it, even becoming fake. An endless scream passing through nature.'
Richey's archive, 1994

On 13 October the band played the Manchester Academy. Tickets were oversold and the venue was densely packed.

'It was dangerously full,' recalls Alan G. Parker. 'A 2,500 capacity packed with 3,000 fans. Factory Records' Anthony Wilson was there milling around and declaring the place a health hazard! There were a lot of gawpers because Rich had just come out of hospital, and all eyes were on him. Everyone was jostling to get to his side of the stage. It was a decent set and you could hear Rich was plugged in and playing more than he usually did. He was wearing this tiny little top with a picture of the Fairy Liquid baby on it, and looked about three stone in weight. I have never seen anybody thinner.

'After the show I spoke to Therapy?'s Andy Cairns and asked him, "How's everything going with the Manics?" and he just gave me a look that said, "Don't go there." When I got to the dressing room to see the band, they didn't seem as tight as they'd been in the past. There was a lot of distance there, a lot of silence. They were on eggshells;

they didn't want to say too much to me or anyone. It was like, if they did, they'd accidently let something out.'

Back in South Wales, on 20 October the band played another sold-out show and the closest to a homecoming, at Cardiff's Astoria. Friends from Blackwood came along to support them, including Richey's former gigging acquaintance Joanna Haywood.

'He came to speak to me and Byron after the show. I didn't know what to expect after hearing he'd been so ill, but he seemed glad to see us. I was drinking heavily and he was propping me up to stop me falling over. He seemed his old self, telling me not to get too drunk and to be careful, because people could take advantage of the fact.

'I remember feeling glad he hadn't changed much, because it reminded me of when we used to hire a van to drive to gigs back in the day, and the time he went nuts when a Chinese businessman offered to buy me breakfast at a service station. He kept telling me, "You think that's all he wants? To buy you breakfast?!" and he sped all the way home down the M4! It wasn't jealousy. It was him being protective. And he still had that natural, in-built concern for people all those years on.'

Before returning to the Continent for the second half of their European tour, the band were given a two-week break, during which Jo successfully contacted Richey for the first time since his suicide attempt that summer. By the end of 1994, they were once again spending time in each other's company.

Photographs in Richey's collection feature Jo at his bedroom window; gazing out over the Bay; in the flat's kitchen eating ice cream; and pulling goofy expressions while posing in front of his wall collages. Another set of images shows the pair at Caerphilly Castle just north of Cardiff, scaling the walls and looking out over the town, and taking selfies as they wrap up warm against freezing winds.

After the disappearance, Jo wrote a letter to Rachel describing their moments together at his Cardiff flat that autumn. 'After he came out of hospital he had changed, without a doubt. Before that, say in the mornings when he was sober, he would be shivering, tearful, gloomy, but he was calm, he could relax, he could talk. This winter, when I stayed weekends – although we were both happy, in good moods, chatting, taking the piss out of each other, watching brilliant films in duvets, gorging on chocolate – he just seemed unable to relax. The TV, the stereo, had to be on. He'd be chain smoking, drinking one coffee after another, writing, eating; he had to be doing something. He had to be occupied. It was as if he let himself stop, if he let himself think, something awful might happen. I know it sounds trivial but it wasn't, it was just awful. I'd end up shouting at him to sit down. I'd be thinking to myself, oh please, please be normal again, come back. It broke my heart, missing him while I was with him.

'One night, I knew he was hiding something from me, he wanted to tell me. It took until dawn for him to say that he wanted to chop off his fingers. This was no joke. He was serious, he was scared. He said he felt like he had no choice! It took hours of reasoning and persuasion for him to rationalise. He felt he had no control over his thoughts. I had never seen him like that before, it was frightening. He kept knives and choppers under the bed, they're still there! Who could I speak to? I've tried talking to the others.'

Richey would further expound on his anxieties to Jo about the American tour that was coming up in the New Year. He was dreading he'd be exposed Stateside as a fraud, due to his inability to master the guitar. He talked of Steve Clark, the ex-Def Leppard guitarist who once broke his own knuckles on a wash basin to evade performing.

That autumn, he also became increasingly fascinated by Dennis Hopper's portrayal of a photojournalist in Frances Ford Coppola's epic *Apocalypse Now* – even buying an exact replica of the camera used in the film and wearing it around his neck in the same fashion. Hopper's character was based on Sean Flynn, son of the legendary Robin Hood actor Errol. After vanishing while on a photo assignment for *Time* magazine in Cambodia, he was immortalised by The Clash with a track called 'Sean Flynn' on their 1982 *Combat Rock* album. Believed to have been captured and murdered by communist guerrillas, Flynn was never seen again. Fourteen years later, his mother had him declared dead in absentia.

'He would have been more than aware of the link between Dennis Hopper's character and Sean Flynn,' says Rachel. 'The year before Richard went missing, Flynn's mother died and his disappearance would have been news all over again.

'By the end of that year, Richard kept going on about *Apocalypse Now* to anyone who'd listen. He'd love telling me how, after filming, Marlon Brando left Hollywood and virtually disappeared. He just gave up on fame and went on hiatus for ten years to live on an island away from everybody and everything – indulging himself by doing whatever he wanted, whenever he wanted, and putting no restraints on himself. He ate constantly, becoming really fat in the process and there was nobody around to judge him or tell him what to do. I think Richard wished he too could go past that point of caring about his own body and appearance, and live a life free from the judgement and scrutiny of others.'

> *'Have you ever considered, any real freedoms?*
> *Freedoms from the opinions of others.*
> *Even the opinions of yourself?'*
> Colonel Kurtz in *Apocalypse Now*

Mark Hambridge had seen little of his friend since moving to Minehead in 1991, but when they were reunited shortly before Richey's disappearance, he, like Rachel, was regaled with Richey's latest passion.

'*Apocalypse Now* was his "last obsession" as I call it, and there must have been some real significance in that. He was very obsessive about things, and always for a reason. Everything always held more layers of meaning for him than the average person. He always made his passions public, because he wanted you to hone in on them, and with Rich the ambiguity of the messages were always there for you to decipher. He'd have a way of layering meaning on meaning, and liking to sit back and watch you figure it out for yourself.'

When asked by *Melody Maker* for his recommended Christmas reading material in December 1994, Richey named *Heart of Darkness* by Joseph Conrad, the book upon which *Apocalypse Now* was based. He told the magazine, 'Any book that has an impact on me, I re-read it and write out all the lines I like and memorise them.'

What might have been the reasons behind Richey's concentrated efforts to draw the attention of his family, friends and fans to these works; a book and film which explored society's corruption and its exploitation of the individual, along with the twin themes of disappearance and exile? With his new-found admiration for the way Brando lived his later years, might Richey also have made the decision to similarly remove himself? Could his methodical and compulsive nature have conspired against his innate sensitivity to facilitate a calculating retreat into his own heart of darkness?

One of the last photocopies Richey printed was of a black-and-white newspaper clipping of Bette Davis and Joan Crawford in the 1962 film, *What Ever Happened to Baby Jane?* The two women portray sisters, former well-known actresses, now hiding in obscurity and living as recluses. Underneath the photograph, Richey wrote out an excerpt from *Heart of Darkness*. He made several further photocopies and kept them in his last known folders of writing.

'Seepy Seepy Bye Bye'
Hubert Selby Jr, *The Demon*
– comment on Richey's set list, 7 November 1994,
Frankfurt, Germany

On 7 November, the band commenced the second half of their tour overseas, supporting the androgynous forerunners of Britpop, Suede. It was during these three weeks on the road that the strains between Richey and the band became even more evident.

In Suede's authorised biography *Love and Poison*, lead singer Brett Anderson remembers his time with Richey during the ill-fated tour. 'He was the only one of the band who wasn't very sociable. I think I spoke to him once. My memory of him is just being withdrawn.'

Suede's newly recruited teen guitarist Richard Oakes recounted that while he made every effort to strike up conversation with Richey, most gave him a wide berth. 'Richey obviously had all his problems and he was always quiet so nobody ever went near him. We were on our bus waiting to go and the Manics' bus was parked next to us and it was bitterly cold. And somebody from our crew came on and said, "That guy from the Manics is sitting outside in his pants!" And everyone was like "Pffff, what a weirdo!"

'I thought to myself, "I'm going to go and talk to him!" I went down and said to him, "Aren't you absolutely bloody freezing?" and he said, "Yes, but I want to be." So I was like "OK ... are you enjoying the tour?" And he had this laminate round his neck with a list of dates and he pointed to the ones he'd enjoyed, this one, this one and this one.

'He said, "This must be amazing for you, you're so young, you've come straight from school, you've got your whole life ahead of you." And I was aware the whole time that while I'm having a great time on my first tour with Suede, this lot are on the point of breaking up. And I'm speaking to the reason that they're breaking up.'

Years later, Nicky Wire would identify this period as an all-time low for the band, telling *Select* magazine, 'It was probably the worst time I've ever experienced in my life. In some respects, it was worse than when Richey actually disappeared, because he was on the verge of madness.

'And James just didn't stop drinking. It was just absolute fucking hell. I said to James one night, "I'm going to leave", and he went out, got wazzed out of his brain and couldn't even fucking remember what I'd said to him. Everybody was totally oblivious to everybody else's needs.

'Every morning I woke up and wanted to go home. Richey had stopped drinking, he'd come out of hospital and he'd just started smoking 65 cigarettes a day. And I can't stand smoke. I'm not having a go at him: he was fucked out of his mind, smoking that much and drinking about 30 cups of coffee a day. Everything was bad.'

James: It's a bad time to go to the tour bus. Richey's teetering. He's always teetering, really.

Simon Price: Has he gone to bed?

James: The abyss.

Sean: Richey doesn't go to bed. He goes to the abyss.

11.45pm. James wants a drink. 'But I can't. Our bus is leaving at 1am, it's not fair to drink in front of Richey, and there's nothing sadder than getting drunk for four hours on a tour bus, then going to sleep.'

12.00am. James: 'I really want a drink.'

12.05am. James is wearing a 'Kill 'em All – Let God Sort 'em Out' T-shirt. 'I feel like a caged animal.'

12.10am. James punches the wall, very hard, very fast. Everyone jumps.

From 'Ooh, Aaah, Street Preach-Ah!', *Melody Maker*, December 1994

With the band and crew maintaining their distance, and the majority of journalists being kept at arm's length, it was halfway through the tour before things reached breaking point. Their appearance at Amsterdam's Paradiso fell flat and left the band feeling more dejected than ever – all apart from Richey, who was oddly upbeat after having carved a gash into his torso and declaring, 'I feel OK now.' With more than a few journalists having made the trip to report on the tour's upcoming finale shows in Germany and Austria, Sean hastily ushered them to a local night-spot and away from the chaos ensuing behind the scenes.

'There was an atmosphere during the whole tour when the journalists weren't around,' recalls the band's roadie. 'I even heard Richey lose his temper and raise his voice, something I'd never experienced before. He and Nicky were having a screaming match on the bus, and Richey was being threatened with being thrown out of the band. He was later given an ultimatum: if he cut again, he'd be out. The atmosphere was beyond bleak.'

Fearing the intra-band tensions escalating, record company affiliates flew from London into Hamburg for the band's penultimate dates. On the morning of 1 December, Richey was found outside the band's hotel in Hamburg, banging his head against a brick wall, his face drenched in blood. The tour was terminated shortly afterwards.

'You read the interviews from the time, and there are unspoken layers of frustration there,' Rachel summarises. 'What with Nick saying he wanted to quit the band, and James punching a wall and stating he couldn't drink because of Richard. The way the band and crew normally toured had totally changed, and it must have been frustrating for them to have to abandon some of their more familiar habits to accommodate somebody who was in recovery.

'It sounded like a hard time for everybody and I imagine Richard felt like a burden. Their friendship was really being put to the test, and because of the commercial failure of *The Holy Bible*, the future of the band was obviously in jeopardy.'

During the last dates of their blighted European tour, Nicky began presenting James with sets of his own completed lyrics. One of these was the future album track, 'Further Away'. Describing it as an 'almost love song', the band would admit after Richey's disappearance that the lyrics represented a moment of freedom, a song the band could never have written in their earlier years. Having mainly co-written with Richey before, Nicky's own ideas for the next album possessed a mellower and more commercial touch; one that was on an entirely different trajectory from Richey's, who at the time slipped the band a note reading, 'Ideas for the next album: Pantera meets Nine Inch Nails meets *Screamadelica*.'

James would later comment, 'Richey wanted to continue with the darkness of *The Holy Bible*, but the rest of us felt that would be falling into caricature. We wanted to breathe a bit more. He wanted complete creative control, and we [the band] would never survive that.'

When the Manic Street Preachers first burst onto the music scene, Richey was considered the de facto band leader. By the end of 1994, was it possible he felt demoted, his opinion now counting for far less? More importantly, to what effect did it determine the decision he would go on to make on 1 February 1995? For a man described by his bandmates as 'adept at dramatic symbolism', could Richey's choice of tattoos during their final tour hold some significance?

Along with his Useless Generation tattoo from the start of his time with the band, Richey added a further three inkings during the autumn of 1994. The first, on his lower bicep, had the words 'I'll surf this beach', which was a line from his fixation, *Apocalypse Now*. The remaining two brandings were inspired by Dante Alighieri's fourteenth-century epic, the *Divine Comedy*. One adorned his upper arm: a sphere of vines and roses, with smaller circles encompassed within, depicting the holy city of Jerusalem at the world's centre, and below it the Inferno and Mount Purgatory. The *Divine Comedy* states that in order to gain passage to Jerusalem, one has to pass through hell and climb Mount Purgatory's seven steps, each representing one of the seven deadly sins, with the implication that man must first pass through hell in order to gain salvation and reach Paradise.

Richey's third tattoo portrayed Dante's ninth and deepest circle of hell, that reserved for the worst kind of sinner – the betrayers and the treacherous. Inscribed in the circle are the words 'Traitors to their Lovers, Traitors to their Guests, Traitors to their Country, Traitors to their Kindred.' Could such a bold statement possibly be read as a forewarning that Richey was to betray his friends and family with his disappearance? Or was it implying that he, himself, was at the mercy of the betrayers? For someone who took the band as seriously as Richey, it's no great leap to imagine him adorning his upper arm with such messages and communicating his sentiments in his usual cryptic manner.

'We didn't speak much about his new tattoos,' remembers Rachel, 'but he did mention wanting to make a pilgrimage to Jerusalem in the New Year. He'd tried to get out of the first part of the US tour in February and asked if Nick could go in his place to do the promotional duties, but [Nick] said he didn't want to go, and perhaps that's because Nick wanted to put distance between himself and the commercial failure of *The Holy Bible*.'

Before the climax of the *Holy Bible* tour, Jo paid one last visit to Richey's Cardiff apartment. Even though it was daylight, he insisted on drawing the curtains and sat her down in front of the television. Before leaving the room, he pressed the 'Play' button on his video player and a pre-recorded VHS of a documentary featuring Joy Division began. It told the story of the suicide of lead singer Ian Curtis, before going on to chart the band's subsequent re-emergence as New Order. Every so often Jo noticed Richey popping his head around the door. Was she taking it all in? Was the message getting through? Such incidents take on greater significance in hindsight, and years later have left those close to Richey attempting to decipher what else he was trying to communicate.

Was this some clue to suicide, or to survival? Was Richey suggesting that, should he commit suicide, the band would inevitably move on contentedly? Or could he have been telling Jo that he was too wise to expect to be loved more dead than alive? Had he thought himself out of the clichéd ending, a step ahead of the game, opting instead for survival and for something better?

In 1996, James told *Melody Maker*: 'One thing I know is that towards the end, Richey became very obsessed with some kind of victory over himself. He really didn't want to be a loser. But, because we haven't got a clue what the fuck happened to him, people can't take that as a testament in blood, that he failed or he succeeded. All I know is that, as I say, towards the end, he was totally obsessed with this idea of victory. Which makes you think ... it's only an assumption, but ... maybe he wanted to divorce himself from every-thing he created?'

'I have always been hated for the right reasons and loved for the wrong ones. All my enemies have been rewarded and my true friends have betrayed me. They've wronged me and persecuted me and if I complained, it was always they were proved right. Sometimes I tried to revenge myself. I could never, never do it. I had too much pity to lay the enemy low. But they had no pity. I would prick them with a pin. They'd attack me with their bludgeons, their knives and their cannon and mangle my bones.'
Richey archive, November 1994

Richey played his final gigs with the band over three nights at the London Astoria. Before these shows, he did something he'd not done since the band's earlier days and invited family, former home-town and university friends, and new contacts from his time at the Priory, to the finale on 21 December.

'He asked me along numerous times but I couldn't go because I was working,' remembers Rachel. 'He was really trying to get Rosie to come along too by any means possible, even though she was away from London at the time. In hindsight, I think he knew it was going to be his last show because of all the effort he went to in trying to get everybody down there.'

The night climaxed in a last release of negative energies. The band trashed all their equipment, while photographer Pennie Smith captured the last ever images of Richey on stage, beating himself about the head with the splintered remains of his hated guitar. He then proceeded to dive-bomb into Sean's drum-kit as the rest of the band exited the stage.

In 1998, Nicky Wire told BBC's *Close-Up* documentary, 'I really felt like "Something's finished here," and it turned out to be the last gig we ever did with Richey.'

In the years that followed, the band were content to allude to a sense of finality after the Astoria gig. It was 2017 before Sean Moore finally confirmed on *Escape from the History* – a documentary detailing the band's successful comeback after Richey's disappearance – that the consensus among the group at the time was that they were as good as finished.

'First *The Holy Bible* didn't do as expected, and we knew we were on the back foot. We were just waiting for that moment for the record company to say that's it, we've spent enough on you. I think with the Astoria when we trashed the gear, I think we thought that was going to be pretty much it for us.'

If Richey was viewing the final night at the Astoria as the end of his time with the Manic Street Preachers, and a full stop on his time in the public glare, then he couldn't have picked a better moment. With his twenty-seventh birthday falling the next day, he would have been all too aware of the pantheon of musicians, from Brian Jones to Jim Morrison, to Janis Joplin, to Jimi Hendrix, who had passed away at the same age and joined the '27 Club'. The recent death of Kurt Cobain had brought this phenomenon back to the fore, and reinforced the number's mythic status in the world of rock and roll legends.

> *'Now he's gone and joined that stupid club. I told him not*
> *to join that stupid club.'*
> Wendy O'Connor, mother of Kurt Cobain, April 1994

One item in Richey's archive is his last personal diary. Gifted to him during the festive season, the Marvel Comics pocket planner spans entries from Christmas Day 1994 through to the first week of the New Year, giving an inkling of what occupied Richey's mind in the lead-up to his disappearance:

December 25th: See Mam. So many kind people + kind presents. Very very kind. Day is so normal. Good cut tonight. Got a throbbing pulsing underneath.

December 26th: Up late. Gave Snoopy a beautiful brush today. Bad phone call.

December 27th: Up really late. Home by 2. Nan. Watch US World Cup. Upsetting memory returns. Buy beautiful Winceyette Pyjamas.

December 28th: Up late again. Can't believe it. No sleep for 3 days now bar a few stolen hours. Go to Bute St. doctors. Unbelievable down there. Go home, good dinner. Everybody is so very kind. I don't deserve it. I am a bad boy. Unworthy. Watch Making of Snow White. Rachel comes around. Watch The Fly, Match of the Day.

December 30th: Get back, nearly crash the car, so tired and sleepy, go to bed at 6 o'clock and sleep til 1 o'clock next day—waking 4/5 times for a coffee / fags / beautiful hearing Jo. Drive to Swansea and visit old places. Feel scared only a little and happy remembering. Panic Panic.

'The Christmas period was very normal,' remembers Rachel. 'A family event, the same as any other year – we exchanged gifts, we watched television and had a traditional dinner. Since the Priory, Richard was taking his commitment to alcohol abstinence very seriously; he didn't even have Christmas pudding because it had the tiniest dash of brandy in it, but he was still restricting his food, so my mam was doing the best she could to feed him up.'

Adrian Wyatt remembers the last time he saw his friend, shortly before the festive season. 'He was painfully thin. McDonald's had just started doing salads, and he told me he was eating one of those every day. By that point he was certainly body dysmorphic. I remember him saying years before that the camera always added ten pounds, and I imagine being photographed continuously by the press couldn't have helped that kind of mentality.

'He was bright enough to be aware of his problems, which can be blessing and a curse. He had a wry sense of humour about it all and knew when to give a little smile. But every time I saw him he was becoming more and more subdued in his interactions. It was like he was having the life sucked out of him gradually and parts of him were fading away.'

On New Year's Eve, Richey turned up on the doorstep of his old friend Stephen Gatehouse, who was still living with his mother. Reaching out at the height of his problems with the band, Richey had only recently made contact again that autumn, six years after Gatehouse infamously wrote into *Impact* magazine under the pseudonym David Geary. Stephen was out, but Richey surprised Gatehouse's mother by staying on the porch for some time and sharing a cigarette with her instead.

The two reminisced over old times, when the Gatehouses' was a hub of activity and usually packed with Stephen's college friends, and former Funeral in Berlin bandmates. Richey apparently appeared grateful for the nostalgia and thankful for somebody to talk to. Half an hour after Mrs Gatehouse said goodnight and shut the door, she gazed outside only to see him still sat there, looking desolate and utterly dejected. Despite being at the helm of one of Britain's biggest rock bands, Richey found himself alone and at a loose end on what would be his last accounted-for New Year's Eve as his diary entry reveals:

December 31st: 'New Year's Eve: Wow. Another Big Wow – I am on my own. Some phone calls. Watch Woodstock and it just makes me sick. Not as sick as Jools Holland tho.

Richey's diary entries cease on 8 January, save for one last scrawl on the 17th, three days after the death of his beloved dog Snoopy. The calendar notes a Lunar Full Moon phase, and Richey writes underneath it 'Killing Moon' – a reference to the best-loved song of one of his favourite bands as a teen, Echo & the Bunnymen. Or had he written it days beforehand, with the vague notion that, at some point between Snoopy dying and the forthcoming trip to America, he would be forced to make up his mind about his future and take drastic action?

'January was the start of a really bad month for Richard, and Snoopy's death was only one of the catalysts,' says Rachel. 'The dog had arthritis in his back legs for a while, but by mid-January he couldn't walk. My mam rang me urgently to come up to the house because the vet was there and said he needed to be put down because he was in so much pain. I rushed up there but it was too late.

'I'll never forget walking into the living room and seeing Richard on the floor, curled into a half circle holding Snoopy's body. He was hugging him tightly and sobbing uncontrollably. He was inconsolable, the most devastated I'd ever seen him. It's one of those images that stays with you for life.'

Snoopy's passing meant further beloved elements of Richey's treasured youth were slipping away, and with them an innocence and happiness he felt he might never experience again. His dog had been by his side during his idyllic childhood and throughout his difficult adolescence, and had now died at the worst possible time. With one of the Priory's councillors having recently identified Richey as suffering with unresolved grief years after the death of his grandmother, this latest bereavement doubtless stirred painful memories for him.

After the disappearance, the band told the *NME* that they'd viewed Richey's mourning of Snoopy as a positive; something tangible and of the real world.

Nicky said, 'He was well on his way before then. It certainly didn't help, but something was gonna give. It gave in the summer, and it was just a question of whether he was gonna change it or not. He didn't seem to get enjoyment from many things by the end. When he cried naturally, it was nothing to do with the Priory, it was just his pet had died.'

'Yes everyone may think I'm daft but I don't give a SHIT. As long as my friends still like me I don't care. When I got back Sat night I suddenly realised Snoopy has been faithful and loyal to me longer than anyone.'
Richey, letter to Mark Hambridge, 1987

When Mark Hambridge caught up with Richey in the days after Snoopy's death, he was one of the first to see his friend's drastic change of image. 'My car broke down in Gloucestershire, so I rang him because he was the kind of person you'd call in an emergency. He got a taxi to pick me up from Tewkesbury Services and take me to his place down the Bay. I'd not seen him since he'd come out of the hospital, and obviously I was apprehensive because of everything that had been said in the press. So, when he opened the door I got a bit of a shock because his hair was totally shaved, and he was wearing these striped concentration camp pyjamas.

'At first, I noticed a distant look in his eyes, but once we started talking, he seemed like his old self, so I thought that the shaved head and the pyjamas were just another look he was experimenting with – nothing profound about it. The Richard I knew was still there, just a little quieter, a little less forthcoming with his words. We picked up where we left off. He didn't speak about the band at all, it just never came up. We spoke about the people we knew in college, our families, my kids. He was always very good around kids, very imaginative, very inventive, he liked children, and you could tell he wouldn't mind having some himself.'

In a 1988 letter to Claire Forward, Richey had divulged why he had shaved his hair in the past and how the act always held a deep level of significance for him: 'I had all my hair cut off after last Tuesday's melting pot of despair. Remember, I said I cut my hair after every emotional trauma?' Therefore, by 1995, to what extent was Richey's newly shorn hair still an outward expression of emotional turbulence? Along with Snoopy's passing and the band's differing trajectory, there was also the emotional trauma of his relationship with Jo reaching breaking point.

In the days before Snoopy's death, Richey visited Jo at her mother's in Walthamstow, east London. He asked Jo to marry him, and she turned him down. He stuck around for less than half an hour, then completed the seven-hour round trip back to Cardiff, after the two had mutually agreed to bring their sporadic four-year relationship to an end.

It was on his arrival back at his flat, in a fit of love-sick anguish, that Richey cut out a chunk of his hair. With a prominent bald patch now on display, Richey had no option but to proceed to shave off the rest of his hair the following day. When he told Nicky what he'd done, his friend's reply was, 'Now I know why they say you've got a personality disorder!'

'Everything was collapsing around him,' remembers Rachel. 'He was shutting down because it was all coming at once – with Snoopy, the band and Jo. He would come home to Blackwood and sit around the house crying. Mam would take time off work to look after him and feel terrible when she had to leave him alone. She kept telling him that he was still young, and there were plenty of other girls out there, but he was adamant that Jo was the only one for him. He was convinced he'd never move on, he thought it would be a betrayal to do so.

'After Richard went missing I spoke to Nick and he told me he'd had to tell Richard bluntly why Jo wouldn't want to marry someone like him – because he'd spent the first two years of their relationship drinking and the rest cutting himself. Richard seemed oblivious as to how unwell he came across to other people.'

'I can't live without you. You can. You love someone because you dominate their life. All masochistic strivings have an aim – to get rid of the individual self. To lose control and to get rid of the burden of freedom.'
Richey's archive, 1993

As we research this book, Rachel brings to our attention a copy of *MOJO* magazine from April 2016. It features a piece about the late Pink Floyd founder and renowned recluse, Syd Barrett. In it, his sister Rosemary Barrett looks back on her brother's intense personality and extraordinary mind, while sharing her belief that he likely had a form of high functioning autism – Asperger's syndrome (AS).

Like Rachel and Richey, Syd and Rosemary shared a bedroom in childhood, and Barrett's sister recalls him 'leaping from his sheets to conduct an imaginary orchestra'. This vivid image brings to mind one of the few family photos Rachel has released of Richey – a teenager at home in Blackwood surrounded by the trimmings of Christmas. He is caught in an unguarded moment, delivering an impassioned soliloquy. Dressed in striped pyjamas and an anti-Thatcher T-shirt, it is a rare view of Richey in the intimate company of his family, in parts vulnerable, yet equally bold and dramatic.

Throughout his time with the Manics, Richey revealed that among the band's many nicknames for him were 'Android' and 'Spock'. AS individuals often say they feel like 'aliens among humans' due in part to their highly logical way of thinking, entwined with a lack of understanding or inability to deal with emotions and protocols when it comes to interaction with others.

Those with Asperger's speak of looking at the world through a different lens, and are often frustrated when they are misunderstood, feeling like they are talking in a foreign language to those around them. While 90 per cent of high functioning Asperger's men lead 'normal' lives, their rigid behaviour can occasionally stand out in relation to their peers.

"It's strange how someone could remember all those quotes ..." Sean reflects.
" ... And the history of the fucking partition of Czechoslovakia ..." Nicky adds.
" ... And could quote In Pursuit of the Millennium *back at you ..."* says James.
" ... And you show him just a little snippet of music that probably doesn't last more than ten seconds," says Sean, *"and within about two or three minutes he'd forget it ..."*
The Face, September 1998

Many with AS tend to interpret words and messages too literally, causing confusion. This correlates in parts with Richey's obsessive nature when it came to analysing the seemingly unnecessary in the most minute of details. Speaking after his release from the Priory, he told the *NME*, 'Nothing else happens in my mind, I just get swamped by one idea. I can just see one little thing on TV and that'll be it. It can be anything, and then I'll just stop functioning. I think, what does it mean? I'm intelligent, why can't I understand that? Just a line in a film or a book, and I've lost it. The last one that happened, when I was hospitalised, was just a tiny little thing on *The Big Breakfast* from Lee Marvin singing that stupid song, "I Was Born Under a Wandering Star". There's a line in that, "Hell is in hello", and for two days, I couldn't do fucking anything. What's it mean, "Hell is in hello"? What are they trying to say? What is the point in that? And then I realised that something was not quite right.'

When it comes to relationships, a great deal of emotional ideology for AS individuals is often learned or copied from television and films. They become obsessed by society's version of 'happily ever after' and grow frustrated when life fails to follows the script. Some bail on relationships altogether because of the level of difficulty involved in processing their emotions, along with the grey area of second-guessing the complicated thoughts and feelings of others.

During Richey's hospitalisation, James commented, 'Richey was always much more into books and films than rock 'n' roll. And I think those art forms are much more idealised. I think they influenced the way he viewed life, and the way he thought it would be.'

Many with Asperger's seem more at ease immersing themselves in books or computers to evade human interaction. Closely related to that is the tendency for those with AS to pursue incredibly idiosyncratic interests, becoming fascinated by narrow and marginal pursuits and obsessions, to the point of confusion to anybody looking on.

Could a form of high functioning Asperger's syndrome explain Richey's renowned intellectual focus and his tendency to immerse himself deeply in the study of anything and everything by deftly applying more layers of logic to his chosen pursuit?

If Richey was on the autistic spectrum, might it explain some of the characteristic behaviours which were of great gain to the early Manic Street Preachers and spurred their meteoric rise to fame? His laser-eyed obsession with the logistics of show business, and his studious research on how to break into the music scene, accompanied by his organised dossiers on journalists, displayed a meticulous attention to detail more often present in the world of academia than that of rock and roll.

James once commented that in addition to Richey being 'a very academic person' who 'loved routines and timetables', he was also 'amazing at giving good copy in terms of soundbites. He knew what to do when somebody put a Dictaphone in front of him.'

Was this micromanagement perhaps a tell-tale sign that Richey was so adept at being the perfect rock star because he had been obliged to enact so much of his life as a kind of performance in its own right? How much of Richey's star quality was assumed naturally, and how much bordered on the studied technique of copy and imitation? The stereotype is that males with AS are far easier to spot than females, the latter having better coping mechanisms and social graces which enable them to cover their difficulties.

Clinical psychologist and Asperger's expert Tony Attwood insists that while a male with Asperger's will present himself as 'agitated, clumsy and immature', a female will be far more convincing at covering her condition through imitation and far better at 'pretending themselves to be normal as an avid observer of human behaviour. She will learn what to do or say, how to copy others and so go unnoticed; unlike the AS boy.' With Richey having a sister so close in age, and a special bond with his grandmother, might he have found it easier to mask his difficulties by mimicking, and copying more percipient female behaviour?

Looking back over his 1994 crisis, Richey commented that he had taken one valuable lesson from it – he had learned to stop putting so much effort into 'being like everyone else'. If there was such an important internal change, mid-year, it may have begun to display itself physically in changes to Richey's outer appearance. In the last months of his time with the band, he appeared to be becoming younger and younger, smaller and frailer. If, in previous years, he had donned the garb of the stereotypical rock star, any traces of that costume were now unceremoniously dumped. What was left was the tiny, frightened, hyper-alert young boy that had perhaps been hiding away in there all along.

The interview Richey gave on Danish TV, his last ever televised interview, recorded in November during the second half of the European tour, seems to confirm this. Outwardly, he looks less worldly than when he first appeared on screen during the band's formative years. Asked by the interviewer how he feels about the future, he gently answers, 'Future. That's a big nasty word, isn't it?' But the rest of his answer suggests that he has found – or is in the process of finding – a way forward for himself.

'We finish touring in December; then, I think, we are going to Asia and America, early next year. And then … you know, being in a band is pretty much routine. Then we'll write, we'll record, and we'll do the same thing all over again. The reason I am doing this is for the two months we have off, where I can just be in the flat on my own and write. I do nine months of touring, so I can get time to write words, that's what I care about. It's very nice staying in hotels, it's very nice doing concerts. But it's not as satisfying as writing something that encapsulates how you feel.'

Was this possible evidence that Richey was re-aligning his priorities? Could he, just a short time later, have concluded that those several gruelling months of touring America were just not worth it after all? It's no surprise to learn that in later years, many with Asperger's syndrome become overwhelmed by life's situations and shut out the outside world as a means of coping, resulting in increased social isolation, and even reclusiveness over the long term.

Rachel reflects, 'I think about my Great Aunt Bessie, who gravitated towards a life of isolation, and how these diagnoses are now being researched as limbic and hereditary, so there's potential "form" there, so to speak. I don't see something like Asperger's as simplifying Richard at all; it just adds another layer of complexity to him altogether.'

With crises in both his personal and professional relationships now forcing his hand, was Richey now at a point where he felt he'd exhausted most of the options for his future?

By marrying Jo, Richey might have thought he had a valid excuse for removing himself from the public eye. Alternatively, marrying and remaining in the band, the pressure of creating a success of a life in music would not be so burdensome, as he would have an existence apart from it; the stigma of failure would not hang so heavily.

'Yet one thing he never let go of was that he was obsessed with creating something perfect,' says Rachel. 'Something that couldn't be faulted by him or anyone else in any way – a band, a relationship, a work of art that was all-encapsulating, timeless and enduring. He was overly idealistic and found compromise very hard and there was a lot of that to deal with in the month before his disappearance.'

'I have a dream of writing a lyric that I think is, flawless really, with no broken edges. That makes sense to me, not anybody else. In fifteen, twenty lines that I've written a lyric that sums up exactly

how I feel about everything. Not just how I feel today but how
I've felt all my life. Everything I've read, everything I've seen,
you know in a few lines, say it all.'
Richey Edwards, last television interview, 1994

By the New Year, the band had hastily regrouped at Surrey's House in the Woods Studios. The place once decried by the Manics as the scene of their previous 'selling out' when recording *Gold Against the Soul* was now firmly back on the agenda, undoubtedly leaving the four with mixed feelings and an unmistakable sense of déjà vu.

Following the commercial disaster of *The Holy Bible*, the stakes were high, with the band later admitting there was a pressure to deliver the goods – and pronto. 'I think possibly the reason we went into the studio so quickly was to carry on with the demos,' conceded Sean. '[It] was probably so we could come away with something fast.'

They spent five days at the studio. While there, Richey handed the band a wedge of lyrics he'd been working on over the festive season. 'They were pretty heavy going,' said Sean. 'There wasn't a lot to put out, to be honest. Most of it was pretty fragmental rambling.'

In the studio they demoed two of Nicky's softer sounding lyrics – 'Further Away' and 'No Surface All Feeling' – along with one of Richey's mellower efforts, 'Small Black Flowers that Grow in the Sky'.

'Also, written [of Richey's] but not demoed, because we ran out of time to do demos, were "Elvis Impersonator: Blackpool Pier" and part of "Kevin Carter",' James told *The Quietus* in 2016. 'I'd played those two to Richey on the acoustic. But it was, you know, "It's a bit like this, I'm not sure yet …"'

James got as far as proposing an initial melody for 'Kevin Carter' and strumming the tune acoustically, but Richey was unimpressed. He said it sounded too much like the bossa nova song 'The Girl from Ipanema' for his liking, telling James, 'I don't want my words to sound like that.' James would later describe this moment as 'an impasse in the band for the first time, born out of taste'.

When asked by *Q* in 1998, 'What would Manic Street Preachers records sound like if Richey had stuck around?' the band replied: 'We'd have reached a compromise situation where we'd do a track for Richey here and there.' Was it possible that, by early 1995, Richey was already feeling that compromise? He had often publicly declared his writing as the core of his abilities, and the bedrock of his self-esteem. Might he have deduced that any future contributions to the Manics would be token gestures of appeasement offered up by his fellow band members?

'When Nicky started writing by himself that autumn, there was a major shift in the band and their principles,' remembers their former roadie. 'The band and Martin suddenly became very career-focused, very fast. After *The Holy Bible* flopped they seemed much more content to be guided by Sony if it meant guaranteeing them a long-term career in music.

'Rich was never in it for that, and I do wonder how that change of direction would have affected somebody who was very much a man of principle – especially with everything he'd said in the press following *Gold Against the Soul*, and the kind of messages he was communicating on *The Holy Bible*.

'I remember thinking at the time what I'd have done if I was in his situation; and how I'd have felt if my friends wanted to change the direction of the band I loved. If it was me who'd worked so hard to bring them to the attention of the media, and got them signed to a major label in the first place, then I'd be pretty pissed that my presence was going to be considered a compromise.'

'I can't help feeling that the band got what they wanted out of Rich when he was around. After the Holy Bible the only thing they could do was change, and it's understandable sometimes in the world of music. I don't hold that against them, but how could they not see how it affected him? To be so utterly demoted like that. They may have let him take control of the fourth album if the Holy Bible sold, but when it didn't ... What happened to truth instead of platitudes? The message first and the music second?'
Jo, letter to Rachel Edwards, 1998

Before the band had even signed to a label, they had always had an impassioned contempt for those who chose a lifelong career in the world of rock and roll. How was Richey to feel now that the band were seemingly content to slog ever onwards up the treadmill to the pyrrhic victory of unit-shifting chart success? Might he have imagined that all that would be left for him and the rest of the Manics to do on the world stage was to become hardened career soldiers, enlisting again and again for seemingly never-ending tours of duty until well past middle age?

> 'He just wanted to go out like a soldier. Standing up.
> Not even like some poor, wasted rag-assed renegade.'
> Willard on Colonel Kurtz in *Apocalypse Now*

Yet creative impasses aside, Nicky claimed that the time spent at The House in the Woods that January was the most tranquil he'd experienced with Richey since the band's earlier years.

'I can honestly say that the five days at The House in the Woods was the only time when I thought he was back to being Iggy/Keith Richards, as opposed to Ian Curtis. But that could have been because he was going.

'I don't think it's been tainted for me. I know it has for James, but I'm glad a phase ended like that instead of the ongoing shit that we'd be going through as a band. In his own way, I think it was Richey making some sort of peace with us. For those two weeks something had clicked in him. Whether he knew what he was going to do or he felt the freedom from it, I don't know, but he was just bang on form, just like he always was.'

Years later, however, Jo was puzzled to hear the band recalling that Richey appeared on a more even keel during their stay in Surrey. 'He seemed *so* much worse at the start of the year, even [than] before we broke up,' she told Rachel in a 1997 letter. 'But the band says he was on top form in the studio, which confuses me all these years on. Does this mean he was trying to control and manipulate me and everyone else by claiming he was powerless? How much control did he have left at that point with the image he was putting out there? I wonder if sometimes he *wanted* different people to see different things.'

Days before Richey gave his last ever interview to the world press, video producer Tony Van Den Ende recalls how Richey paid him a surprise visit at a studio just off London's Oxford Street. There, Van Den Ende was editing the rushes for the American release of the 'Faster' single, in the presence of Sony's Rob Stringer and the band's manager, Martin Hall. The producer had worked with the Manics before.

'I met the band when I did their first "You Love Us" video in 1991,' Tony recalls. 'Richey was this amazing piece of eye candy, an almost walking Warhol piece like the old studio stars. I'd seen them play a few times after that, and was really excited by their music and message, so I was desperate to work with them again.'

In October 1994, Tony was invited to the band's Cardiff gig, where he was introduced to a group of representatives from Sony USA. By the end of the night it was agreed that he'd film the video for 'Faster', live from the Astoria, two months later.

'As well as recording at the gig, we had to do some filming in the day for close-ups,' remembers Tony. 'It wasn't a very positive shoot; Nick got really fed up quite soon into the process, wanted to "move things along", whilst Richey was just milling around by himself. He stayed away from the band and crew, and just came onto the set when he was called. The other three hung around between takes, doing the usual things you do on a shoot – chatting, drinking, eating – but what struck me the most was that all their passion and energy had totally dissipated. It just seemed joyless, like a job they didn't want to do any more.'

Now, in January 1995, Van Den Ende witnessed consternation on the part of the record company about their investment in the band. 'Martin Hall and Rob Stringer were already there in the editing suite when Richey suddenly pitched up with his shaved head, and what I can only describe as Belsen-style pyjamas. It was the middle of winter.

I remember looking down at his feet to see he was wearing slippers. He must have been absolutely freezing! It reminded me of that story about Syd Barrett and Pink Floyd, and how after leaving the band, he went to see them in the studio – but because Syd had shaved his head, and changed his look so drastically, it took a while for them to recognise him.'

Richey stayed at the London studio for 45 minutes, viewing the video twice and complimenting Tony on his efforts. However, before he departed, Rob Stringer asked him to step outside for a chat.

'I don't know what was said out there, but once Richey left, questions were raised,' recalls Tony.

'It went off quite heavily for about five minutes after that. I think back to the argument, and it was like witnessing one at a bar – there's stuff in the past, there's stuff entangled in there and you're just getting small parts of a bigger picture. It wasn't Martin or Rob's style but it erupted because of one person – Richey. When you put yourself in Rob's position and all the money Sony were losing, it was business. To me it was like Warhol all over again, amazing people and the odder the better, but to him as a professional maybe it was too out there.

'I think someone mentioned the way Richey looked in the end, otherwise it's the elephant in the room. It was undeniably a concentration camp vibe, and he must have still had it in him to know the shock he'd cause looking like that. Was he doing it to wind people up? Would Rob have found that almost confrontational, for Richey to be depicting a Holocaust victim, especially if Rob has Jewish family members himself?'

'I am a man of peace, but when I speak, they are for war.'
Psalm 120, 'A Song for Ascents', 120: 7
Richey Edwards set list quote, Cologne, 3 December 1994

Days later, on 23 January, London-based rock journalist Midori Tsukagoshi of Japan's *Music Life* magazine received an unexpected phone call from Richey, actively seeking a last-minute interview shortly before the band's American departure. 'Can you get a train to Cardiff right now?' he asked. When Tsukagoshi's train pulled into Cardiff Central Station, she spotted the instantly recognisable yet markedly changed Richey waiting on the platform, still in Belsen-style pyjamas. If Rob Stringer or the band's management had let it be known to Richey that his new uniform was not conducive to sales, he was not toeing the line.

During the interview, Richey reaffirmed his long-held views on the music industry, and seemed eager to get them off his chest in the bluntest way possible, freely condemning professionals in the record industry and their treatment of artists. 'Most people in this business are totally insensitive. Most are downright evil. I personally don't know anyone who is in a band that I respect. And no one at the record companies really cares about the bands.'

Midway through the interview he took off on another familiar tangent, keen to discuss one of his favoured topics, love and relation-ships. Perhaps desiring to control a particular image of himself until the very end, he played down the notion of his past interpersonal rela-tionships. 'The longest one was a girlfriend I had when I was younger, and that lasted about four days, I think? Since starting the band only one girl. I can talk to her easier than with anyone else. That's really important to me. But even to her I've never said, "I love you" or anything. I've known her for a few years, but I've kissed her once, no, twice, that's all. Really, that's it. When you're in love, I think there's a feeling of being trapped.'

Given his relationships with both Claire Forward and Jo, was Richey shying away from reality – or was he trying to maintain control of his narrative arc, right up until the end?

Apart from his interview for the Japanese publication, Richey's last documented week before disappearing consisted of both ordinary behav-iours and some that have since been scrutinised as to their significance. Unusually he made four separate visits to Cardiff's Queen Street, where he withdrew £200 from cashpoints on 20, 21, 23 and 25 January. Some of his acquisitions are itemised in his receipts – morning breakfasts in Marks and Spencer, comics and books from Forbidden Planet, and films (including duplicate VHSs of Mike Leigh's *Naked*) from Virgin Megastores. It would also be the final time he paid a visit to his Blackwood family home.

'The last time I saw him, he seemed flat, but with that, he was calm,' says Rachel. 'He'd brought flowers up for Mam like he often would, and had his camera with him. He was taking photos of me just sitting on the sofa and of Mam doing the ironing, which I thought was odd at the time.

'When I got up to leave, he made a point of looking me up and down, like he was taking me in for whatever reason. So I said to him, "What's the matter? Is there something wrong with my belt?" and he just said, "Nothing." But it was obviously something, and by then I think he'd definitely made some kind of decision in his head.'

Before James and Richey's scheduled departure for America on 1 February, the band reconvened for two days' rehearsal at The House in the Woods. During that time, Rob Stringer visited and reported on Richey's apparent new enthusiasm for the upcoming trip – something at odds with what Richey had been telling those closest to him.

On the evening of 31 January, as the band were leaving the studio, Richey gave them each a gift – a magazine for Sean, a CD for James and a *Daily Telegraph* and a Mars bar for Nicky.

'I just saw it as an act of kindness for the fact that he'd been pretty difficult,' Nicky told the *Guardian* in 2009. 'So the *Daily Telegraph* and the Mars bar, I just saw it as a little "Things are going to be OK". Which maybe, in his mind, that's what it was.' He sighed. 'But different meanings of OK, I guess.'

While Nicky and Sean headed to Blackwood and Bristol respectively, James and Richey made their way to the Embassy Hotel, in London's Bayswater.

'We'd just bought a band car, the Vauxhall Cavalier,' said Nicky Wire later, 'and the ashtray in it was like the mountain in *Close*

Encounters ... It was terrible. Sean hated it and I hated it because we're anti-smokers. And it was only three months old. So James and Richey drove the Cavalier to the Embassy Hotel and that was it. I remember them leaving, and it was one of those dark, dark nights. And that was the end, really.'

Chapter 11

The Vanishing

Richey Edwards was dreading going to America. Shortly before ringing his mother to tell her of his trepidation, he and James hung back in the underground car park of the Embassy Hotel to listen to some of the demos recorded at The House in the Woods.

'I said, "Which one's your favourite?"' James told *Q* magazine in 2016. 'And he said, "The others are OK but Small Black Flowers is the one I really like." With a shrug of the shoulders, he was a bit ambivalent about the rest.'

The pair checked into adjoining rooms and Richey made his way to room 561. They arranged to meet later and venture out to explore the local cafés, pubs and eateries along nearby Queensway.

'He rang my mam that evening, and told her he didn't want to go to America,' Rachel recalls. 'It was the last conversation she had with Richard, but she never picked up on anything being seriously wrong.'

By the time that James Dean Bradfield knocked again, Richey had changed his mind and told him he'd prefer to stay in and have a quiet night instead.

In the version of events presented to the public, James Dean Bradfield was the last person to see Richey alive. However, between the time James went out and came back, Richey had received a guest at the hotel. Much of what the Edwards family learned of the subsequent hours came from the band themselves. That evening, as confirmed to Rachel by the band, Richey was in his room with a female named Vivian.

With only a passing mention of her by the band, Rachel has been unable to ascertain Vivian's relationship to Richey. She was not mentioned in any of the official police files Rachel accessed in the nineties. She is believed to have been a fan turned friend, yet all of Rachel's subsequent attempts to track her down have proved fruitless. As well as the mysterious Vivian, the Edwards family are still unsure exactly who – from either the management or the record company – was at the Embassy that fateful night, preparing to travel to the States.

'We still don't know exactly what happened that night,' says Rachel. 'I've spoken to other people with family members who have gone missing, and normally they have received a much fuller picture of the last known 24 hours of their loved ones. For us, though, even after all these years, there's new information being revealed about the night Richard vanished. It was only after reading a magazine interview with James that we discovered the two of them spent time listening to new songs in the Embassy basement.'

It is not clear at what time, and for how long, Richey's visitor, Vivian, was in his company that evening, or whether or not he left the Embassy with her.

The following morning, James waited in the hotel lobby for his friend. Richey, normally prompt and punctual, failed to appear. James became concerned when he received no answer from Richey's room, and requested that a member of staff use a master key to unlock it. On entering, there was no sign of Richey. They found a bath full of water and a gift box that contained several items; videos, books, photographs and a note, simply reading 'I love you.'

This was addressed to, and later passed on to, his former girlfriend, Jo. Wrapped like a present, the box was decorated with literary quotes and a collage of cryptic photographs which included everything from cartoon characters to decaying mansions.

Richey's receipts show that the day before the box's discovery, he had spent £9.60 at a Surrey printers. Might that have paid for some of the photographic decorations on the box? If so, for how long had Richey been planning to leave this parting gift for Jo?

Twenty-four hours later, band manager Martin Hall filed a missing person report at Harrow Road police station. Staff working at Hall or Nothing were granted access to Richey's address book, and began phoning around his contacts. Nobody had heard from him.

Rachel recalls that Graham Edwards was initially reluctant to ask many questions. 'My dad was of the opinion that the police are there to solve crimes, and he was a bit uncomfortable with it all. He put an article in the *Daily Mail*, saying, "Please make contact, Richard", and went on Red Dragon Radio to appeal. My dad felt Richard was an adult and had made his own decision ... but then he also knew he was ill, so was it his own decision?'

James travelled to the States alone, while Nicky Wire made calls to various British hotels to ascertain whether Richey had checked in. On 15 February, Cardiff Police issued a public statement appealing for information regarding Richey's whereabouts:

Police are anxious to trace Richard James Edwards, a member of the pop group 'Manic Street Preachers' who has been missing from the London area since Wednesday 1st February, 1995 when he was seen leaving the London Embassy hotel at 7.00am.

It is known that on the same day he visited his home in the Cardiff area and is still believed to be in possession of his silver Vauxhall Cavalier motorcar. Registration – NO: L519 HKX.

Richard's family, band members and friends are concerned for his safety and welfare, and stress that no pressure will be put on him to return if he does not wish to do. They stress that his privacy will be respected at all times.

Police are asking anyone who has seen Richard, knows of his whereabouts, or have seen his car, to contact them at Cardiff Central Police Station on 0222 22211 and ask for the Crime Desk or CID office.

Should Richard himself hear or see this appeal, his family and friends are anxious for him to contact one of them or the Police to let them know he is safe and well. They again wish to stress that Richard will not be urged to return or reveal his whereabouts if he does not wish to do so.

A few days later came the news that Richey's car had been found. The Vauxhall Cavalier was discovered parked at Aust Services on the English side of the Severn crossing. Inside were photographs that Richey had taken of the family after the Christmas period. The ticket attendant who reported the car on 17 February claimed he had first noticed the abandoned vehicle three days earlier, on St Valentine's Day.

It was reported there were signs that someone had been staying in the car for some time. Nicky Wire believed Richey had been sleeping in the vehicle. Its battery was flat and inside was an empty wine bottle, rubbish strewn everywhere, and, in the cassette-deck, a Sex Pistols tape.

The discovery of the car outside Bristol saw a third police force become involved. In addition to London's Met and South Wales Police, the Avon & Somerset force also joined the search. Graham Edwards was told by the latter that it was his responsibility to pay for the car to be towed back to the family home. It seemed apparent that the vehicle was not viewed as crucial evidence.

'The police didn't want to know anything about the car,' says Rachel 'They never investigated the car; never looked into why it may have had a flat battery, or the circumstances around that. I don't believe they took anything out of there to look at. What my dad brought back in the car was a hold-all bag, an empty bottle of wine, the photographs, Richard's medication and a cassette tape.'

Richey's passport, his Severn Bridge toll receipt and some spare change were found at his Anson Court property. Richey – or somebody else – must have visited and had placed the items in full view of anybody entering the flat.

A review of Richey's bank statements and receipts from the days before his vanishing, showed that he withdrew cash in two further

223

transactions after January 25. He firstly visited an ATM in Cardiff, taking out £200. A day before his disappearance, he withdrew a further £200 from a cash machine in Surrey. From the total amount, £44.40 was spent on new pyjamas and presents for the band, while he paid the printers £9.60. This would have left him with £346 – a substantial amount of cash to be carrying around in 1995. The money was never found or accounted for.

Three weeks after Richey had vanished, on 25 February, the Edwards family home received a surprise visit at 3.20am from the local Gwent Police, apparently at the behest of London's Met. 'They searched all through the property and out into the back garden,' says Rachel. 'My mam and dad were really disorientated and alarmed. The police didn't really say why they were doing it; just that it was in relation to Richard going missing.'

Following the announcement of his disappearance, the sightings began to flood in. Rachel travelled to London to see the police file and made some photocopies. She brought back two statements given to the police, with two days separating them, detailing reported encounters with Richey in Newport, Gwent.

The first, dated 21 February 1995, was a witness statement by 19-year-old David Anthony Cross, a second-year student at Gwent College, Caerleon.

A friend of mine named Lori Fidler, an American girl is friendly with Richie [sic] James Edwards who is a member of the band called Manic Street Preachers. Lori has been a friend of mine for three years. In that time she has visited Britain on four occasions from New York in America where she lives. The Manic Street Preachers were or are Lori's favourite band. When she has visited Britain particularly on the last occasion she followed their tour. Lori has often shown to me photos of the band as well as photos of Richie James Edwards taken with her. Although I do not follow the band I know what Richie James Edwards looks like having seen the photographs.

CHAPTER 11

Cross relates how, on Sunday, 5 February, he caught a bus from campus to go to the gym. Arriving at Newport bus station at 10am, he turned towards a newsagent shop.

As I approached the newsagent's shop I saw stood outside this newsagents Richie James Edwards. He did not appear to have come out from the shop. He was stood alone near to a silver grey coloured car, the make of which I did not know. It looked similar to a Vauxhall Cavalier. Although I did not know him I spoke to him, I said to him, 'Hello Richie, I'm a friend of Lori's.' He said to me, 'How is she? How is she doing?' He looked at me and said, 'I'll see you later.' I was about to enter the newsagents when I saw him get into the driver's seat of the car and drive away in the general direction of the bus station. There were no other persons in the vehicle. I am positive it was Richie James Edwards from the photographs I have seen. The only difference was that his hair was shaved very short. I recall he was wearing a dark blue coloured jacket which had a white pattern to it. When I spoke to him, although briefly I noticed he looked withdrawn and pale. I then went into the shop. I did not or have not seen him since.

An August 1995 article in the the *Sunday Times* reported that journalist Sue Reid was granted access to the police files on Richey's case. Among the '15 slim folders' she perused, she located information which showed an incorrect assumption by police that the box of gifts Richey left at the Embassy was not for Jo, but for the same Lori Fidler. Nobody knows how the journalist made that assumption.

Among Richey's private collection of photographs, we find a picture that has also been distributed online among fans. In the online version, Richey and Lori stand side by side in late 1994. In Richey's personal copy of the picture, Lori's half of the photo is torn off and her image no longer present.

There was also a 23 February witness statement from a Newport taxi driver, Anthony Edward Hatherall. At about 7am on Tuesday,

7 February, two days after the David Cross sighting, he received a call to pick up at the King's Hotel on High Street.

I parked outside and went into the reception area and asked at the desk for the person who had requested a taxi. The female receptionist stated that she would inform him and I returned to my taxi. A male person came out and sat in the rear nearside of the car. I would describe this person as being male, white, approx 5' 10' / 6' tall, slim build, dark brown collar-length hair which was all one length, clean shaven, gaunt face, wearing a black polo neck top and blue jeans. He had a Walkman (personal stereo) attached to his jeans and he had headphones on. On getting into the taxi he said, 'Can you take me to the Uplands in Rogerstone?' I agreed and drove on. I noticed that he spoke with a cockney accent, but it sounded very much put on. He asked me if he could lie down in the back seat and I stated I had no objections.

This person did not appear to be drunk or under the influence of drugs. There was no conversation between us until we got to Uplands when I asked him where he wanted to go exactly. He produced some paper with directions on it which he said he had got from the hotel. He read from it stating he wanted the A4591 to Risca, Crosskeys and Cwmcarn. I stated that I could not go on a longer run until I had some money up front. He then handed me £40 in two £20 notes. I asked him for his exact destination but he stated that he did not know at the moment. He said he was looking for his boss who had driven a lorry to South Wales from London and had broken down somewhere in Gwent. I thought that this was extremely strange and if he had not paid would not have gone any further.

The passenger asked for a road map of South Wales and about various railway stations. The driver told him the nearest station was Blackwood bus station, and they drove there.

For the rest of the journey he sat quietly in the back until we got to Blackwood Bus Station. It would have been about 7:50pm at this time. As we entered the bus station he said, 'No, this is not the place'. He asked again where the nearest Railway station was and I explained there was on in Newport and one in Pontypool. He then requested I take him to Pontypool Railway Station. At Pontypool station he got out of the car and asked me to wait for him. A short while later he returned and stated he had phoned the London office and been told to go to Aust Services which is on the English side of the Severn Bridge. He requested I go via the 'scenic route', not driving along the motorway because he stated he is always driving along the motorway.

There was very little conversation until we got to the Severn Bridge. At first he stated he wanted to be dropped in the motel at the Severn Bridge Services but then changed his mind. I eventually dropped him off at the café area of the Services. He paid me another £20 and then I drove away. Before I left he asked me for a receipt for the fare. The actual fare was £68 but he asked me for a discount which I gave him. I made the receipt out for £70 to Buster Haulage.

Hatherall later spotted a piece in the local paper about Richey going missing, and felt his photo looked familiar.

I thought he looked similar to the male person I drove to the Severn Bridge services. My suspicions were heightened by the peculiar events of that night and the strangeness of the person.

These statements conclude that two separate witnesses claim to have spotted Richey in the same location two days apart. Yet was the person in the back of Hatherall's cab really Richey? How likely is it that somebody five foot seven in height could pass for somebody six foot tall? Then there is the hair. Richey recently gave himself a closely cropped crew-cut; was his 'collar-length hair which was all one length' a wig?

Also, the issue of the London accent. Was there perhaps someone in contact with Richey from the south-east of England who fitted Hatherall's description? A contact from within the music industry perhaps, or even an old friend?

If the person was Richey, perhaps he was searching between Newport and Blackwood, in disguise, for a missing contact crucial to his plans. That would explain the passenger's furtive behaviour, lying low in the back seat and preferring less busy roads – plenty of local people could recognise Richey. But there is perhaps a likelier hypothesis which takes into account some of the detail of Hatherall's statement and that of David Cross.

David Cross apparently saw Richey on Sunday morning, a stone's throw from the King's Hotel. Two days later, Hatherall picked up a passenger who was either staying at the King's Hotel, or possibly seeking out somebody staying there. Was Hatherall a witness to the individual's frantic search for a missed connection? Bearing in mind this was in the era before mobile phones, was Richey meant to have met someone but failed for some reason to make the rendezvous?

Years later, purported sightings of Richey were a lot further afield. In late 1996, Vyvian Morris, a 48-year-old musician from Swansea, was on holiday in India, when, as he reported several months later, he thought he spotted Richey mingling with others on the hippie trail and clothed in the generic uniform of the globe-trotting hippy.

We were on a visit that day to the hippie market in Anjuna. It was early in the afternoon, and we had just got there when we saw this group of hippies coming out of a cafe and getting on a bus. I immediately thought, that's Richey Edwards. He looked a bit the worse for wear. He was very sun burned and had matted long hair, like it hadn't been cared for. He was wearing a kaftan, jeans and had a tote bag, like all the hippies. He got onto the bus and I just managed to ask another of the hippies living in that commune, who the other guy was. He told me: 'That's Rick'. I asked him how long he had been with them and he said: '18 months'. It was too much of a coincidence. Then, they got on the bus and were gone. My girlfriend and I had got separated and she had the camera. I just wish I had got a picture of him. The full significance did not hit me until I got back home. I only told a few members of the band I am in, no one else. I did not want to go to the police then because of his family – they must have had their hopes dashed so many times, and I did not want to be the one who raised them up to be dashed again. Because of that, I tried to put doubts into my mind. Without speaking to the man, I could never be 100% sure it was Richey, but I do think it was him.

Morris, who was also a Media Studies lecturer at Neath College, later claimed to have regretted going public with the information, causing stress and palaver for Richey, who 'had worked so hard to gain this anonymity'.

This remorse was too late. Inevitably, tabloid journalists flew out to Goa, hell-bent on a scoop and a photograph for their front page. However, they got little joy from Goa's community of hippies, who doubtless viewed the hacks as emblematic of the kind of tawdry life they were escaping.

The Met in London said they would be relying on local police in the former Portuguese colony for help in following things up. For his part, the British Ambassador to India remarked how easy it is to disappear in that part of the world: 'People do it all the time.'

In November 1998, a barmaid in Corralejo, Fuerteventura, reported seeing Richey at the Underground Bar where she worked. British-born Tracy Jones told a local Tenerife newspaper, the *Island Sun*, that one of the bar's customers had stared at a man and shouted, 'You're Richey from the Manic Street Preachers!' The individual he accosted ' ... just started to run towards the door and within seconds he was gone.' It was a persuasive story, and Richey's old friend and confidante from the Priory, Rosie Dunn, also flew out to Fuerteventura.

'I went with my husband to check out the sighting, at this hippy commune,' she recalls. 'The *Sunday Mirror* sent us out there, and I spent a week trying to track him down. But I think it was a nasty hoax. We did extensive work with the family and media, followed tips and used investigators.'

After Christmas that year, the Edwards family received a letter from a Mrs Ambrosini on the neighbouring island of Lanzarote.

[On] Boxing Night we were returning to our apartment when we spotted a young man playing a guitar very quietly and singing to himself. It was a very quiet spot and we stopped to look, because we thought it odd that he should be sat on the floor and playing and singing in this manner. He did have another man with him; he was doing nothing but hanging around. This was down by the Old Port, opposite the Victoria Inn, in Calle. Above some Council buildings there is a paved area and he was in there playing. Lanzarote is just a short boat ride from Fuerteventura.

Several years later, in October 2004, holiday-maker Lee Wilde felt that he had spotted Richey, again in Lanzarote, on the island's surfing hotspot Famara Beach.

I know people will find this difficult to believe and that they'll think I'm some sort of crackpot, but I am convinced that is who I saw. Everyone I've mentioned it to just gives me that quizzical look with a raised eyebrow, but I know what I saw and I'm totally certain of it. He didn't do anything very much, we smiled and chatted briefly – you know, just hello and some small talk. He was looking out across the water with half closed eyes because of the sun, but he still watched me approach. Before I could say hello back, he just said something like 'It's beautiful isn't it?' all while staring ahead. He was talking about the view obviously but I was more intrigued by his appearance. There was something quite different about him. He was incredibly thin, skinny would be a good description, a drawn complexion and greying hair. Then there were his arms. They were wrapped in leather bracelets and

Richey and
Martin Hall in
a health farm
sauna, 1993.

1. FROM DESPAIR TO WHERE?
2. DRUG DRUG DRUGGY
3. SLEEP FLOWER
4. NOSTALGIC PUSHEAD
5. LIFE BECOMING A LANDSLIDE
6. GOLD AGAINST THE SOUL
7. ROSES IN THE HOSPITAL
8. SYMPHONEY OF TOURETTE
9. LA TRISTESSE DURERAM
10. YOURSELF,

lyrics typography like:
VIOLATOR C.D

John Menzies
Prod. Ref. 29397

What really stood out in Richey's *Gold Against the Soul* folder was the sheer
volume of visual material, cut-outs from magazines, newspapers and posters.

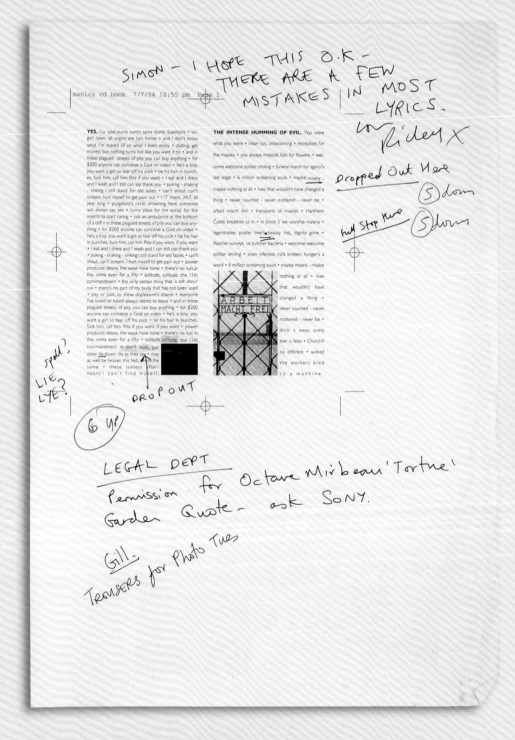

Richey's *Holy Bible* corrections, 1994. 'He was still working despite being in hospital' recalls Rachel. 'He was making phone calls to the album designer and re-arranging lines ready for the printed lyric sheets.'

4st. 7lb. Days since I last pissed • cheeks sunken and despaired • so gorgeous sunk to six stone • lose my only remaining home • see my third rib appear • a week later all my flesh disappear • stretching taut, cling-film on bone • I'm getting better • Karen says I've reached my target weight • Kate and Emma and Kristin know it's fake • problem is diet's not a big enough word • I wanna be so skinny that I rot from view • I want to walk in the snow • and not leave a footprint • I want to walk in the snow • and not soil its purity • stomach collapsed at five • lift up my skirt my sex is gone • naked and lovely and 5st. 2 • may I bud and never flower • my vision's getting blurred • but I can see my ribs and I feel fine • my hands are trembling stalks • and I can feel my breasts are sinking • mother trys to choke me with roast beef • and sits savouring her sole ryvitta • that's the way you're built my father said • but I can change, my cocoon shedding • I want to walk in the snow • and not leave a footprint • I want to walk in the snow • and not soil its purity • Kate and Kristin and Kit Kat • all things I like looking at • too weak to fuss, too weak to die • choice is skeletal in everybody's life • I choose, my choice, I starve to frenzy • hunger soon passes and sickness soon tires • legs bend, stockinged I am Twiggy • and I don't mind the horror that surrounds me • self-worth scatters, self-esteem's a bore • I long since moved to a higher plateau • this discipline's so rare so please applaud • just look at the fat scum who pamper me so • yeh 4st. 7, an epilogue of youth • such beautiful dignity in self-abuse • I've finally come to understand life • through staring blankly at my navel.

DIE IN THE SUMMERTIME. Scratch my leg with a rusty nail, sadly it heals • colour my hair but the dye grows out • I can't seem to stay a fixed ideal • childhood pictures redeem, clean and so serene • see myself without ruining lines • whole days throwing sticks into streams • I have crawled so far sideways • I recognise dim traces of creation • I wanna die, die in the summertime • the hole in my life even stains the soil • my heart shrinks to barely a pulse • a tiny animal curled into a quarter circle • if you really care wash the feet of a beggar • I have crawled so far sideways • I recognise dim traces of creation • I wanna die, die in the summertime • I have crawled so far sideways • I recognise dim traces of creation • I wanna die, die in the summertime

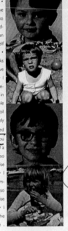

(handwritten annotations:)
letter rites here?
FD
?
this line straight
8Y
WORDS DROPPED HERE
10-12Y
death — Phil/Nigel.

12 STEPS OF A.A.   Scarface!

1. We admitted we were powerless over alcohol — that our lives had become unmanageable.
2. Came to believe that a Power greater than ourselves could restore us to sanity.
3. ~~Some~~ Made a decision to turn our will and our lives over to the care of God AS WE UNDERSTOOD HIM.
4. Made a searching and fearless moral inventory of ourselves.
5. Admitted to God, to ourselves, and to another human being the exact nature of our wrongs.
6. Were entirely ready to have God remove all these defects of character.
7. Humbly ask Him to remove our short comings
8. Made a list of all persons we had harmed, and became willing to make amends to them all.
9. Made direct amends to such people wherever possible, except when to do so would injure them or others.
10. Continued to take personal inventory and when we were wrong promptly admitted it.
11. Sought through prayer and meditation to improve our conscious contact with God AS WE UNDERSTOOD HIM, praying only for knowledge of His will for us and the power to carry that out.
12. Having had a spiritual awakening as the result of these steps, we tried to carry this message to alcoholics, and to practice these principles in all our affairs.

WE ARE GENETICALLY DISEASED, X FACTOR GENE = PHYSICAL POWERLESSNESS that RULES OUR LIVES, sacrifice everything to repeat 1st experience getting high.

THE URGE IS ALWAYS THERE, CANNOT STOP IF WE TAKE 1st DRINK
   PHOTO COPY Addiction & Recovery.

WE CAN'T USE & WE CAN'T QUIT
DESTROYED PHYSICALLY EMOTIONALLY SPIRITUALLY

GIVE YRSELF, ADMIT YR POWERLESS, NO MORE DENIAL.

The Disease is not our personal responsibility but we are personally responsible for recovery.

Richey's '12 steps of AA', The Priory, 1994. For Richey, the hardest part of his treatment was the Alcoholics Anonymous Twelve Step programme. It is frequently accused of having religious connotations, with confession and restitution at its commandment-like core.

All I am Giving Up is Misery, Pain, Discomfort, mere existance.

REMORSE + GUILT = DEFEAT.

WE NOT ALCOHOL ARE THE DEMONS.

SELF CENTRED. FUCK YEH. IMMATURE. FUCK YEH.

SELF-DEFEATING- FUCK YEH.

Burns my temper tantrums — cant hit out at anyone else.

┌───┐
│ REMEMBER STEP I ALWAYS.   │
└───┘

SUICIDE IS PAINLESS

Dying voluntarily implies that you have recognised, even instinctively, the ridiculous character of that habit, the absence of any profound reason for living, the insane character of that daily agitation and the uselessness of suffering.

One must brush everything aside and go straight to the real problem. One kills oneself because life is not worth living.

It is essential to die unreconciled and not of ones own free will. Suicide is a repudiation. No. 1, 8

Richey's personal notes, The Priory, 1994. Its many dense pages capture a mind hurtling towards a deep existential crisis, fast losing faith in all around him.

Robin Morgin - PORN IS THEORY, RAPE THE PRACTICE.
Irelands 'Lunatic Fringe' has existed for a century. } Epiphany

Disillusionment the most purful political movement of the past 25 yrs.
Even MY generation embrace teh own youth - changes.

Indecent Proposal no kind of Moral Dilemma.
Spoof Movies get their laughs at expense of pop audience

1950's - Austere - value everything, boil cabbage.
  60's - Idealistic - RNR Revn, Pol Salvation.
70's/80's - Nihilistic - beyond caring - produced the most reactionary post
       war govt.
    90's - Aesthetic - only care/value trivialitis. 1st generation to reach
       20 and reject adult values. Disciplined conversations about
       changes.

Why Am I So Scared. · WHY AM I SO SCARAD
Savagery Beats Humility.
'The Still Pt of a Turning Universe.'
She Shivers when She Gets Out Of Bed, She is a Poet Soon-to-be, oh baby,
I'm here. Drips, plasters, stitches, dried up cunt, split split.
I need pornography to justify my failure.
No emotional satisfaction unless you pay for it.
I couldnt hurt you now even if I tried.   BITCH-WIND.

Just Another, blowing holes in one another - poetry of America.
   Jerk off at an ad about dietary dog food.
   Rubber Gloves and syringes.
A Spine of Self-Loathing, Bite my cheek till it bleeds.

Man-in-Control. Big Deal. Hendrix Fuck & Kill. So you an Pidgeon.
How much can a mother Hate her child - dress a boy as a Sailor/man.
He's gonna wish his Ma had haddan abortion insteadda him.
Why fight a War. To answer that you have to know why yr living.
The only thing worse than torture is waiting to be tortured.'
'The syllable that rhymes with breath.'
'Love belongs to desire & desire is always cruel.'

'I hate the whole fucking planet, myself, my failure, my self-pity.'

She Wasnt As Strong As I Wanted Her to be.

The lure of hedonistic experiences, whether through drugs, self-harm, or
other means is often known to give a semblance of identity and feeling
back to the borderline patient.

Taxi Driver
Made in Britain
Midnight Cowboy
Whatever Happened to Baby Jane
Streetcar Named Desire
Cat on A Hot Tin Roof
Who's Afraid of Virginia Woolf
Apocalypse Now
Johnny Suede
This Sporting Life
Kes
Loneliness of the Long Distance Runner
Saturday Night & Sunday Morning
Rumblefish
Last Picture Show
State of Grace
10 Rillington Place
Planet of the Apes
Last Exit to Brooklyn
Breakfast at Tiffanys
Treasure of the Sierra Madre

Little Foxes, Sunset Blvd, All About Eve
The Entertainer, The Dresser, Meantime.

Small Craft Warnings / Suddenly Last Summer
Go Ask Alice   Sassan Poetry
Bell Jar   Baby Doll etc
Season in Hell   No Longer Human - Dazai
Junky   The Trial / Metamorphosis - Kafka
PRIMO LEVI   Frisk - D Cooper
Myth of Sisyphus / Outsider / The Fall / The Plague
The Boy Looked at Johnny - Burchill / Parsons
Mystery Train - Greil Marcus
Awopbop - Nik Cohn   Elvis - last 48 Hours / Lives of Lennon - Goldman
1984
Lolita - Nabokov   Notes from the Underground - Dostoyevsky
Another Country - James Baldwin   Beautiful Boy & Her Hair - F Scott Fitzgerald
Jonathan L Seagull - Bach   Black Rain - Ibuse
Borstal Boy - Behan   Thirst for Love - Mishima
Less Than Zero / American Psycho - BEE Dorian Gray - Wilde
Lord of the Flies - Golding   Miracle of the Rose - Genet
Brave New World - Huxley   1982 Janine - Alasdair Gray
Cuckoo's Nest - Kesey   Crash / Atrocity Exhibition - JG Ballard
Desolation Angels - Kerouac   Blown Away - AE Hotchner
Prick Up Y Ears - Lahr   Dance with the Devil - Booth
Dice Man - Rhinehart   Knots - RD Laing
Invisible Man - Ralph Ellison Under the Volcano - Lowry
Catcher in the Rye - Salinger Wasteland - T.S Elliot
Birdy / Pride - Wharton   Torture Garden - MIRBEAU
Naomi - Tanazaki   Runaway Soul - Brodkey
The Fire Next Time - James Baldwin Any Blake / Larkin

Richey's list of his favourite things, 1994. Throughout Richey's archive, he would write out – sometimes repeatedly – quotes from favourite books, films, and albums in order to memorise them off by heart. Like many borderline patients, he often felt that others could define his thoughts and the contradictory opinions that inhabited his mind more succinctly than he could himself.

Richey performing at the Manchester Academy during the 1994 British tour. Tickets were oversold and the venue was densely packed. Backstage, the band were on eggshells.

Snoopy's passing in January 1995 meant further beloved elements of Richey's revered youth were slipping away, and with them an innocence and happiness he felt he might never experience again.

had something to say. He said it. Since I had peeped over the edge myself, I understand
better the meaning of his stare, that could not see the flame of the candle, but was
wide enough to embrace the whole universe, piercing enough to penetrate all the hearts
that beat in the darkness. He had summed up — he had judged. "The horror!" — this
was the *expression* of some sort of belief; it had candour, it had conviction, it
had a vibrating note of revolt in its whisper, it had the appalling face of a glimpsed
truth — the strange commingling of desire and hate — a vision of greyness without
form filled with physical pain, and a careless contempt for the evanescence
of all things — even of this pain itself. True, he had made that last stride, he
had stepped over the edge, while I had been permitted to draw back my hesitating foot
And perhaps in this is the whole difference; perhaps all the wisdom, and all
truth, and all sincerity, are just compressed into that inappreciable moment of time
in which we step over the threshold of the invisible. Better his cry — It was an
affirmation, a moral victory, paid for by innumerable defeats, by abominable terrors, by
abominable satisfactions. But it was a victory! — I found myself back in the sepulchral
city resenting the sight of people hurrying through the streets to filch a little money from
each other, to devour their infamous cookery, to gulp their unwholesome beer, to dream
their insignificant and silly dreams. They trespassed upon my thoughts. They were intruders
whose knowledge of life was to me an irritating pretence, because I felt so sure they
could not possibly know the things I knew. I had no particular desire to enlighten
them, but I had some difficulty in restraining myself from laughing in their faces,
so full of stupid importance. I daresay I was not very well at that time. I tottered about
the streets — there were various affairs to settle — grinning bitterly at perfectly respectable
persons — It was not my strength that wanted nursing, it was my imagination that
wanted soothing — I offered him the report on the "Suppression of Savage Customs," —
"This is not what we had a right to expect," he remarked. "Expect nothing else," I
said. — He had faith — don't you see? he had the faith. He could get himself to
believe anything — anything — I remembered his abject pleading, his abject threats, the
colossal scale of his vile desires, the meanness, the torment, the tempestuous
anguish of his soul — I — I alone know how to mourn for him as he deserves. —
"He died as he lived." "His end was in every way worthy of his life."

One of the last photocopies Richey printed was of a black-and-white newspaper
clipping of Bette Davis and Joan Crawford in the 1962 film, *Whatever Happened
to Baby Jane*. Underneath the photograph, Richey wrote out an excerpt from *Heart
of Darkness*. He made several further photocopies and kept them in his last known
folders of writing, 1995.

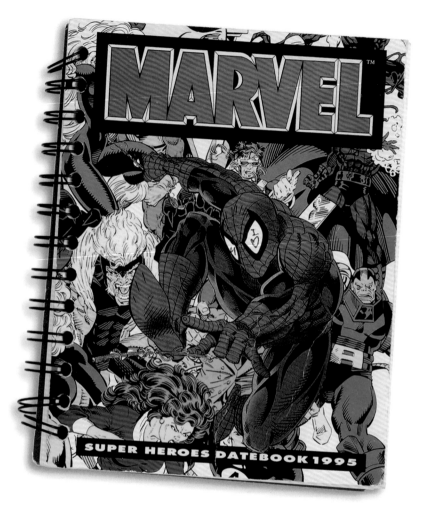

Richey's final diary, 1995. The entries span from Christmas Day through to the first week of the New Year, giving an inkling of what occupied Richey's mind in the lead up to his disappearance.

Left: Richey's change of image in 1995 which shocked close friends.

'Kevin Carter' lyrics, 1995. James and Richey disagreed over the melody for 'Kevin Carter' which James would later describe as 'an impasse in the band for the first time, born out of taste.'

Richey in 1995, sporting his changed image soon after Snoopy's passing, the band's differing trajectory, and the ending of his relationship with Jo. He wrote 'I cut my hair after every emotional trauma'.

fabric that looked like rags — but in a fashionably untidy way, I don't think they were bandages. But on the areas of his arms that weren't covered you could make out scars which looked worse than they really were because of his tanned skin.

Although many people are desperate to believe any evidence of Richey's continued existence, it is fair to say that a large degree of scepticism surrounds the majority of these reported 'sightings'. They are each largely based on one person's reportage, and who knows how credible these witnesses may be, and how much their testimonies have been shaped by (possibly subconscious) wishful thinking?

The only safe conclusion is that this variety of post-disappearance sightings from all over the globe is testament to the continued general fascination with Richey Edwards. It leads us to the central, over-arching question of this book: just what happened to him? And, specifically, and not over-fancifully, is it possible that the clues that he apparently scattered during his life could even help us to unravel the mystery of his vanishing?

Chapter 12

The Narrative Verdict

'Meanwhile, the water suffers, though appearing to sleep
And feels passing through its melancholy lethargy,
The thousand shadows, with which it trembles endlessly,
And which opens, in its surface, an enlarged wound.'
Georges Rodenbach, 'The Enclosed Lives'

In his 1974 Pulitzer Prize-winning work, *The Denial of Death*, Ernest Becker writes that humans live not just in the world of matter but in symbols and dreams: 'His cherished narcissism feeds on symbols, on an abstract idea of his own self-worth, an idea composed of sounds, words, and images, in the air, in the mind, on paper. And this means that man's natural yearning for organismic activity, the pleasures of incorporation and expansion, can be fed limitlessly in the domain of symbols and so unto immortality.'

As conscious beings, says Becker, we are defined by our fear of death; our response is to pursue our own cosmic significance, in heroics. Human cultures are hero-systems, with various designated roles catering to varying degrees of heroism.

Central to this book's view of Richey Edwards has been precisely this aspect: namely, his blatant efforts to pursue his own transcendent symbolic meaningfulness, via the modern medium of rock music. Richey

certainly knew the mechanics of the processes this involved; his sensibility emerging from academia and more broadly in postmodernity, a
very self-referential and textually aware moment in our culture's history.

But Richey's vision for what the Manic Street Preachers could signify
was more deeply embedded in immortality-games and heroics than his
three band members. By the third album he had parted narrative
company with the other Manics, dissatisfied with their search for record
industry success.

For Richey, racked with lower self-esteem than his colleagues, the
fear of death and its remedy in immortality were pressing matters of
great urgency. Disillusionment with the less precarious path the band
were taking saw him plunge into deep depression – his idealised self,
defined by the drama and tragedy of a full-stop departure from the
game, was incompatible with such mundanity.

'Mental illness,' says Becker, 'is really a general theory of the failures
of death-transcendence. The avoidance of life and terror of death become
enmeshed in the personality to such an extent that it is crippled, unable
to exercise the "normal cultural heroism" of other members of the
society.'

As we know, Richey's personal mythology aimed far higher than his
peers. But its failure, its coming apart, was all too public, and all the
more painful for that. As James Dean Bradfield has said on many occasions, Richey just feared being thought a loser: 'One thing I know is
that towards the end, Richey became very obsessed with some kind of
victory over himself. He really didn't want to be a loser. But, because
we haven't got a clue what the fuck happened to him, people can't take
that as a testament in blood, that he failed or he succeeded. All I know
is that, as I say, towards the end, he was totally obsessed with this idea
of victory.'

In the first half of 1994, leading up to his suicide attempt, it is
possible to trace the deepening of his dread sense that his strategy was
coming apart. He was faced with the prospect of keeping his head down
in a mid-ranking careerist band in which he was not even the best
guitar player. It would have been an excruciating compromise.

We know that he had attempted suicide before, and so he may have done so again on 1 February 1995. The burning question now is whether we feel Richey spent the second half of 1994 reimagining his 'hero-system' in a way that allowed him to exit the band and survive. Imagining the specifics of what may have happened, there are many options, but they essentially boil down to three fundamental hypotheses.

The first one, and the 'common sense' view of Richey's fate that is held by the public at large and most Manics fans, is that he parked his car at the Severn Bridge and jumped into the waters of the Bristol Channel, his body drifting off never to be found.

Richey's condition in the months prior to February 1995 lends great weight to this suicide hypothesis. But it may also be thought to provide something of an alibi.

The remaining Manic Street Preachers' private opinions on Richey's likely fate appear to be quixotic and somewhat self-contradictory. Strangely, they have managed to simultaneously hold to the firm conviction that he is likely still alive, while apparently not trying everything to trace their vulnerable friend and bandmate.

James has commented, 'I never think he's dead. If it's true, you feel like there's got to be a body. It's too easy to imagine that he's not dead, that there's been a rebirth of sorts. I've always been in love with rock 'n' roll mythology, and I know I'm over-imaginative, but the scenario in my head is very vivid indeed.'

In this, the Manics seem to be relying on several hopeful thoughts: that, placed beyond public view, Richey's health problems did not worsen; that some harm has not been done to him by others; and that their own vivid imaginings in rock mythology have, in this instance, become a self-fulfilling prophecy.

Apparently, the band hope Richey has overcome all obstacles in his desire to become a mythical figure. Yet in the weeks before disappearing, he was smashing his head against walls, lacerating his torso, and walking around London in slippers and pyjamas – very visibly unwell. What evidence is there to support their belief?

This alternative theory that Richey Edwards survived is, of course, far more attractive, tantalising, and yet still impossible to prove.

In 1991 comments for Vivid TV, Nicky Wire shared an intriguing vision of his future: 'I just want a number one album in America, and then [to] retire to a concrete bunker like J.D. Salinger.' Only a couple of years later, a member of his own band would pull off a disappearing act. We would be wilfully blind not to consider the obvious connotations.

In the wake of *The Catcher in the Rye*'s phenomenal success, J.D. Salinger sought a completely private life, publishing his last fiction in 1965, and giving few interviews. His absence sparked the popular imagination, with numerous books and films charting attempts to track down the mysterious author. His self-imposed exile became a pillar of the Salinger mythology. Prior to Richey's disappearance, the band mentioned Salinger more than once, always in relation to his bunker retreat.

Speaking in 1991 to *EP* magazine, Richey said: 'One of the best things I've ever read is J.D. Salinger. After his big success, *The Catcher in the Rye*, he locked himself away in a basement for twenty years. But he was still writing. He's got stacks of manuscripts on his shelves, but no one's ever seen them.'

The interviewer asked: 'Could you see yourself doing that?' Richey replied: 'I'd like to think so.'

Is there a single instance of a rock band advertising the desire to suddenly vanish from view? It seems unprecedented. And yet, that one band who we know did indeed express such desires, and very clearly so, then went on to lose one of its members in circumstances of great mystery.

Mythologising disappearance as a positive action was an idea very evident in the life and work of another of Richey's favourite writers, William S. Burroughs. Anyone as familiar with Burroughs's story as Richey knows that considerable stretches of his adult life were spent in exile in countries other than his native United States.

Burroughs made a virtue of the act of 'cutting'; not just textual or pictorial cutting, for which he was renowned, but severing ties with his immediate surroundings. Extending 'cutting' into the realm of personal relations, he pursued a personal freedom that involved leaving behind all that is familiar: one's environment, closest people, previous life.

Yet of all the writers, thinkers and cultural figures that Richey referenced, the likeliest candidate for a mythic typology that he may have emulated is French poet Arthur Rimbaud.

Rimbaud completed his main work between the ages of 16 and 19, before turning his back on his life as a man of letters and vanishing from public view. He travelled the globe and settled in Abyssinia (now Ethiopia), where he worked for an export company. Returning to France years later, to have his leg amputated, he passed away at the age of 37.

James Dean Bradfield is sure that he personally introduced Richey to Rimbaud: 'There is a kind of terrible irony there, because I remember I bought into the whole enigma of Arthur Rimbaud, the poet, when I was young. One of the only books I'd given Richey that he hadn't read was A *Season in Hell* by Rimbaud, the book that created this interesting myth around the poet.'

The remark seems to suggest that, had Bradfield not introduced into Richey's consciousness the mythology of the exiled poet, things might have turned out differently. For the exile of writers like Rimbaud, Burroughs and Salinger suggest a route by which a living writer may experience a flavour of immortality while still alive.

In those last months, Richey took definitive measures to link himself with Rimbaud. On tour in France in November 1994 he was interviewed for *Melody Maker* wearing a white boiler suit covered in lines of Rimbaud verse. As he peered into a tomb in Montparnasse Cemetery in Paris, the letters scrawled across his back read: 'Once, I remember well, my life was a feast where all hearts opened and all wines flowed. Alas, the gospel has gone by. Suppose damnation were eternal! Then a man who would mutilate himself is well damned, isn't he?'

Was this, in hindsight, a deliberately placed pointer, left for those seeking answers after his disappearance?

Richey was also pictured wearing his Rimbaud overalls in the catacombs, a centuries-old series of labyrinthine tunnels dug beneath the streets of the French capital. Urban legend says the catacombs serve as the entrance to hell. Richey would have likely known that their officially designated entry-point, at Place Denfert-Rochereau, was chosen on account of the square's original name: Barrière d'Enfer (Hell's Gate).

In the section of *A Season in Hell* entitled 'Bad Blood', Rimbaud distances himself from bourgeois standards, likening himself to various exotic races: Vikings, Mongols, Africans. He is compelled to overseas adventure: 'My day is over; I'm leaving Europe. The sea air will burn my lungs … I will be lazy and brutal.'

These references prove Richey was at the very least cognisant of disappearance as a romantic trope. And on the day that he vanished, Richey left at the Embassy Hotel a box of texts which, blatantly and unequivocally, he knew would be deciphered in context with his vanishing that same day. The level of disappearance- and exile-oriented content in that box is extraordinary.

If we make the assumption that the texts left in the Embassy gift box serve as a black box recording salvaged from the closing seconds of Richey's journey as a Manic Street Preacher, then their contents provide details of his mind's parting flight path.

In a letter to Rachel, Jo listed the box's contents from memory:

1. Camino Real with Kilroy underlined (Tennessee Williams).
2. Nietzsche.
3. A rubbish book by a young middle-class girl telling me to write a book as an example of what could be published.
4. Some sort of testament to socialism don't know who the author is. An extract. Brilliant I thought.
5. Photos of us, and W.B. Yeats' house.
6. Equus.
7. And, of course, the Vadim Maslennikov note beside his bed. The author who disappeared without a trace! A book I regret giving him, just before the Thailand dates. He said in one of his letters that it was mind-blowing. Unusual for him to say something like that, I thought.

One startling item is the 'rubbish book by a middle-class girl', with Richey's accompanying recommendation that Jo write her own book. Presumably he meant a memoir, culminating in her time with him. This lends credence to her suspicion that Richey may have been 'manipulating' his experiences, even their moments together, to the point of 'acting out' for narrative effect.

Tennessee Williams's play *Camino Real* (1953) is a mythical-allegorical tale of trapped romantics caught in a small town surrounded by desert. Several are figures from history and literature – Lord Byron, Casanova, Don Quixote. The town, Camino Real, is both literally and metaphorically the end of the road for its characters, suggesting they are imprisoned in purgatory, or one of the circles of hell. But they retain some hope; if they stay alive, there is at least the potential for escape. As the Byron character says: 'Make voyages. Attempt them. There's nothing else.'

Richey underscored lines spoken by one character, Kilroy. He is an anti-hero but the audience roots for him. He neither understands nor accepts the rules of the situation and rages against his confinement, embodying American optimism and boldness. Before he becomes 'an undistinguished member of a collectivist state', Kilroy yearns to escape via the only possible way out – an aeroplane named *Il Fugitivo*.

Peter Shaffer's play *Equus* (1973) evidently held great importance for Richey, having also, as we have seen, been chosen as the vessel for his earlier suicide note the previous year. In the play, a mentally troubled youth, Alan Strang, blinds six horses by gouging out their eyes. The story revolves around his discussions with a psychiatrist, Dr Dysart, and Alan's impact on the doctor, who comes to realise that his own life is safe, unimaginative and lacking passion. Alan, by contrast, has created his own mythology around ritual worship of the horse-as-god.

A psychiatrist's role is to render the abnormal normal, but the doctor admires Alan. Dysart has the option to 'make this boy an ardent husband, a caring citizen, a worshipper of abstract and unifying God', but comes to realise that straightening Alan out in this way is 'more likely to make a ghost!'

Nicky Wire reckons Richey arrived well-prepared for his dealings with psychiatrists, and his use of *Equus* prior to entering the Priory suggests as much. It also adds to the list of texts Richey referenced dealing with mental hospitals, psychiatry and madness – leading even his sister to question whether he may have willed himself into certain institutions.

Another major theme is the relationship between young Alan and his parents. He divulges to the psychiatrist that his parents' repressive nature forms the background to his sexual-religious worship of horses. The issue of a repressive Christianity plays a part, something that Richey hinted at several times in retelling his own upbringing, despite Rachel's denial that any of the family attended church in Blackwood as much as Richey suggested.

The theme of parent–child difficulties reoccurs elsewhere in the gift box. Jo's item number 7 refers to *Novel with Cocaine* (1934), written by M. Ageyev, the *nom de plume* of a Jewish-Russian author, Mark Levi, then living in Istanbul. The teenage first-person narrator, Vadim Maslennikov, is self-absorbed, cruel, vicious and dislikeable – but completely honest. He has disdain for his mother, often lashing out at her. Jo recalls handing the book over to Richey at around the time of the Manics' trip to Thailand in spring 1994, and says it became a shared favourite.

Novel with Cocaine has fascinated Richey fans for the fact that its author handed over his manuscript for publication then fled without trace, never to be heard from again. Was this a duplicate scenario – Richey leaving a blindingly obvious heavy hint of his survival?

If that notion seems tenuous, we can reveal an even more remarkable parallel. When Ageyev delivered his manuscript to a friend in Paris, he also gave them his passport. Similarly, on the evening before he disappeared, Richey was in his hotel room with a female friend, Vivian, and, according to reported remarks by Nicky Wire, made repeated offers for her to have his passport. Take it, he kept saying, he wasn't going to need it. Surely no coincidence, considering a copy of the Ageyev book was lying right there in the room?

Jo's list failed to give more details on the book she described as 'some ode to socialism'. Whatever it was, we could take it as a counterbalance to the kinds of politics usually associated with Friedrich Nietzsche.

Nietzsche's fabulist masterpiece, *Thus Spoke Zarathustra* fits perfectly with the running theme of exile, evident from its opening line, when a 30-year-old Zarathustra leaves his home for a new life in the wilderness. The prophet lives an ascetic existence for ten years, but – crucially – feels the strong compulsion to return, with new insights for humanity:

From all mountains do I look out for fatherlands and motherlands. But a home have I found nowhere: unsettled am I in all cities, and decamping at all gates. Alien to me, and a mockery, are the present-day men, to whom of late my heart impelled me; and exiled am I from fatherlands and motherlands.

Nicky Wire has openly pondered whether Richey adopted a similar role for himself, half expecting him to return after years of working on a literary masterpiece, ready to blow everyone away with a work of great genius.

In his January 1995 lyric, 'Judge Yourself', Richey tapped into his current fascination with the writings of Nietzsche. In the line about 'Dionysus' and the 'Crucified', he refers to Nietzsche's opposition of Christian values with those of the Greek god of wine and theatre.

When Jo listed 'Nietzsche' among the gift box of items, her handwriting then began to spell out 'The Antich ...', before crossing it out. She later confirmed that this was the book she was left by Richey.

In *The Antichrist* (1885), Nietzsche wrote: 'The most spiritual human beings, as the *strongest*, find their happiness where others would find their destruction: in the labyrinth, in severity towards themselves and others, in attempting; their joy lies in self-constraint: with them asceticism becomes nature, need, instinct.'

Supposing Richey pursued such a life of asceticism as a positive option in 1995 – would that not require his becoming a completely transformed person? Nietzsche offers a possible explanation, resolved around the name Richey placed in that final lyric, that of Dionysus.

Nietzsche says: 'The word "Dionysian" means: an urge to unity, a reaching-out beyond personality, the everyday, society, reality, across the abyss of transitoriness: a passionate-painful overflowing into darker, fuller, more flowing states.' The German philosopher described himself, in *Beyond Good and Evil*, as the 'last disciple of the god Dionysus'.

Automatically, we think of the various reported sightings of Richey internationally – in Asia, off the African coast; bedraggled, barely recognisable, but in his very survival somehow embodying all the points listed above. Richey may have had strong pangs of guilt, but his new passion, Friedrich Nietzsche, gave great encouragement in overcoming them.

The hero, says Nietzsche, yearns to become his opposite, his anti-self. 'He gains from this creative conflict with the opposite of his true being. The intellectual thus becomes the anti-intellectual man, of "perfect bodily sanity".'

Nietzsche's philosophy of 'self-overcoming' offers us some explanation for how Richey may have become such a barely recognisable person, post-disappearance – that is, if any one of the purported sightings are true.

How conscious was Richey of all this 'Nietzschean superman' theory as he counted down to retirement? For Christmas 1994, he received a card from the band, with pop-up Marvel Comics characters, and an accompanying 1995 diary on the same theme. Nietzsche's influence on the two-dimensional pop-culture superheroes of comic books is well documented. Was Richey alert to the obvious analogy with what he was about to do, donning a mask and transforming into a new persona?

We examine Richey's *Marvel Superheroes Datebook 1995*. On its front cover is a picture of Spiderman in action; in the white of his eyes, Richey has written the same message he apparently left for Jo: 'I Love You'. Turning the page, the inside cover has a monochrome picture of

Spiderman, and Richey has written a speech bubble for him, saying: 'Spidey say, Call myself Lyla-May'.

This may have been idle doodling, yet we wonder whether it may show Richey had not lost his sense of humour and perspective – it could be saying he knew he was about to launch himself into a probably self-defeating transfiguration.

Was he heading into a less public existence, where he might find the necessary space to explore what it was he needed to become? These were high stakes indeed. The Manic Street Preachers may have gone on to become heroes to many millions, but Richey would become … what? A superhero? Even if only to those willing to receive the signs, and with the wherewithal to interpret them. As Nietzsche said of his own writings, they served as 'fish-hooks' designed to catch only a rare few.

The Embassy gift box also contained photos Richey had taken around London, including several of the outside of a house with a blue plaque, formerly the residence of Sylvia Plath, and earlier still of Irish poet W.B. Yeats.

Jo sees Yeats as the likely inhabitant of interest. There is an obvious overlap between the work of Nietzsche and Yeats; the German philosopher profoundly influenced the Irish poet, as well as the new generation of fascists across Europe. Supposing, then, that Richey *had* been consciously referencing both Nietzsche and Yeats, in the context of his disappearance, which elements common to the both might be relevant?

Following Nietzsche, the heroes of Yeats's plays embody the Dionysian 'insistence on strength of will, passion, self-sufficiency, solitude and boundless self-overflowing'. Nietzsche and Yeats, considered together, add fuel to the theory of pre-meditated disappearance.

Yeats's famous poem 'The Second Coming' also feels like it has much in common with where Richey's mind was travelling through that final year. The early-to-mid-nineties were chock full of millennial angst and what seemed at the time to be a gathering series of nightmare news events presaging apocalypse. *The Holy Bible* and his subsequent lyrics seemed to want to capture that atmosphere.

We visit Cardiff University Library in the hope of digging out the link we instinctively know is there between Yeats and other references from Richey's last known year. Something relating Nietzsche with Yeats with millenarianism? Or possible content linking heroic exile, mythology, modern history and the occult?

Numerous titles catch the eye – *Yeats's Quest for Eden*; *Yeats, Neoplatonism and the Aesthetic of Exile*; *Yeats, the Man and the Masks*; *Yeats, the Poet as Mythmaker*; *Yeats and Nietzsche – An Exploration of Major Nietzschean Echoes in the Writings of William Butler Yeats*.

Sitting surrounded by decades of research on Yeats, the relevance becomes obvious to us, and it feels certain that Richey took a photograph of the Yeats commemorative plaque outside the poet's former residence in London with some definite sense of purpose.

We find a book called *Yeats and the Poetry of Death – Elegy, Self-elegy, and the Sublime*. *The Poetry of Death* was Richey's first suggested title for what became *The Holy Bible*. And Yeats's 'The Second Coming' ends with this apocalyptic couplet: 'And what rough beast, its hour come round at last / Slouches towards Bethlehem to be born?'

Bethlehem. In his last weeks, Richey spoke repeatedly of wanting to go to Israel. Why? Calling your last album by that title, poring over countless religious texts, plans for a journey to the Holy Land – are those the outlines of a personal mythology Richey was assembling for himself?

Of course, the less delicate answer would involve something along the lines of his acquiring a 'Messiah complex', and losing sense of reality completely. In a 1995 letter to Rachel, Jo told how Richey feared losing his mind at Anson Court in late 1994.

'I know I should have asked him about the voices. Can't come to terms with the fact I could see he wasn't coping, but still I left him. Perhaps that was part of the reason for his panic about being left alone in the flat. It was as though he felt he had no control over his own thoughts: "Something bad is going to happen if I stay in this flat."'

This is Jo's testimony; a witness account from the person closest to Richey. Had he become psychotic or schizophrenic by the end? His friends, including the band, have suggested as much.

While Richey's photograph showed the blue plaque memorial to W.B. Yeats outside the poet's home, we should not forget that the same house was also where Sylvia Plath committed suicide on 11 February 1963. Richey would have been aware of both and of the ambiguity in leaving behind such a photograph. As with so many other pointers, that picture may be read in favour of both hypotheses – suicide *and* survival.

So, perhaps Richey pursued spiritual interests abroad? Researching this book, we happened across someone who had heard this theory many times. A resident of Cardiff since well before 1994–5, she was acquainted with its music scene and had long known the city's various tattooists. We approached her not to enquire after disappearance theories but to find out about an aborted tattooing session that Richey had booked in January 1995.

As we talked, the woman said: 'Most people think he went to Israel, don't they!'

'*Do they?*' we asked.

'Yes, living on a kibbutz.'

We gave this theory no particular credence until Rachel raised the same idea: yes, Richey had been going on about heading to that part of the world just before he vanished.

Richey was acutely aware of the counting down to the end of the millennium. From this thought shoots a wild theory: had he indeed looked to get to Israel, could he have planned on remaining there until around the turn of the century, before making a dramatic return, perhaps armed with his new literary masterpiece, or manifesto, or memoir?

Is this too fantastical? Well, there is further supporting evidence in Richey's late 1994 tattoo – a diagram of the entry to Hell, below Jerusalem, based on an illustration from a 1949 pressing of Dante's the *Divine Comedy*.

Dante's work had become intrinsic to Richey's efforts to relay his predicament. Many photographs taken of him in those last few months show him deliberately sporting his new inkings for the camera. There is one snap of him leaning against railings outside Anson Court, upper arms flattened out as they drape over his knees; another of him wearing a sleeveless hoodie, and awkwardly squaring out his shoulders to show off the deltoids. There even exists a blurry photo, evidently taken by a fan gazing up from street level, of Richey on the Manics' tour bus. Through a misty window, he is captured pushing aside his sleeve to show the Jerusalem shoulder.

Was he perhaps anticipating that people would later scrutinise and interpret just these kinds of clues?

Dante Alighieri famously wrote the *Divine Comedy* following his enforced exile from Florence in 1302, the result of political rivalries. He is yet another name in that long list of authors Richey name-dropped who had lived or written about a life of exile.

When we pore over Richey's own bookshelves, they offer similar clues. We find a work by an American poet, Hart Crane, whose best-known work, *The Bridge*, was often referenced by Richey. Crane committed suicide by jumping into the sea, so it is easy merely to assume that Richey identified with this suicide component. Yet, as we leaf through its pages, one corner is folded over. Richey had marked a poem named 'Exile'. And his literature collection continues to yield potential clues.

The main character in James Hogg's *The Private Memoirs and Confessions of a Justified Sinner* (1824) is a young man who meets another, very similar to himself, and falls under his spell. A series of murders follows – has the narrator been tempted by the Devil to carry out his mission, or has he gone insane? Part psychological thriller, part satire, there is also an element of meta-fiction, or the ironic use of standard tropes to show the work's self-awareness as a constructed narrative. Very Richey.

Richard Bach's *Jonathan Livingston Seagull* (1970) tells the story of a seagull who ventures beyond the routine lives of other gulls.

He encounters two fellow gulls who show him the way to a 'higher plane' through the perfection of knowledge. 'I don't mind being bones and feathers,' he says 'I just want to know what I can do in the air and what I can't, that's all.' Perhaps Richey also read Bach's best-selling sequel, *Illusions: The Adventures of a Reluctant Messiah* (1977)?

Six Miles to Roadside Business (1990), by Michael Doane, develops on from the cult components in *Apocalypse Now* and Richey's known interest in the Reverend Jim Jones and the mass suicide at Jonestown, Guyana. Main character Vance Ravel goes off into the desert wilderness of Utah to discover his true self and becomes the reluctant leader of a small hippyish cult. Images come to mind of that dreadlocked Richey spotted in Goa or the Canaries.

Also on the bookshelves are several copies of Albert Camus's *A Happy Death*. Richey had snapped up an armful and had begun distributing them to friends before his disappearance. In the book, Patrice Mersault goes on the run from Algiers, seeking happiness and a meaningful life. He discovers that these are found not in relationships, nor in money alone, but happiness is possible, given two criteria – sufficient solitude, and sufficient time.

Mersault gives up on hedonism and nihilism, and arrives at an answer betraying Camus's obvious debt to Nietzsche: 'You make the mistake,' says Mersault, 'of thinking you have to choose, that you have to do what you want, that there are conditions for happiness. What matters – all that matters – is the will to happiness; a kind of enormous, ever-present consciousness. The rest – women, art, success – is nothing but excuses. You know the famous formula: "If I had my life to live over again?" Well, I would live it over again just the way it has been.'

As we progress through Richey's book collection, it becomes clear we could locate messages in nearly all of them, and many of them would be highly fanciful.

Yet Rachel sees the point of this line of enquiry, 'Why would you take a box of all those books, videos and pictures to a London hotel?

The things he thought symbolised him. It seems a bit pre-planned with whatever he was going to do.'

James Dean Bradfield has admitted to often being left perplexed by Richey's lyrics. One line, however, from 'Peeled Apples' (*Journal for Plague Lovers*) about a dwarf taking his cockerel out of a fight made him laugh out loud. Could the image have perhaps been lifted from another source? A dwarf, cockfighting; instantly, scenes come to mind from one specific novel, noted as one of Richey's favourites, Malcolm Lowry's *Under the Volcano*.

Were the Manics conscious of this reference? Certainly, the work has been documented as playing a place in the band's genesis, setting off Nicky Wire's long journey into serious reading after his mother, Irene, brought a copy home from Blackwood Library. It later became important to Richey, too.

Under the Volcano (1947) tells of the last hours in the life of the British consul in Mexico, Geoffrey Firmin. Lowry's original plan was for a trilogy of works based structurally and thematically on Dante's the *Divine Comedy*, with *Under the Volcano* as his 'Inferno'. Its message is clear: hell is a state of mind.

Fully aware of his impending death, the consul, consumed by alcohol, nevertheless retains his ability to articulate his interpretation of the world around him as filtered through his unique perspective. This was said of Richey himself, and it is easy to see how Lowry's novel became important to him and Nicky Wire.

Something about Lowry and his masterpiece suggests it was as relevant as any work by Dante, Conrad, Rimbaud or Blake, and the Faust legend, to understanding Richey's final months. Indeed, *Under the Volcano* references other written works in the same way Richey did – in fact, precisely the same authors. It was postmodern in referencing and being shaped by other works by previous writers; an element also to be found in works by the Manics, especially those of Richey prior to his disappearance.

Was Richey quietly using Lowry's incomplete trilogy as a model for his work, much as Lowry himself had used Dante? Was *The Holy Bible* album his 'Inferno'? Were the writings left over to the band in early 1995 intended to become his 'Purgatorio'? And was there maybe then a third installation, an album corresponding to Dante's 'Paradiso', to be delivered when Richey returned home, possibly at the turn of the millennium?

Does all of this evidence suggest Richey's disappearance was not just the predictable falling apart of his time in the music industry, but the apex of his entire approach from the very beginning: his semi-detached knowingness and theoretical alertness? Does the disappearance constitute Richey's wresting intellectual control over proceedings, rather than the end of him mentally? The issue essentially revolves around the extent to which we feel Richey retained a masterful authorship throughout.

Was he writing this whole story?

Our intuition regarding the truth about Richey Manic draw us to these kinds of answers. Very little has been done in terms of a proper official full-scale search for Richey, and thus no progress made in learning the empirical facts of the case. What we are left with is this, the narrative verdict – the narrative that emanates from Richey's words and actions and seems to imply a planned disappearance and exile.

Yet how does the survival theory respond to the grave doubts about Richey's ability to survive in hiding, cut off from those he knew and loved, all the while having the latter's suffering on his conscience?

In *The Denial of Death*, Ernest Becker writes: 'One of the key concepts for understanding man's urge to heroism is the idea of "narcissism" … It is one of the meaner aspects of narcissism that we feel that everyone is expendable except ourselves. We should feel prepared … to recreate the whole world out of ourselves even if no one else existed. The thought frightens us; we don't know how we could do it without others – yet at bottom the basic resource is there: we could suffice alone if need be, if we could trust ourselves.'

Is it realistic that Richey could reduce his life so drastically, and stay alive? Not only is it possible, but Richey had been repeatedly expressing the desire to minimise his life. He had also publicly craved a life of reclusion and exile. He may have managed both.

How, though, might we square the facts of his mental and physical fragility with such a venture? Social withdrawal is often a basic fact of depression; utterly fearful of death, yet too scared to live, the depressive retreats into a kind of living death – clearly, Richey's degrading relations with his life in music demanded such a departure.

Yet as a rock star, his retreat was not that of your average citizen. Richey's disappearance supplied him with a solution to his failing heroic status: now all at once simultaneously everywhere and nowhere, he had gone from being a media face to being a universal spectre flitting through the ether. His vanishing permitted him the otherwise impossible: an immortality upgrade.

One final theory on Richey's vanishing invites the reader to question beyond the standard options. There are the 'known unknowns' but also inevitably those 'unknown unknowns' that seldom occur to us.

Nicky Wire ventured this way when he shared his personal fears that something bad might have happened to Richey at the hands of someone else. It was brave of him to broadcast what may appear to many fans to be a strange thought. Wire would know, if anyone would, the state of play at the business end of the music industry; its high stakes, the huge profits that hang in the balance. Any future investigations into the Richey case ought to strive to thoroughly probe a range of possibilities; something we have tried to kick start with this book.

Our attempts to access official records and persons of interest inevitably went through Rachel Edwards, who we would expect to have the right to see important documents and to be able to speak with those people relevant to the case. Yet as we progressed with the writing of *Withdrawn Traces*, the title gradually took on a new and unintended meaning.

Over the course of more than two years, we saw endless delays from the police. The Richey file went missing then suddenly reappeared. One minute Rachel had the right to access information from her brother's file; the next, the police claimed she did not. Phone calls were not returned. New officers were continually put in charge of the case.

Even more disrupting were the many Manics-related people who were initially very happy to talk to us, only to then withdraw co-operation. Frustrating as this was for us, we were nonetheless only experiencing second-hand, and in a limited way, the long years of thwarted efforts on the part of Richey's relatives.

The following chapter details Rachel's search, which has been truly exhaustive, certainly compared with the apparent lack of effort that has been expended by official investigations.

Chapter 13

Rachel's Search

'*And I said, "That last thing is what you can't get, Carlo. Nobody can get to that last thing. We keep on living in hopes of catching it once and for all."*'
Jack Kerouac, *On the Road*

As the official search for Richey began to lose impetus, Rachel was determined that her brother would not become a forgotten statistic. She was desperate that his very essence would not be consigned to a few dusty files, which would gradually disappear beneath a stack of other, seemingly unsolvable cases.

In the 24 years since Richey left the Embassy Hotel, the passage of time has cast its mist over certain events and decisions taken in the immediate aftermath of his vanishing – but possible lines of investigation remain.

As the years have passed, Rachel has witnessed many failed initiatives, inadequate responses and missed opportunities on the part of the police as she attempted to unravel the truth behind her brother's disappearance.

'Immediately after hearing about Richard going missing, I was under the impression the authorities were doing the best they could to trace him,' she remembers. 'I was young, and my parents came from a generation who believed the police would do everything in their power to find a highly vulnerable individual. Sadly, that wasn't the case.'

As the police investigation progressed, she became aware of a lack of cohesion and attention to detail, and formed the impression that her brother's disappearance was being viewed as little more than a stunt from a publicity-hungry rock star.

With no experience of police procedure, Rachel was uncertain as to how a missing person search should be organised, but over the years following Richey's disappearance she has begun to question certain aspects of their investigation.

Former Wiltshire Police Officer Detective Superintendent Stephen Fulcher was involved in many such investigations. Although not involved in Richey's case, he has raised his own concerns about how the police generally instigate and carry out searches.

In 2011, the vastly experienced Fulcher was leading an investigation into the disappearance of a young woman, Sian O'Callaghan, who vanished after leaving a Swindon nightclub. A suspect, taxi driver Christopher Halliwell, was arrested five days into the hunt. DS Fulcher believed that there was a chance that Sian might still be alive, and so, mindful that time was of the essence, he abandoned police protocol by authorising an urgent interview with Halliwell – without a legal representative present.

Not only did Fulcher's actions result in the discovery of Sian's body, but also in Halliwell leading him to the remains of another victim, 20-year-old Rebecca Godden. Halliwell was given a life sentence. Fulcher, however, was suspended from his job for not following official police guidelines for questioning suspects, and was found guilty of gross misconduct. In response to this, he resigned from the force.

Fulcher feels that an obsession with police procedure diminishes the bigger picture: 'The public needs to know what the police *won't* do if their daughter went missing. People need to be informed.'

Drawing on his knowledge of missing person cases, Fulcher believes that investigations into Richey's disappearance fell short of even the most basic police procedure. He explains how vital it is to account for an individual's last known 24 hours as soon as possible: 'That 24 to 48-hour period from when you hear about the disappearance is the time you act. That's when you can gather the most important information before a large part of it is lost.'

As Richey was not reported as missing until over 24 hours after he vanished, time was crucial. Yet Rachel is unaware of any interviews conducted with James and Vivian, the last two people to have seen her brother alive. Nor has the person who apparently checked Richey out of his hotel at 7am been formerly identified or interviewed.

'We, as a family, never spoke to Vivian or even knew her last name,' says Rachel. 'Just a few people were aware of who she was, and we were never put in touch with her. Only she knows the full extent of the conversation that she and Richard had that night. Nick told my parents he was trying to give her his passport, and that could carry some weight somewhere in the investigation.'

> 'The last person to see somebody alive, they're going to give that detailed account of someone's mind-set prior to them going missing. They are the key to an investigation and they should be spoken to as quickly as possible. They are always interviewed.'
> Reported Missing, BBC One, 2017

Rachel believes that other vital opportunities to gain a fuller picture of Richey's last known hours at the Embassy Hotel were missed, whether through a lack of police endeavour or through oversight. 'Did the police look at incoming and outgoing calls to his hotel room? Surely the hotel would have kept a guestbook detailing who was coming in and out? Richard could have been in communication with someone other than Vivian that night.'

Rachel soon discovered that the greater the number of police forces involved, the more complicated the process became. Becoming aware of the ineffective communication between the three forces has proved to be deeply frustrating for her.

'There seemed to be no accountability, no one would take responsibility, and we were always being passed from pillar to post. It certainly wasn't advantageous to have more forces involved – it was quite the opposite. When the car was found, the police took photos of it but two years later destroyed them. That was evidence they destroyed. Have you ever heard of that happening in an unresolved case before?'

The discovery of an abandoned car near the bridge would normally mean the deployment of a coastguard and a Severn Area Rescue Association (SARA) search to the nearby river, yet for some reason the police failed to authorise one in Richey's case – despite two recent searches having been undertaken the previous month when the abandoned cars of two missing people were found in the Severn area.

'A search when a car is discovered near the Estuary is standard procedure,' says Mervyn Fleming, station commander at SARA. 'It was unusual we were never contacted, and this incident was never recorded with us.'

The Severn Estuary has the second highest rise and fall of tide in the world, and the movement of the water within it is very complex. If a body were washed down into the Bristol Channel, it is highly unlikely it would travel out into the Atlantic for some time, as the incoming currents are stronger and faster than those flowing outwards.

In his 2002 book, *Disasters on the Severn*, Chris Witts describes how the vast amount of silt moved back and forth each day with the tides could easily submerge a body in the sediment, hiding it forever. If a search had been made of the river earlier (or at all), would there have been a chance of Richey's body being retrieved?

'Along with search boats being sent out, shallower parts of the Severn have been dredged in these cases,' confirms Fleming. 'So there's always a possibility, even a remote one, of finding something in the weeks after an individual makes it into the water.'

Rachel started contacting agencies to try to understand what might have happened to her brother's body had he entered the water. 'I spoke to the National Rivers Authority, the Maritime and Coastguard Agencies and the Hydrographic Office, and we discussed the details of the tides on the date Richard disappeared. They all gave conflicting answers about the arrival of the spring tide, and the strength of the current that February. There wasn't anything conclusive I could really take from them.'

Rachel continued writing letters to coroner's offices throughout the UK requesting details of any bodies washed up in their region. She also wrote to the monasteries of Ireland, England and Wales enquiring whether anybody who matched her brother's description had taken refuge there. The replies fill up an A4 file and show that her efforts drew a blank.

'It was soul destroying, and no matter what I did, it never felt like enough,' she says. 'I spent days driving around Cardiff, looking for any clues after Richard vanished. I checked his diary and saw he went to a tattoo parlour in Cardiff the month before. When I went there, they told me they remembered him, and he'd asked for a tattoo of Jo's name to be put on his arm. They refused because as a policy the shop didn't ink names.

'Then I saw some receipts for the Marriott Hotel, which was close to his flat. I know in the past he'd spend nights there because he hated being alone, but this time the receipts were for massages. The staff there remembered him. They told me how his legs and back were scarred from self-harming, and how disturbing it was to see. I also drove down to Swansea and spoke to some of his old lecturers. But nobody there had seen him.

'When the trail ran cold, I'd go down to the riverbank in Bristol and just stare into the water, wondering if his body was beneath it, submerged in the sediment. My head was everywhere. There is no ten-step process for grief when someone you love goes missing. You are constantly flipping back and forth, between hope and hopelessness, just waiting for the next piece of news or pivotal information.'

A short while after Richey disappeared, the officer in charge of the case, Detective Sergeant Stephen Morey, set the tone for the investigation: 'At every street corner there is potentially a Manics fan who would recognise [Richey]. He has so many out there. It is not as though he was just an ordinary unknown who has disappeared. Every fan is unwittingly looking for him. He has drawn no money since he left the hotel six months ago, nor asked his parents for any. In these circumstances, I have to move towards the theory that Richey is no longer with us.'

Such discouraging comments seemed inappropriate for an ongoing, active search for a vulnerable adult. Richey's original missing person report revealed that he had a previous psychiatric history. As a high-risk case, his details should have been immediately circulated to forces nationwide via the Police National Computer system. However, it was only in April 1996 that Richey's information was finally shared nationwide. Why a delay of 14 months?

At the time of Richey's disappearance, the lack of a UK-wide police database for missing persons resulted in families suffering the most painful emotional trauma. There were many tragic instances where parents of missing children may have had their suffering unnecessarily prolonged due to the non-transmission of information between forces. In the same decade that Richey disappeared, another three young men who had also gone missing were featured in local news stories. Unlike Richey, their bodies were eventually found. Nevertheless, a disproportionate amount of time passed before their families were notified.

In 1998, the *Independent* highlighted police failings in identifying the bodies of the three young men. Sixteen-year-old Christopher Goodall disappeared from his Stockport home in October 1997. An ardent Manic Street Preachers fan, Chris had recently broken up with his girlfriend. When she received an angry letter from him, stamped with a South Wales postmark, his parents quickly realised its significance. Recalling the news stories about Richey, his mother, Joan Battersby, immediately feared the worst. 'Even before the letter, it came to me in the night that he might be heading there,' she recalled. 'He was such a fan, he thought it was so cool [Richey] getting out like that when life became too much.'

The family contacted Derbyshire police and left for Bristol immediately. A publicity campaign was launched across the south-west to try to find Christopher. Several police forces became involved but, sadly, it was all too late. Christopher's body had already been found, washed up out of the Severn River at Beachley, just over the Gloucestershire border. His remains lay unidentified on a mortuary slab in the county from November until the following March.

Discovered at a location bordering three police forces – Avon and Somerset, Gwent, and Gloucestershire – the body was taken to the latter county. Unlike the other two, this police force had not been informed by Derbyshire police. It was only after an appeal made by Gloucestershire police in February's *Police Gazette*, requesting information about the teenage body in their mortuary, that the connection was made.

Appropriate inter-force communication, or contact with the National Missing Persons Helpline (NMPH), would have meant that Christopher's body could have been identified far sooner. In fact the NMPH would later become instrumental in solving the case of a missing 21-year-old care worker, Simon Allen.

Simon, from Keighley, Yorkshire, had suffered from depression and had recently spent three months in a psychiatric hospital before he vanished in early 1994. Due to his mental health history, his parents wasted no time in reporting him missing. Their relentless search, including a television appeal by his father, unfortunately yielded no information.

Simon had jumped from a bridge in Leeds, just 20 miles away and within four hours of leaving his home. His body was retrieved immediately. However, it took the police three-and-a-half years to identify his body and inform his parents. This only occurred by chance when the NMPH became aware of an unidentified body in Leeds, and requested photographs from the police. Despite Simon dying so near to his home, the system still failed to identify him. His family's grief was further compounded in the knowledge that their son had been buried in an unmarked grave with three other unidentified people.

Most disturbing of all – and of possible significance when considering the fate that may have befallen Richey – was the case of Anthony Calveley, whose body was discovered in central London in January 1996.

Suffering from longstanding drug and alcohol addictions, the 35-year-old succumbed to bronchial pneumonia. His body was found in the city on a freezing winter's night. Originally from Birkenhead, Calveley had been sleeping rough in the capital for many years, busking with his guitar to survive. Unlike Christopher and Simon, he was immediately identified as his birth certificate was among his possessions. He also had a criminal record, with his fingerprints contained in the police database.

This should have made it easy for the authorities to contact his family. Their name, Calveley, was an unusual one. Also, his mother still lived in the area identified on Anthony's birth certificate. Yet still two years passed before she was notified of her son's death.

Again, the NMPH discovered that Anthony had died, and incredibly, despite a positive identification, four months later Lambeth Council disposed of his body. His family were distraught when informed that his remains had been cremated and his ashes buried in a London cemetery.

Anthony's sister, Chris Hibbs, explained that her mother had great difficulty coming to terms with her son's death, especially given the inaccuracies in the post-mortem report and because the family were never able to see his body.

'The post-mortem examination said he had yellow nicotine stains on his left hand, but Tony was right-handed,' she says. 'It said he was under six foot. But Tony was six foot tall. If there was a body, we could have done a DNA test. She [Mum] couldn't even have a funeral for him or have a get-together for his friends – the little things that make grieving easier.'

The National Missing Persons Helpline charity, re-named Missing People in 2007, has expanded considerably following the Fred and Rose West case in 1995. Once reports of multiple female bodies being dug up at 25 Cromwell Street in Gloucester became public, the charity was inundated with calls from people who believed that their missing loved ones could have been among the couple's victims.

John Bennett, the Detective Superintendent who led the West inquiry and later received the Queen's Police Medal, has since suggested that rather than unidentified bodies being buried in a shared grave, each person's remains should be interred separately. This would enable them to be exhumed in order to extract DNA, if necessary. Graves with multiple remains cannot currently be opened to exhume a body without the permission of all the families concerned.

With such traumatic stories coming to light, where families hold out false hope for months and even years, it is not surprising that Rachel has spent much of the past 24 years in despair, wondering what might have happened to her brother. 'I get distraught thinking that Richard might have been one of the nameless bodies that wasn't identified, who ended up in an anonymous grave somewhere,' she says. 'Or, worse, that his body was cremated, which would further limit the chances of ever finding out the truth of what happened to him.'

Rachel has also expressed her concern at having to take the initiative in providing a sample of Richey's DNA to the police in 2005, in order for it to be cross-matched with unidentified bodies on the police database. 'They never asked for it, or even told me that the option was available. I just happened to see something about it on a television programme and rang the police myself to plead with them to take a DNA sample from his toothbrush and comb. They had ten years to obtain it and they didn't. It seems beyond careless.'

Shortly after Richey's disappearance, Anna Bowles, an undergraduate from St John's College, Oxford, proposed an interesting theory to the Metropolitan Police. Based on Richey having written songs about the Holocaust, she suggested that he could have travelled to Germany on a visitor's passport to mark the fiftieth anniversary of the atrocity. She also voiced concerns that the discovery of his body may have resulted in a spate of suicides similar to those that occurred following the death of Kurt Cobain.

Bowles stated, 'I am interested in protecting those among my friends who are vulnerable and hope that this theory would help to do so, for, providing no body is found, it permits the extension of rational hope until mid-May.'

Her reference to the possibility of an epidemic of copy-cat suicides, should Richey's body be found, poses a thought-provoking question: could someone have found his body and decided that for the greater good he should remained unidentified?

'Emotionally it is very difficult, because from one day to the next, I have differing thoughts on what could have become of him,' says Rachel. 'People say the evidence obviously points one way, but when you're at the centre of it, the film reel in your head doesn't stop. There's nothing left unturned in your mind when someone is missing.

'On the dark days, you do think about so-called conspiracies, you do think about cover-ups, because absolutely anything could have happened, and Richard or his body, or ashes, are still out there somewhere, in whatever form they now take. I always think that someone, somewhere *must* know something.'

> 'You used to watch television. Now it watches you.'
> Phil Patton, *Wired* magazine, January 1995

Closed-circuit television cameras and their use to monitor our daily existence are arguably reaching a peak today, but even in 1995, CCTV cameras were already in operation from what were considered strategic viewpoints.

Cameras put in place on the Severn Bridge to identify vehicles crossing in and out of Wales remained unchecked by police in the search for Richey. This oversight was highlighted by the 1997 radio programme *Eye on Wales*, in which reporter Tim Rogers sought to shed light on the way missing person cases were investigated, drawing particularly on Richey's disappearance and the use of CCTV cameras.

As Rachel explains, 'Tim Rogers spoke to a member of the Metropolitan force involved in Richard's case during the programme. Detective Inspector David Snelling informed him that there was no footage from the bridge, and if it did exist, it would have been destroyed by 1997. Yet Tim Rogers easily obtained the recordings from the operators of the bridge. It appears to be something else the police overlooked.'

The Edwards family and the police would later view the tape salvaged by Rogers from the bridge's control room. It contained grainy footage of what appeared to be an individual on the bridge's footpath during daylight hours on 1 February. However, the weather conditions were dreadful with the cameras covered in rain. This made it impossible for Rachel or the police to make a positive identification.

'It was hard to decipher if it was even a person because of the heavy rain, yet it was a line of enquiry that needed to be investigated and eliminated,' states Rachel. 'In hindsight, I wonder if another opportunity was lost by not viewing footage taken either side of 1 February to elicit how often the footpath was used by pedestrians. If it showed little usage, then there is [more] probability that what we thought was a figure could well have been Richard.'

There were other opportunities for the police to investigate CCTV recordings in trying to establish what happened to Richey. Given the mystery surrounding his passport (in that he had reportedly tried to give it away the night before he vanished and it was later discovered in his Cardiff flat after he went missing), surely some consideration should have been given to the two separate witness statements that placed him in Newport in early February 1995, just around the corner from Wales's main Passport Office.

If Richey was seeking to obtain a new passport, it would have been relatively simple in 1995. One-year passports were still being issued, and they required the minimum of security checks. Should Richey have made his way to the Passport Office, surely CCTV cameras would have been present? With two statements placing him nearby, wouldn't those in charge of the investigation have wanted to view such footage?

'I know CCTV wasn't as prevalent then as it is now,' Rachel deliberates, 'but because of the police overlooking something as obvious as the bridge footage, it makes me wonder if they checked if the Aust Services station had any cameras, or even the business parks next to the river's walkway.'

Conversely, it could be argued that Richey may have been well aware of cameras along his route and so decided to avoid them. Even so, a toll ticket in his Cardiff flat suggests otherwise, since he would still have needed to drive across the bridge from east to west to have obtained the ticket. Did the police interview the staff manning the tollbooths on 1 February? Perhaps one of them may have remembered a shaven-headed, gaunt young man, or even recognise him as a member of the Manic Street Preachers.

The Severn Bridge toll receipt raises further questions concerning Richey's disappearance. The timestamp reads 02:55.

Unsure as to whether the ticketing machine on the Severn Bridge had a 24-hour clock format, we managed to track down Ian McCray. He was the owner of the company, Channel Time, which installed the ticketing systems on both of the Severn Bridges.

'The tickets the old bridge produced were definitely telling the time in a 24-hour format,' he told us. 'There had to be a way to distinguish a.m. from p.m. for all kinds of reasons. Some people would need the receipts for expenses and VAT purposes. They could be used in crime investigations. I even installed these systems for the South Wales Police so they could clock in and out with a specific time when they brought people into their stations for questioning. I worked for 37 years with those clocks, and a receipt stating 2.55 means the early morning.'

McCray points out that, today, anyone travelling across the bridge into Wales would have to ask specifically for a receipt, as the normal procedure is that payment is made and then the toll barrier is raised. While he is unsure whether this was the case on the bridge in 1995, he feels it quite possible that Richey – or whoever was driving the silver Cavalier – would have needed to request a receipt: 'To be honest, the police have contacted us before about our ticketing system with regards to certain crime investigations, and I was quite surprised when we didn't hear from them about this particular high-profile case.'

For Richey's vehicle to have crossed the Severn Bridge at 2.55am, he would have had to leave the Embassy Hotel at some time between midnight and 1am. For years, the official timeline had been that Richey had checked out of the hotel at 7am on 1 February and that seven hours were unaccounted for beforehand. It now transpires that this was never the case.

Rachel is stunned at receiving this news, realising that a difference of 12 hours could change the way Richey's disappearance had been treated from the very outset. 'The first thing I want to know now is: who on earth said they checked him out of the hotel at 7am? Or, who drove his car over the bridge earlier at 2.55 in the morning? He can't have done both.'

DC Fulcher acknowledges that Rachel's frustrations are justified, and while he admits the police aren't miracle workers, he believes that every possible lead should have been followed. 'The police are taught that every missing person's case should always be treated as a potential homicide until you know otherwise. You just never know. But the problem is, the police only want to deal with murder if there's a body.'

When one considers that the timestamp on the bridge receipt was totally misinterpreted and that this oversight has only recently been unearthed after over twenty years, it begs the question – can any more information be salvaged when it comes to investigating Richey's disappearance?

'Only approximately 1 in 2,000 missing persons results in suicide. The suicide theory is one of the first to suggest itself in a disappearance case. Statistically, however, it can be shown that the odds are greatly against the suicide solution. Disappearance is motivated by a desire, to escape from some personal, domestic or business conflict. Murder, the unspoken fear of the relatives, and the police, must always lie in the back of the investigator's mind as a possible explanation.'
Charles E. O'Hara, *The Fundamentals of Criminal Investigation,* 1956

In 2004, Ian Halperin and Max Wallace published an investigation, *Love and Death: The Murder of Kurt Cobain.* Cobain had been registered missing for four days in 1994 before the discovery of his body in the garage of his home in Seattle. In their book, Halperin and Wallace claim that Cobain did not in fact kill himself, but that his death was a staged suicide, and should therefore have been treated as a murder enquiry by the authorities.

During their research they interviewed Vernon Geberth, retired commanding officer of Bronx Homicide Task Force. He said: 'I can show you a list as long as my arm of murders that were staged to look like suicide. All death investigations should be handled first and foremost as murder cases until the facts prove differently. The issue is not – could this conceivably have been a suicide? It is: could this conceivably have been a murder?'

In an interview following Richey's disappearance, Nicky Wire expressed the deepest fears over the fate of his missing bandmate. 'I just hope nobody has harmed him,' he told the music press. Usually too hard-headed to air such ideas publically, Nicky was nonetheless making it clear that even he hadn't ruled out the possibility that Richey might have been involved in some sort of foul play.

In January 1995, one month before Richey's disappearance, Angela Bradley vanished from her parents' home in Gloucester. She had been suffering from depression and anorexia. Twenty-one years later, Community Protection Inspector Andy Matheson of the Gloucestershire Police re-opened the case as a murder investigation.

'Angela's car was found parked and abandoned at Mythe Bridge, which crosses the Severn at Tewkesbury,' he says. 'The keys were still in the ignition and the obvious conclusion was that she went into the river. But there is no evidence to say either way. You can't rule out foul play. She was a very vulnerable woman and you can make these connections, and believe that she came to some harm, as she seems to have vanished so completely.'

Well placed to offer perspective from the police viewpoint, Matheson admits that officers do not have the time and resources to explore the spectrum of possibilities when someone vanishes. 'There's more to consider than just the two options of suicide or somebody relocating elsewhere. I've got outstanding missing persons' cases and in an ideal world they would all be looked at, but unfortunately most will never get the attention they deserve.'

CHAPTER 13

With such obvious similarities between Angela and Richey's disappearances, there remain several investigative procedures that should be addressed.

'People have commented in the past how staged the discovery of Richard's abandoned car appeared,' says Rachel. 'He hadn't had a drink since he left the Priory the previous year and yet there was an empty wine bottle in the car – no receipt for it although there was lots of other rubbish. The steering lock was left on the vehicle, but if someone is in a chaotic state of mind and intending to kill themselves, it seems unlikely they would care to do such a thing. Maybe he or perhaps someone else put the lock on to ensure the vehicle *was* discovered. In hindsight, the steering lock should have been fingerprinted to eliminate this possibility.'

In 2011, Rachel was contacted via a social media website by an ex-postman, David Ramus. He claimed to have spotted Richey on the Severn Bridge footpath on 1 February 1995.

'I had no transport and the only way I could access the bridge was the footpath,' he said. 'I am convinced without a shadow of a doubt that the young lad on the Aust Tower side who looked extremely surprised at my presence was your late brother.

'I was so concerned at his state that I made a detour to the bridge office and reported it. The person who spoke to me did not ask for my name, and I think he was just night security. I have no idea if it was even logged.'

With his slight and vulnerable appearance, Richey might well have fallen into the wrong hands. Should he have been in a desperate state of mind – as Ramus's description seems to suggest – he may have put his trust in people who took advantage of a random opportunity, as may also have been the case with Angela Bradley.

The unexpected deaths of Jim Morrison, John Lennon and Michael Hutchence have each been fertile soil for those perferring to explore conspiracy theories about how such musical icons met an untimely end. Rather than it being a case of Richey being in the wrong place at the wrong time, might someone closer to home have been plotting Richey's removal for their own gains?

'He didn't like the direction the music was taking – he wanted to
play blues – and he didn't want to tour America anymore.'
Anna Wohlin, girlfriend of Brian Jones, 2013

In a 1993 fanzine questionnaire, when Richey was asked who his favourite ever rock star was, he answered, 'Brian Jones.' He strongly identified with the tragic story of Jones, whose image crops up repeatedly in his private files. One inscription, in a folder of university history work, reads simply, 'POOR BRIAN JONES'. The personal act of scribbling in the margin, perhaps during a dull lecture at Swansea University, dates Richey's fascination with Jones to a time well before the Manics. And 1994, the year before Richey vanished, was a particularly bumper year for news about Jones.

Two books published that year investigated Jones's life and the mystery surrounding his 1969 death. Geoffrey Giuliano's *Paint It Black – The Murder of Brian Jones* and Terry Rawlings's *Who Killed Christopher Robin? The Truth Behind the Murder of Brian Jones* each laid out new information claiming that Jones had been murdered; drowned in his outdoor swimming pool at Cotchford Farm, East Sussex, by one Frank Thorogood, a builder working on the property.

Richey would already have been abreast of the speculation surrounding Jones's death, but now there was a new public focus – his death was being treated as a crime. The authorities had reassessed events at Cotchford Farm and a plea for further information had even been made on the BBC's *Crimewatch* programme. Richey would have known all this. For him, Brian Jones's case was evidence of the mystery, allure and intrigue surrounding rock music at the highest level: the mythic level.

In the absence of a murder conviction, theories still swirl darkly around whoever was responsible for Jones's death. Many could be said to have motives – financial or otherwise – for his removal. He had many enemies in the business. Had Richey, too, made enemies that were closer to home?

Known for his provocative nature, might Richey Edwards have overstepped the mark by seeking confrontation with powerful people, or even just the wrong kind of people?

There sill remains the possibility that, possessing a remarkable insight and perception – as well as an ingrained showmanship – he may have purposefully made an exit before he became a victim of the industry, leaving those who adored him pondering: murder, suicide or escape? Was all this a part of his own, self-creating, over-arching narrative?

After his disappearance, James described Richey as being 'adept at dramatic symbolism'. Intimately aware of the myth-making craft, was it in his character to layer his own story, and leave it floating in mid-air; a huge and deliberate question mark over what might have befallen him?

Conversely, Richey may have had an accomplice or accomplices participating in his disappearance, and, if so, what might have happened next? If this were the case, surely there would have been a meticulously thought-through plan? Perhaps he had been inspired by his Uncle Shane, who while not deliberately aiming to distance himself from his family, had fallen out of contact for five years before re-establishing links with those at home. Alternatively, Richey's questionable mental state at the time he vanished could have led to his demise through other factors, while in the care of those who had sought to assist him.

Richey might have been suicidal in the days, months or even years to come, driven to the brink by his use of substances, his mental illnesses or even by the frailty of his body. The implications for his fellow conspirators would have been immense had he subsequently passed away in their care – by whatever means – and it would be unlikely that anybody who had assisted him would step up and speak of such events in the fear of being incriminated themselves.

'I know people could see it as clutching at straws, but I saw a documentary on Netflix called *Who Took Johnny*,' says Rachel. 'The outcome was that the missing person [Johnny] was forced into disappearing because if he went home, he'd be endangering the lives of his family. Things like that get into your head, thoughts like – did Richard have enemies? Could he have been forced to disappear? Is he maybe with somebody who's supporting him right now?'

Since 1995, Rachel has become an active campaigner with Missing People UK. Founded in 1986 after the disappearance of estate agent Suzy Lamplugh in south-west London, the charity offers social and emotional support for those affected by the disappearance of a loved one.

'They were a lifeline when Richard disappeared,' says Rachel. 'I don't know what I'd have done without them. It's a unique situation to find yourself in; in terms of what to do next logistically, and how to deal with it emotionally. To have a port of call in terms of advice and support was invaluable.'

Rachel became a representative for the charity in 2010. The same year, she helped launch the Missing Rights campaign, alongside Peter Lawrence (father of missing chef Claudia) and Gerry and Kate McCann (parents of missing toddler Madeleine), urging the government to implement laws to improve the support for the families of those who are missing. The campaign had certain aims:

Aim 1 – Families of missing people should know everything possible is being done to find their missing loved one: Every region should have a local missing persons' coordinator who will hold local services to account. Every family should have a named single point of contact in the police force dealing with their missing loved one. All unidentified bodies should be cross-matched with missing person reports.

Aim 2 – Families affected by a disappearance should have access to support: Every family of a missing person should be signposted to Missing People's free emotional, practical and legal support services by the police. A network of specially trained counsellors should be developed to support the unique needs of families of missing people.

Aim 3 – Families left behind should be spared the pain of unnecessary financial and legal bureaucracy: A Presumption of

Death Act for England and Wales (already in place in Scotland and Northern Ireland) – this has been achieved. A legal guardianship mechanism that would enable families to become trustees of a missing relative's affairs.

Rachel's involvement in the implementation of Aim 3 was very close to her heart, as the Edwards family found declaring Richey legally deceased a difficult and heartbreaking process.

'We had the opportunity to begin the procedure of declaring Richard dead in 2002, seven years after his disappearance, but we held out,' says Rachel. 'My dad was always sure Richard was going to come back after five years just like Uncle Shane did, but as those years passed … you could see it in Mam and Dad's faces, they had nothing left to say.

'Then my dad became ill with cancer, and he knew the latter part of his life was approaching. He didn't want to leave Richard's unresolved affairs for my mam and I to deal with alone, so we started the proceedings to obtain a death certificate towards the end of 2005.'

At the time, when families are coping with unresolved grief, the law regarding death *in absentia* did little to ease the burden for relatives, either financially or logistically.

'As well as dealing with what I call "suspended loss" there are the logistics of handling the missing person's everyday affairs,' says Rachel. 'It's the small things you wouldn't even think about, like sorting their finances, insurance policies, mortgages and, when it came to Richard and his line of work, his publishing rights. After he went missing his direct debits were still going out, his flat was sat there rotting, and we couldn't let it or sell it. When someone disappears, you realise that banks and other institutions have no system to address the affairs of clients who go missing and are now presumed dead.'

During this time, Rachel and her father sought advice from several legal experts who found it hard to counsel them adequately on their predicament. With no legal framework in place, it took the Edwards family three years, and significant financial outlay, in order to obtain a death certificate for Richey.

On 24 November 2008, Richey Edwards was legally declared dead.

'I went into the solicitor's office with my dad and we had to swear on the bible that we thought Richard was deceased,' she says. 'It was a horrible situation for us as a family because it felt that in doing this we were giving up on him. But it wasn't about that: it was about the practicalities. Mam and I will never give up the search for Richard, or the hope of finding out what happened to him.'

In September 2011, Rachel gave evidence to Parliament's Justice Select Committee about her family's ordeal. The Presumption of Death Act 2013 was passed and became law in October 2014.

As a result, families are now able to approach the courts for the right to declare their missing loved one deceased. The legal power of the certificate enables those left behind to resolve the affairs of the departed in a speedier and more succinct manner. The achievement of Rachel and the charity allows further legal clarity for professionals who work with the families of missing persons, and also for other agencies involved in administering assets.

'It's such a harrowing procedure, not just emotionally but bureaucratically,' she explains. 'With the Missing Rights campaign, I thought if I could help spare other families the same long-drawn-out process, then some good could come from the situation.'

A year before the Bill was passed, in the autumn of 2012, Graham Edwards sadly succumbed to cancer at the age of 77.

'There aren't really any words that do justice for the heartbreak my dad carried before he died,' says Rachel. 'He passed away with the biggest uncertainty hanging over him. Not knowing makes it so much worse. It's more painful than grief: it was a prolonged bereavement that ate away at him for years. There was never any closure for him. I don't think any parent could imagine a worse torture than never finding out what became of their child. I don't think he ever reconciled himself with that.'

'Doubts are crueller than the worst of truths.'
Molière, *Le Misanthrope*

270

CHAPTER 13

While Rachel desperately sought to discover what had become of her brother, the band would re-invent themselves and find fame and fortune following the loss of their chief lyricist.

> *'The band have never given you or me the opportunity to hear what they had to say off camera, in person, to people that mattered to him, at least. Only to those who contributed to his unhappiness.'*
> Jo, letter to Rachel Edwards, 1997

In the years since Richey's disappearance, the Manic Street Preachers have gone on to sell millions of albums, pick up numerous awards, and become firm favourites of the British musical establishment. A year after Richey vanished, their comeback single, 'A Design for Life' reached number 2 on the singles chart and their accompanying album, *Everything Must Go*, has since gone triple platinum.

Having achieved great mainstream success in Richey's absence, the band's mentions of him throughout the past two decades have primarily taken the form of public praise for him as a rock star, with Nicky Wire admitting that he misses Richey's input as a co-writer, or repeated references to how 'cool' Richey had always been. For the Manic Street Preachers, the band's own narrative appears paramount, and the Richey story seems to find its place within this larger one.

'There's definitely a public and a private side when it comes to the band and my brother and his disappearance,' says Rachel.

> *'Formed in the Valleys, ner ner ner ... Inspired by Guns N' Roses and Public Enemy, ner ner ner ... Bloke went missing, ner ner ner ... Have I really got to read that shit again?'*
> James Dean Bradfield, *Independent*, 2004

Since 1995, it's fair to say that the Manic Street Preachers appear to have carefully policed the boundaries of received wisdom on the topic of their former bandmate. A central tenet of this effort to retain control of the narrative has been their guarding against prurient interest or speculation for fear of hurting the feelings of those most immediately impacted by Richey's disappearance – the Edwards family themselves.

This is a noble stance to take, and one aimed at steering away from exploiting deep personal hurt and family tragedy. Rather than inviting fans and commentators to engage in wild speculation on Richey's whereabouts, and instead of actively encouraging their hundreds of thousands of fans around the world to look for Richey, the Manics have drawn a boundary around the matter in the name of good taste.

'When I speak to journalists to highlight Richard's anniversary, some ask me about the band, if they're in touch or what they've done for the Missing Persons charity,' says Rachel. 'When I tell them, nothing that I'm aware of, they're aghast and tell me they're really surprised.'

However, there is a sizeable gap between the band's narrative on Richey's disappearance and Rachel's interpretation of events. Rachel feels that the lion's share of the attempt to find him has been left to herself.

As Rachel sees it, the band and those surrounding them could have helped her more with the search.

Richey's old friend Adrian Wyatt also remains unhappy about what happened after his disappearance. He feels more could have been done to help find Richey.

'There were interviews when James was saying he wouldn't talk to Richard if he came back and hinting it was best that he stay away as it was "obviously working for him" being wherever he was,' says Adrian. 'I remember thinking it was such an odd thing to say about a friend. You'd do anything for someone to come back, you'd grit your teeth and lie because you'd be worried about the safety of that person.

'To be honest, it seems as if they did and said as little as possible. They ticked certain boxes, but I felt they showed little emotion or passion. It didn't feel right. I liked to think at the time they were unable to talk about it, but now I wonder whether there was something more to it.

'My feeling is what propelled them into the spotlight was Richard going missing. They may have had massive success since without input from him, but in my view they wouldn't have even got the attention of a mainstream record label in the first place without him.'

In the weeks following Richard's disappearance, the band got in touch with Rachel and asked her to go down to his flat to retrieve a folder with a Bugs Bunny cover from his shelves for them. She asked them why and was told it was because they wanted to look for clues, and that it was the property of Sony Records, and they had to have it back.

'I wasn't able to think straight at the time and just handed it over,' remembers Rachel. 'I know there were some sheets with lyrics on them inside, but I hadn't got a clue whether Richard had said it was OK for the band to take them. The stuff in there could have had his private musings on them: stuff he wouldn't have wanted published.'

With the permission of Graham Edwards, the band would go on to use the lyrics that Richey left in that folder in early 1995 on 2009's *Journal for Plague Lovers* album.

'Not only that, but the pictures on the folder itself were used for the inner sleeve for the *Journal for Plague Lovers* album, and that was his personal file,' says Rachel. 'I think he never left the Bugs Bunny file for them as they claimed. I think it was about how they could market it as Richard's lyrics. They'd already used some of his lyrics on a 2005 track called "Picturesque" without notifying us, or asking for permission.

'I've seen people on internet forums commenting about how different what Nick sings on "William's Last Words" is to the actual words Richard wrote on the accompanying paper. Again, it's the band's structured narrative of four best friends until the end.'

The Manics' missing bandmate now tends to appear as a footnote or an afterthought in any post-1996 documentaries or interviews.

'It was odd that the band never responded to a letter which Jo sent them about the poem she had written called "Edit the Sky", which formed part of the song, "The Girl who Wanted to be God".'

Surprisingly, the Edwards family were never contacted by the band's record company after Richey's disappearance, and Rachel and her parents were sad not to have been able to speak to anyone personally.

Rob Stringer – the CEO of Sony Records at the time of Richey's disappearance – is quoted to have said that his relationship with the band has been at the core of his career and that he is close friends with the remaining members. 'They changed record labels with me. As much as anything they've been the reason why I do this job, and I speak to all of them at least once a week and have done for 15 years. We've had lots of ups and downs.'

In an interview with the *NME* in the same month that Richey disappeared, Stringer had talked about how well-informed Richey was about suicides. 'Richey is a very ritualistic person. He doesn't act arbitrarily. And the scary thing is, he's the most well-read person I've ever known – he would be able to tell you the last words of all the world's famous suicides, he would know the content of Kurt Cobain's suicide note off by heart, and he would know twenty different ways to disappear completely. He will have planned it. He may be in Tibet for all I know ...'

Rachel says, 'I even wrote to [Stringer] recently, asking for more information about him saying that Richey was obsessed with the perfect disappearance. I received nothing back.'

Both Rachel and Jo have over the years felt excluded from the Manics' inner circle. In a letter sent by Jo in 1997, she wrote, 'Nobody ever said a word to us. That was the biggest insult. What a betrayal. What would Rich have said?'

Only last year Rachel tried to contact the Manic Street Preachers' management to view the findings of a private investigator that the band hired immediately after Richey's disappearance.

'I was told by the management that they couldn't remember the name of the person who did it, or where they'd placed his written findings. Also, if the PI didn't speak to me, my family or Jo, some of the last people to be in contact with Richard – who *did* he speak to?'

'The Band should know that if you love someone and lose them, all you want to do is find them again. It's so simple, and it's more important than

the band, the press, fame or anything. Love and death is more
important than any of that.'
Jo, letter to Rachel Edwards, 1996

Ultimately, only the remaining Manic Street Preachers know exactly how they feel about Richey Edwards and his disappearance. His loss must have hit them incredibly hard, and to their credit they have continued to play all their shows with an empty symbolic mic on Richey's side of the stage. However, how Richey felt about the band towards the end is, in truth, open to interpretation.

In a 1994 interview with the *NME*, Richey described himself as having a 'very childlike rage, and a very childlike loneliness'. Having bequeathed the song 'Elvis Impersonator: Blackpool Pier' to the band shortly before his disappearance, could its lyrics be considered a pre-emptive strike at any future incarnation of the Manic Street Preachers, hell-bent on pursuing a decades-long career without him?

Richey was notorious for his arcane lyrics, some of which were indecipherable even to his bandmates. Do such lines in 'Elvis Impersonator' contain some of the venom and 'childlike rage' attributed to Richey by those familiar with his more spiteful side?

The song is purportedly a thinly veiled attack on the ongoing Americanisation of the entertainment industry. Yet some lines certainly leave room for interpretation. Who was Richey calling out as so 'fucking funny' in his pointed refrain?

Occasionally referenced by Richey, the writer Michel Foucault, was frequently described by friends as being possessed of a similar sardonic nature to the missing Manic. In a documentary, *Michel Foucault Beyond Good and Evil*, author James Miller stated: 'As always with Foucault, you never know if he's being ironic or serious, it's always a thin line, and I tend to think he's usually smiling ... so you have to keep the irony, and take seriously what's being told to you with the smile.'

Rachel Edwards is the first to admit that, in the same way, there were always many multi-faceted, sometimes undecipherable layers to her brother.

'When I think about what might have become of him, and the not knowing, I sometimes believe this was his intention all along,' she reflects. 'To never be found. Because there are ways of doing that. He's not living as an ex-member of a band like Syd Barrett was, or he's not dead like Ian Curtis. In a way, it cheats people of an opinion of him.

'The only certainty in life is death, and with Richard we don't even have that. He was such a complex person, and from speaking to others who knew him and trying to piece together who he was from their memories, it seems obvious that nobody ever really knew him as well as they thought they did.'

Whether he opted for suicide or survival, the likelihood is that the mystery of the disappearance of Richey Edwards will only ever be definitively solved in the event of his sudden reappearance, or in the discovery of a body. For now all that remains is an enigma – a shadow of a man and of an artist who touched the lives of those who loved him deeply.

'He gave so much as an artist, a poet and most of all as a person,' says Rachel. 'He was my brother and I will never give up searching for him. I think of him first thing in the morning and last thing at night. Until we find out what happened, I'll never be able to live my life properly. Until Richard's body is found, I will not be convinced that he is dead. Without that finality, I can't give up and I will continue to search until I discover what has become of him.'

'I think of him every day. Even after all these years. Every new place I go to, I wonder what he would think of it. I think about the way he thought and his opinions, which I can see in a different light now I'm older. I think of him that winter, when he was in such a mess, trying to find something to make me laugh, saying, "I just want to see you smile, Jo." It just makes me cry. I'm not being silly or romantic, I haven't, and I don't think I will ever meet or feel that way about someone again. I really don't. You just don't meet people like him. Not remotely like him. Despite his faults – and bloody hell, everyone has millions of faults – you knew he was gentle, he was quiet and emotional with me on good days. He

just talked quietly and sensitively. He listened. Just things like laughing at things like dumb cartoons or something was so nice. Everything was going wrong, yes. But he was gentle and loving and incredible. He was warm, just so soft. That just never seems to come across.'

Jo, letter to Rachel Edwards, 1998

Acknowledgements

Amanda Roberts, who made writing this book possible.

Jan Noakes for exploring the Edwards family tree.

Simon Molyneux and Mari Ellen Roberts for always being ready to read a draft.

Guy Mankowski, for being the voice of reason.

Emma Forrest, who years ago believed in my writing from the beginning.

Kevin Pocklington, for being the best agent a writer could ask for.

Ian Gittins, an editor and a half and patient throughout.

Lorna Russell and Lucy Oates at Virgin Books for believing in this book and Richey's legacy.

Thank you to all contributors: Simon Cross, Alistair Fitchett, Adrian Wyatt, Mark 'Den' Hambridge, Greg Noble, Alice Forward, Claire Forward, Rosie Dunn, Joanna Haywood, Jemma Hine, Tony Van Den Ende, Richard James, Richard Fry, Benji Webbe, Rachel Parks, Colin Blowers, Stephen Fulcher, Ian McCray, Andy Matheson, and the team at SARA (Severn Area Rescue Association).

Most of all, thank you to Rachel Edwards. A best friend and a true inspiration to us all.

Appendix

Letter to Mark Hambridge (Den), 1987. Richey talks about attending gigs and his love for music.

NEUADD MARY WILLIAMS
ROOM 407
UNIVERSITY COLLEGE S'SEA
SWANSEA
SA2 8PP

Dear Den, Thanks for the letter.
It was CLASSIC on Thursday. After you left a group of people gathered around the PRIMITIVES [WOT A CONCERT] dressing room but they only let me & THE MONKEE'S in. They headed for the rest of band walking right past Tracy — probably something to do with their similar haircuts. I talked with Tracy (who equals SEX) and she is even better looking close up than in photographs [WOW! HOW IS THIS POSSIBLE?] She signed a photograph for me

"TO RICHARD,
WITH LOVE,
KISSES AND
HUGS
(TRACY PRIM)"
XX

O₀ R₀ G₀ A₀ S₀ M₀ → (she didn't say 'Orgasm' it's just the way I felt)
It would have been brilliant if you'd stayed. We stayed almost till the end bopping the night away. The Monkees may even have scobbed a lift home although I doubt it. NEARLY FORGOT- Tracy shared her ORANGE

JUICE with me and I've still got the carton as a souvenir. [imagine her lips have been all over it and then I drink out of there ~ WOW] She also gave me a signed PROMO 7" of OCEAN BLUE b/w NIGHTMARE CITY... I left it in their dressing room for safe keeping ~~to~~ and after they left I went to dance until the driver of the minibus was ready but then when I went back to get the treasured artifact ~~the thing~~ the dressing room was locked and the cleaner had gone home with the only set of keys. OH NOOOO.

I felt a bit upset but then cheered up cos I still had the most important thing of all, something no one can ever take away, steal, lose etc ... I'm of course referring to GOOD TIMES in MEMORY CITY and unless MR AMNESIA hits me the PRIMS in P.TALBOT will be an A1 GOOD TIME.

PORT TALBOT could turn into the stuff dreams are made of if they continue to get some good bands.

WHAT do you think of 'the Cure' - I think it's OK but & I'm disappointed because it could be so much more BETTER. It could have been a CLASSIC instead of another adequate Bunny tune.

I hope you saw CLARE on 'ZTT'S WICKED'. She didn't look that nice - because it was raining and dead windy but on video we are talking one "HORNY FUNKYBITCH" as the Rugby

I expect to beat someone up.
I've heard he's one nasty dude
lads say

I hope you had a good night out
with BREAKER. The last couple of nights
have been quite boring down here due to
Exam fever. I've only got 4 exams left
and then I'm off to visit SMASHED CITY
for a couple of days. We will be talking
alcoholic poisoning, and some poor sod
walking below the window of 407 getting
a mouthful of SICKY all over him.
"IT'S A LAUGH THOUGH, EH JOHN."

I'm glad you liked my tape. Did you
like the Clouds? and the Jam? I'm
well impressed with your tape especially
'Spin the Web', 'Brother', 'A Gentle Sound',
'Splash', '1969', 'Jennifer Wants' and 'Almost
Prayed'. We'll have to do each other another
set of tapes when I come home next.
After my exams finish on 11 JUNE [General
Election Day. I hope Mag the Bag doesn't
get in] I'll probably pay B'wood a flying
visit on SATURDAY and go back SUNDAY.
Are you going to see 'My Bloody Valentine'?
'Cos I am if they organise a Minibus or
you, Adrian & Gradehouse come down so we've
got 4 for a kick. I doubt if Adrian will
come down because I think he's got an
exam. The same probably applies to G'house
so it looks as if we'll have to give MBV
a miss.
        "Never Mind, Never Mind"
I think Ad & Becki will be seeing each
other for a long time yet.
        LUCKY BASTARD.

Oh well, must go and do some work.
I saw Clare today looking extremely
munchy
"Sky is painting a rainbow /round (her)
head like a halo"
GOOD BYE

Richard

X

PS   I enclose a review done by the
HATED STUDENT UNION of TWP gig

PPS   Keep in touch + don't be a stranger

PPPS   I, G'house still pissed off over Belli

PPPPS   I heard your getting along rather well
with a certain girl called Angela (?)
Well, I'm not sure that's her name
but am I on the right track.

286

Letter to Mark Hambridge (Den), 1988. Richey encourages his friend Den to start a band.

161 KING EDWARDS ROAD
BRYNMILL
SWANSEA

YAH DENNY,

HOW DID THINGS GO ON MONDAY. TITS, BUM, FANNY — THE LOT. I HOPE YOU BEHAVED YOURSELF YOU DIRTY ROTTER. SERIOUSLY THO — I HOPE IT WORKS OUT. I HOPE YOUR DRUMMING BUY ALSO GOT BACK UNHARMED.

TODAY ITS A COLD MISERABLE PISSING DOWN FRIDAY NIGHT. EVERYONE HAS GONE DOWN TO THE PUB BUT I CAN'T SEE THE POINT ANYMORE. I DON'T WANT TO GET PISSED, I DON'T WANT A GIRLFRIEND I JUST WANT TO BE A GUITAR HERO IN A NEW MUSIC-SOCIAL-POLITICAL REVOLUTION. ANYWAY, SEEING AS MY FUTURE DEPENDS TO EVERY EXTENT ON MY GUITAR ABILITY I'VE GOT TO DO LOTS OF PRACTICE AND I LOVE THE PROSPECT OF IT. OF ACHIEVING SOMETHING WORTHWHILE - OF INJECTING SOMETHING INTO SICK WRISTS OF YOUTH — IN TEN YEARS TIME I WANT KIDS TO LOOK AT BLUEBEAT AND WISH THEY COULD HAVE BEEN AROUND WHEN THIS GENERATION GENERATION TAKES OFF. AND IT WILL.

THIS WEEK I GOT A BRILLIANT BOOST FROM ALL THE MUSIC PAPERS. THE MISSION WON ALMOST ALL AWARDS. IT JUST SHOWS THAT YOUTH STILL WANTS A BASIC GUITAR BAND. THE PRESS / PEEL ELITE CAN SHOVE PIXIES / BUTTHOLES / ACID ETC DOWN THEIR THROATS BUT THEY STILL WANT TO ROCK. AND I FEEL GOOD. I HATE CLUBS, I HATE DANCING TO DANCE RECORDS I HATE THOSE WORDS THAT SAY NOTHING. GOD IT WAS BRILLIANT SEEING THE PRESS. WE CAN SUBSTITUTE ALL THAT GOTHIC BULLSHIT FOR A BEATIAC CRESCENT OF AWARENESS, OF CHOICE. WE ARE A SUBURBAN CUT TOO DEEP TO HEAL, A STRAIT JACKET TO TIGHT TO BREATHE. PEOPLE WILL TRY TO WRITE US OFF, PUT NO FAITH IN US, LAUGH AT US. WE ARE A STATE OFFENCE COS WE CARE. WE CAN SUBSTITUTE ALL THIS ACCEPTANCE / APATHY FOR POSITIVISM. OK I KNOW THERES NOTHING WORTHWHILE HAPPENING IN THE WORLD BUT WE CAN TAKE IT DOWN

AND MAKE IT HAPPEN. I MEAN I JUST ~~THE~~ SAW
BIGGEST WASTE OF TIME EVER ON TOP OF THE
TOPS. SO - - NME RECKONS THE DARLING BUDS
ARE A GREAT HOPE. BULLSHIT. ~~THEIR~~ THEIR
PERFORMANCE DID NOT INSPIRE, THEIR LYRICS
REEKED OF SUGAR-SWEET MONEY GRABBING
VACUUM. TO CHANGE SOMETHING, TO CHANGE
PEOPLE YOU EITHER HAVE TO ANTAGONISE/~~ABUSE~~
OR ENERGISE THEM. MAKE THEM WANT TO
START A BAND, QUIT THEIR JOB, CUT THEIR
HAIR EVEN. IF YOU DON'T DO THAT YOU FAIL.
AND DARLING BUDS FAILED OH-SO-BADLY.
MANIC STREET PREACHERS HAVE NEXT TO NO
SONGS ABOUT GIRLS AND THEY, WE, WILL
NEVER HAVE ANOTHER ONE. FROM ~~NOW ON~~ KNOW
ON THERE WILL BE NO ROMANTIC LYRICS OF
LOVE OR UNREQUITED LOVE, NO PERSONAL
STATEMENTS JUST DIRECT, HARD STATEMENTS
ABOUT THE STATE MACHINE. ABOUT THE
REPRESSION OF VIOLENCE, OF THE OPPRESSION
OF DISAFFECTED YOUTH, OF STUPID IDIOTS WHO
BEAT EACH OTHER UP, OF A GOVERNMENT THAT
SELLS MISERY AS IF ITS A COMMODITY THAT
WE NEED (AND MAKES A MILLION WHILE DOING
IT).
    OH WELL, TIME TO GO.
LOOK → WE NEED ANOTHER BAND MORE
THAN ANYTHING ELSE RIGHT NOW. GO
DOWN BUNS, GET BUN TO COME UP - GET
 SOME LYRICS, GET PRACTICING. BE READY TO
PLAY SOON. YOU'VE GOT TO DO IT ~~xxxxx~~
DEN. IF NOT FOR YOURSELF THEN FOR THIS
GENERATION THEY NEED YOU. WE NEED YOU.
ONE BAND CAN'T CHANGE THE WORLD. TWO CAN.
SO DO IT.
        TAKE CARE
         LOVE
          Richey
           X

DROP YOUR LIFE AND PICK UP YOUR SOUL.

Letter to Mark Hambridge (Den), 1988. Richey's passion for starting a band can be evidenced in this letter to friend Den.

161 KING EDWARDS ROAD
BRYNMILL
SWANSEA

YAH YAH DENNY,

HOPE THE POUNDS ARE STILL POURING OFF YOUR BODY. EVERYONE'S NOTICING YOU KNOW – LAST TIME I PHONED HOME MY MUM SAID SHE HAD SEEN YOU WALKING THROUGH BLACKWOOD AS SHE PASSED BY IN A CAR BUT EVEN AT A ZILLION MILES AN HOUR SHE STILL SAW YOU HAD LOST WEIGHT. HOW HAVE YOUR WEEKENDS BEEN? TITS/BUM/FANNY THE LOT, NO DOUBT GIRLS – I DUNNO. WORRA PILE OF SHIT. ALWAYS SEEM A BIT UNINTERESTING TO ME – BOREDOM, PUKE, SHAPELESS, BULLSHIT, IMITATION – BUT THEY ALSO LOOK SO FUCKING BEAUTIFUL. I MEAN SOMETIMES IF I SEE A GIRL I'VE BECOME OBSESSED WITH IT MAKES ME FEEL BRILLIANT ALL DAY. CLARE MADE ME FEEL BRILLIANT BUT I JUST COULDN'T LET THINGS SHE SAID NOT BUG ME. EVEN ON A REALLY LOW LEVEL OF IMPORTANCE – SAY MUSIC. THEY JUST LIKE A TUNE – I WANT MORE. ALSO EVERYTHING GENERALLY THEY WANT DIFFERENT THINGS. ON SATURDAY THIS REALLY HORNY GIRL CAME UP AND JUST AS I THOUGHT 'FUCK, SHE'S HORNY' SHE ASKED ME TO DANCE TO THE CULT. STUPID AIN'T IT AND THEY THINK I'M STUPID FOR WANTING TOO MUCH.

DID YOU SEE ALL THAT CREATION STUFF ON RAPIDO AND DID YOU SEE GREAT ROCK N ROLL SWINDLE AND HOWS THE JOB HUNTING GOING. FUCK KNOWS WHAT I'M GONNA DO AFTER UNIVERSITY. I HOPE TO GET A VAN AND TOUR THIS SHITHOLE COUNTRY DRIVING LE PREACHERS TO FAME AND FORTUNE. WHAT IS HUW GONNA DO AFTER THE FINALS. I GUESS NO ONE WANTS TO SETTLE DOWN YET.

HAVE YOU SEEN BEN MUCH. I STILL HAVEN'T HEARD FROM HIM YET AND I'VE STILL GOT THIS THINGY TO SEND HIM.

289

OH YEAH - YOU SAID SOMETHING ABOUT
CLARE MARSH SENDING ME A LETTER
BUT I HAVEN'T HAD ANYTHING. SAYING
THAT I KNOW FOR A FACT THAT SOME
OF MY MAIL HAS GONE MISSING. MOST
RECENTLY A LETTER FROM COLLEGE
AND FROM THE LIBRARY.
     ANYWAY - SORRY THIS LETTER IS SHIT
AND SHORT BUT I'VE GOT UNTOLD AMOUNTS
OF ESSAYS TO DO BY DECEMBER 1ST(BUT
I'M GONNA TRY + COME HOME ONCE BEFORE
THEN - HOPEFULLY AROUND NOV. 5TH) IF
I DO I'LL RING YOU BEFORE THEN.
     LOOK SORRY THIS LETTER IS SHORT
BUT I'VE REALLY GOT TO GET DOWN TO
SOME WORK. OH YEAH. NEARLY FORGOT-
DID YOU SEND ANY WORDS TO SCOTT L.A
RICKENBACKER. I NEVER SEE HIM BUT I
THINK HE'D LIKE IT. I THINK IT WOULD
BE QUITE A GOOD LINE UP ACTUALLY
   DRUMS - YOUTH EXPLOSION (DRUM Machine
                unless Suitable Keith Moon Rocker
                comes along)
  BASS - BUM THE MIGHTY
  LEAD - SCOTT L.A RICKENBACKER
  VOCALS - DENNY B
  I MEAN EVEN IF YOU ONLY ONE OR TWO
SONGS TO START WITH IT WOULD ~~BE~~ STILL
BE BRILLIANT TO DO A CONCERT WOULDN'T
IT AND WHAT BETTER PLACE TO DO A 1ST
CONCERT THAN WITH MSP IF YOU COULD
PLAY TOGETHER IT WOULD BE LIKE A
PERFECT PERFECT EVENING. LIKE AT LAST
A DEFINITE COMMUNITY OF FEELING. WITH
BANDS AROUND LIKE SPINELESS· WHITE NOISE-
NO IDENTITY/BELIEF-& HATELESS - BULLSHIT
ETHIC ACQUIRED TASTE IT'S REALLY
DISHEARTENING. AND F.I.B ARE JUST HEAVY
METAL. WITH YOUR BAND IT WOULD SEEM
MORE ALIVE. TWO BANDS ALWAYS GIVES
MORE CREDENCE, MORE AURA - MORE
PUBLIC ACCEPTANCE THAT IT IS NOT A
HYPE. & THAT IT IS A GENUINE BELIEF
SO DO IT - NOW. IMAGINE JUST

DRIVING INTO TOWNS, FLINGING OPEN COLD,
MECHANICAL VAN DOORS AND OUTPOURING
THE ENERGY OF YOUTH. ~~AS~~ TWO BANDS
— A BELIEF — A FEELING —
 OF ENERGY
 OF HATE AND WAR
 OF LOVE AND PEACE
OF ATTITUDE
— RICKENBACKERS AND LES PAULS.
DIVING ONTO STAGE CAPTURING
BODIES TRICKED BY ACID HOUSE,
RE-ESTABLISHING THE BONDS OF YOUTH,
ACCENTUATING GENERATION GAPS.
VITAL AND BURNING.
GO ON STAGE AND KICK THEIR ZERO
WHITENESS INTO SUBMISSION. MAKE THEM
FEEL LIKE YOU DID WHEN YOU SAW YOUR
BEST EVER CONCERT.
 ESTABLISH AND REACTIVATE.
 DESTROY AND RE-BUILD.
 ENERGISE THE SULTRY CHEEKBONES
OF NO-CHARISMA. MAKE PEOPLE
WANT TO BUY RECORDS AGAIN.

OH JEEZ I'M~~E~~ AT IT AGAIN. ANYWAY —
IT WOULD BE GOOD WOULDN'T IT? SO
GET SCOTT ON A BLUE HOTWIRE TO
SWANSEA AND BANG HIS RICKENBACKER
INTO GEAR. GET SOME SONGS, GET
SOME NOISE AND, AS KEVIN ROWLAND
 SAYS, FOR GOD'S SAKE BURN IT DOWN

 LOVE
 Richey
 X

PS PLEASE COULD YOU SEND BEN'S ADDRESS AS
 I'VE LOST IT.

Letter to Mark Hambridge (Den), 1989. Richey talks about joining the Manic Street Preachers.

RICHEY

39 STUDENT VILLAGE, HENDREFOLIAN, SWANSEA
SA2, 7PG

DEAR DENNY,
                    LISTEN!
"THEY WERE EXACTLY THE SAME MORONS THAT
LAUGH LIKE HYENAS IN THE MOVIES AT STUFF
THAT ISN'T FUNNY. I SWEAR TO GOD, IF I
WERE A PIANO PLAYER OR AN ACTOR OR
SOMETHING AND ALL THOSE DOPES THOUGHT I WAS
TERRIFIC, I'D HATE IT. I WOULDN'T EVEN WANT
THEM TO CLAP FOR ME. PEOPLE ALWAYS CLAP FOR
THE WRONG THINGS. IF I WERE A PIANO PLAYER,
I'D PLAY IT IN THE GODDAM CLOSET."
            — J. D. SALINGER —
I FEEL LIKE THAT., I ONLY RESPECT BLUEBEATS
OPINIONS AND THAT IS HARD TO RECONCILE, KNOW-
ING THAT IF YOU ARE IN A BAND SO MANY
TWATS WILL EVENTUALLY LOVE YOU AND TRY
AND DISPLACE YOUR BELIEF, WATER IT DOWN INTO
SOME POXY IDEA OF THEIR OWN MAKING. MAYBE
THATS WHY YOU HAVE DECIDED TO WRITE AND I
CANT BLAME YOU FOR IT IS PURE, MUCH MORE
PURE. YOU ONLY HAVE TO ANSWER TO YOURSELF
AND AS SUCH DON'T EVER HAVE TO COMPROMISE.
                                    THINK
SAYING THAT THO I DON'T MANIC STREET
PREACHERS WILL EVER COMPROMISE. AS SUCH WE
ARE THE GREATEST BAND EVER.
"THAT'S THE THING ABOUT GIRLS EVERYTIME THEY
DO SOMETHING PRETTY, EVEN IF THEY'RE NOT MUCH
TO LOOK AT, OR EVEN IF THEY'RE SORT OF STUPID,
YOU FALL HALF IN LOVE WITH THEM, AND THEN
YOU NEVER KNOW WHERE THE HELL YOU ARE. GIRLS.
JESUS CHRIST. THEY CAN DRIVE YOU CRAZY. THEY
REALLY CAN."
            — J. D. SALINGER —
DON'T KNOW ABOUT YOU BUT I'VE JUST ABOUT GIVEN
UP. I THINK YOU MUST TOTALLY CONCENTRATE
ON AMERICA JUST AS I MUST JUST TOTALLY
CONCENTRATE ON MY GUITAR. WE MUST BOTH HAVE
COMPLETE BLINKERED VISION AND NOT ALLOW ANY-
THING TO INTERFERE IN IT. WE KNOW WHAT WE

REALLY WANT - YOU AS THE GREAT BLUE WRITER
AND ME AS A GUITARIST - AND WE MUST DO ALL
WE CAN TO GET THERE. IF WE FALL IN LOVE WE
WILL, SO HAPPY AND CONTENT AND THO'WE WILL
NEVER ENJOY THE SAME THINGS AS THE REST
WE WILL ULTIMATELY BE IN THE SAME POSITION
AS EVERYONE ELSE. WE WILL HAVE GIVEN UP THE
CHANCE TO AFFECT ANY KIND OF CHANGE.
"BREAK THE CHAINS OF YOUR THOUGHT, AND YOU
BREAK THE CHAINS OF YOUR BODY, TOO."
- RICHARD BACH - JONATHAN LIVINGSTONE SEAGULL -
WE BOTH KNOW WHAT WE NEED TO DO AND WE
MUST NOT ALLOW ANYONE TO STOP US. EVERY HASSLE
I HAVE AT THE MOMENT SEEMS TRIVIAL WHEN
COMPARED TO WHAT WE CAN ACHIEVE. HERE I AM
STUCK IN HENDRE AND I HATE IT. IT IS TOTAL
PRISON. BUT IT DOESN'T MATTER. LIKEWISE
THINGS SEEM TO BE GOING COOL FOR YOU, LOSING
WEIGHT, JOB ETC - BUT WHETHER WE ARE HAPPY
OR SAD WE BOTH NEED SOMETHING MORE. NOTHING
MATTERS TO ME AS MUCH AS SEEING SOME
BLUE TOTALNESS ABOLISHING ALL THE WRONGS
OF THIS SOCIETY. IF WE DO NOT DO THIS THEN
WE WILL REGRET IT FOR THE REST OF OUR
LIVES.
"REPRESSION IS A SYSTEM"
- BANKACCOUNT REALITY -
I'M SORRY THIS LETTER IS SHORT BUT I JUST
WANT TO KNOW WHY THE LETTER YOU SENT HAD
RICHEY SELLOUT ON THE TOP. I HOPE I HAVEN'T
DONE SOMETHING WRONG. ALSO WHY DID YOU SEND
IT TO NICK? DIDN'T YOU GET THE LETTER I
SEND AS SOON AS I MOVED TO HENDRE?
"HOW DOES ONE BECOME MEDIOCRE. BY MAKING
CONCESSIONS."
- VAN GOGH -
NEVER STOP WRITING DEN, NEVER STOP BELIEVING
THAT WE CAN CHANGE ALL THIS ALONELESS, THAT
WE CAN REESTABLISH A FEELING, PUT BACK
HOPE INTO OPPRESSION, LIFT UP DEPRESSIVE
BOREDOM WITH A PURE BLUE SPEED BOLT OF
CATALYSTIC YOUTH. NEVER GIVE IN.
LOVE
Richey
Zero

Letter to former girlfriend Claire Forward, 1988. Richey's letter shows his love and devotion to Claire.

TELL ME ABOUT [...] — UNE
DON'T KNOW WHAT QUESTIONS
TO ASK

①

BABEY BABEY CLAIRE LES TWOL,
SORRY I'M SUCH A
HOPELESS CASE AT FRENCH — I KNOW THATS NOT
HOW YOU SPELL 'LES TWOL' BUT IT SOUNDS SORT
OF LIKE THAT. PAH — GO AHEAD SLAP ME. I'M
SO SORRY. SORRY SORRY WELL, UM, ER,
BANG WHOOSY RAMBLE WHOOSH KERPLOOSH
GOODIGY BODABA. NOT MUCH TO SAY. I MISS
YOU MISS YOU MISS YOU. AN AEGIS OF
YEARNING. HUNGER APPETITE. AN AMPUTATED
HEART. SINCE YOU LEFT REALITY HAS BEEN
ONE LONG FUCKER. PISSHEADSVILLE. A MALINF-
ORMED EMBRYO OF DESOLATION.
    YAAATAH. DESPONDENCY, DESPAIR, STARK-
EYED DESIRE. I NOW HAVE NOTHING. NOTHING
AT ALL. EMPTINESS. SINCE WEDNESDAY I
HAVE BEEN NOWHERE.
    APOLOGIES — MOMENTARY COLLABORATION WITH
FAITHFUL DIARY
    THURSDAY — COOKED NICK, JAMES, SEAN A
MEAL — 'WHITE TRASH' — MY OWN INVENTION.
IT CHUCKLED, IT SHOULD HAVE ZOOMED.
    FRIDAY — NO FUCKING-WHERE
    SATURDAY + SUNDAY A [crossed out]
WEEKEND OF TOTAL NAUSEA. DIDN'T WANT
TO GO OUT WITH ANYONE, BUN PHONED BUT
RISCA DOES NOT APPEAL. PARIS DOES.
BABEY BABEY PARIS SATELLITE. AN ORBIT
OF BAREBACKED GENTLE TENDER LOVE.
[crossed out] A MOTIONLESS ATMOSPHERE OF
TRANQUILITY TODAY WAS ALSO SO VERY
DIRE. NO JOB NO JOB — MOMENTUM
INADEQUACY GROUND TO A HALT IN
THE DHSS. THE SEDUCTION OF PENNILESS
EXTREMITY, THE DISTORTED METAPHOR OF
AFFLUENCE. THE COUNCIL SAID FUCK
OFF. THIS DIALECTIC YOUTH NOW HAS
NOTHING TO OCCUPY GREY DAYS OR
NIGHTS. BOREDOM. APATHY. REJECTION

ALL HAUNT ME. I WAKE UP AND
CATCH LONELY REFLECTIONS OF MYSELF
IN MY BEDROOM MIRROR. THE DAY
PROGRESSES IN A SIMILIAR MODE.
AAWWWWWW W   I JUST HATE THIS
INTRANSIGENCE. IT BREAKS ME. NO SOUL
NO SPIRIT. I TRY TO SIGN THE LOVE
OF ENERGY ON MY FOREHEAD BUT SINCE
YOU LEFT I CAN DO NOTHING. EVERYTHING
IS VAPOURISED. ENTHUSIASM SINKS EVER
FURTHER INTO MY MEMORY.
    I DECLINE
    I DECLINE
DEN TRIED TO DRAG ME FROM DEATHBED
INSOMNINIA ON THE WEEKEND - HE STAYED
DOWN THERE ALL WEEKEND (YAH - I HATE
IT WHEN I REPEAT WORDS) TOTAL
ALL-CONSUMING REJECTION - I HAVE NO
NEED TO GO TO SOME STUPID NAIVE
FESTIVAL. HIPPY FUCKING SHIT. LONG
GREASY HAIR SHADOWS ILLETERACY.
SOME OH-SO-POXY-MID-70S-CONCEPT
AFFAIR. SO I STAYED IN. NICK AND
JAMES + SEAN SAW THEIR BABEYS AND
THEN WENT BACK TO WATCH VIDEOS.
OBVIOUSLY I COULD DO NEITHER.
AS I FEEL NOW I PHYSICALLY COULD
NOT SIT DOWN AND WATCH SOME FILM.
MY MESS OF A BODY IS DYING FAST.
STREAMING ACQUIESCENCE. POSSESSION,
SCEPTICISM IS A FORGOTTON DREAM, AN
ABANDONED ETHIC. BARRACKED
RAINBOWS INCLINED TOWARDS THE
MONOTONE. PLEASE PLEASE PLEASE
PAINT THE SKY RED WHITE AND
BLUE. TOUCH THE SEA. TATOO THE
SKY WITH LOVE. WASH THE CHEAP
COLOURS AWAY SPLASH YOUR
BEAUTY LIKE COLOUR. BURN HURRICANE
COLOURS THAT CAPTIVATE THE MOON.
I WANT TO WAKE UP TOMORROW AND
SEE YOUR REFLECTION IN THE
SKY. PATHETIC AND HOPELESS I MAYBE
BUT I WANT TO SEE YOU

A POLOROID WILL DO . NO FUCKING
FRENCH BOYS ON THERE. THO.
RELAPSE 1/ → WHEN I SAY 'FUCKING'
I DO NOT MEAN IT IN A VIOLENT
MASS CONSCIENCE WAY — NO SKINHEAD
POWER HERE — RATHER I MEAN A
SPITFIRE 'FUCK', THE KIND OF 'FUCK'
DENNIS HOPPER WOULD SAY, THE KIND
OF FUCK YOU'D SAY WHEN YOU PASS
YOUR DRIVING TEST E.G [I HATE
EXAMPLES — THE I CAN DEFEAT
YOU WITH KNOWLEDGE, VERBOSE AND
UNNECESSARY TECHNIQUE] "FUCKING 'ELL
TREV, I PASSED" THAT IS A GLORIOUS
GOLDEN, CASCADING 'FUCK', A FUCK
OF MOMENTOUS IMPORTANCE I.E. IF THERE
IS A SYNTANNED RAW RED MAN-BEAST
OF BURGEONING (?) VITALITY IN THE
PHOTOGRAPH THEN I WILL BE FUCKING
PISSED OFF. THE YOU-KNOW-WHY
EFFECT "JEALOUSY IS A DANGEROUS
THING" SAID THE JUDGE.
"YES" I REPLIED ... "I JUST HAD TO
STICK THAT BLADE THROUGH HIS HEAD..
DUM-DUM-DE-DUM. WHISTLE MISGUIDED
HATE AND KISS ME VERBALLY.
I STROKE YOUR THIGH, CARESS
(I NEVER SPELL THAT RIGHT — PHLUMPF)
YOUR HAIR, KISS YOU ALL OVER EVERY
NIGHT. MANIAC DREAMS. RICOCHOLET
AWAKENINGS ON THE CRESTFALLEN
ABYSS. TIMELESS AWE-STRUCK MEMORIES.
MY ONE LAST GASP VICE.
NO MORE CONTRADICTION — I MISS YOU.
DYNAMITE ACHING. NO SAFETY NET
STANDARDS. WHEN I FALL IT HURTS.
CUT ME I BLEED. I JUST WISH I
COULD GET A NEW CRYSTAL BALL.
I SEE MY FUTURE FLESHED IN
PAIN, BITTERNESS — PARASITE FEAR
A LABYRINTH CLOWN. YOU ARE
GOING TO CAUSE ME SO MUCH
PAIN AND HURT AND I HAVE NEVER
BEEN HURT BEFORE — HURT. HURT.

HURT — VICIOUS POVERTY, SQUALID INTELLECT, MISERY — ALL DEAD ROADS TO ME. I HAVE NEVER ALLOWED MYSELF TO GET HURT. I HAVE RUN AWAY FROM ALL EMOTION, I HAVE RUN AWAY FROM LIFE, REALITY ALWAYS LOOKED SO UNAPPEALING, A LAST FUNCTION MADNESS — STREET DECAY. I SAW SO MANY PEOPLE GETTING HURT, TEARS, PAIN — HURT HURT HURT. IT IS OF DESPERATE SIMPLICITY — I DID NOT WANT TO EXPERIENCE THOSE EMOTIONS. AS IT WAS IT JUST FELT LIKE I MISSED OUT ON EVERYFUCHING THING. WHO WILL SWALLOW LIFE? I SPAT IT BACK OUT AND LANGUISHED IN MY BEDROOM.

I HAVE NEVER CRIED.

YOU WILL MAKE ME, SMASH ME ON ALL FOURS, CRAWLING, BEGGING, TEAR LADEN. SOBBING INCANDESCANT, A PALLID STAIN OF INSOLENCE, A CARDIAC ARRESTING BULLET. SYMMETRIC WATER THEFT, AN ERUDITE FURY. DON'T DO IT BABEY — A RESIDUAL DESTROYER OF FORMER YEARS I DO NOT NEED. 20 YEARS WERE NOT A SHAM — THEY WERE NECESSARY FOR THIS VERY MOMENT. SELF INFLICTED BARBED WIRE CELIBACY IS NECESSARY, COMPLETELY AND UTTERLY, FOR SOUL AND EMOTION. GUILLOTINE ADDICTION DEAD AND GONE.

SOON YOU WILL GROW WEARY OF ME, TIRE OF EVERYTHING, RETURN TO SCRAPS OF LIFE, GORGE YOURSELF ON ADULTHOOD. I WILL BE LEFT WITHERED AND DECAYED. MY HEART HANGS SENTINEL-LIKE ABOVE PARIS — DO NOT SHOOT IT DOWN. I AM NOT INCENDIARY PROOF.

YOU HAVE OPENED DOORS FOR ME — I KNOW WHY I LACK SO MANY THINGS. FOR THE FIRST TIME I

TRULLY THINK. FOR TOO LONG I HAVE
PERSONALISED EMOTION, INTERNALISED
EVERY FEELING. TRUE SELFISM ONLY
EVER SLIPPING OUT UNDER ALCOHOL
STIMULUS.
 RELAPSE Z/ FLOWER COVERED DRESSES
HIDE DARK PEARL SECRETS - REMEMBER
THE ONLY TIME I SPOKE TO YOU WAS
IN A PISSED STATE. HOW VERY MIDDLE
CLASS - I APOLOGISE, I PAPER OVER
ENORMITY WITH SELLOTAPED FAMILIARITY.
SORRY SORRY SORRY. I SPOKE TO YOU
WHEN PISSED, I KNOW - NUMBED BRAIN
CELLS ARE NO MORE WORTHY THAN REPRESSION
BUT IT IS NECESSARY. I KILLS
TURMOIL, CATCHES ONTO SHYNESS
AND KILLS IT STONE DEAD.
 ANYWAY I FINALLY KNOW YOU
RESTRICTED EMOTION IS DEAD HOPEFULLY
I SHALL SOON BE ABLE TO KISS
SUNBURST HONESTY - SAY THE
THINGS I ALWAYS WANTED TO SAY.
I DO NOT UNDERSTAND LOVE - IT
IS A TRICKEY DEFINITION. I ONLY
REALLY UNDERSTAND LONELINESS BUT
I THINK, IF MUTILATED COUNTLESS
LITERATURE IS TO BE BELIEVED, I
LOVE YOU. YES I DO.
 MAYBE I CAN TRUST PEOPLE FROM
NOW ON BUT I DUNNO. I REALLY DON'T.
WHATEVER I FEEL IS OF NO IMPORTANCE.
DIMINISHING SPECIFICS. SOON YOU
WILL HATE ME POUR SCORN AND
INVECTIVE ON ME. BUT I HOPE NOT
REMEMBER - EVERYTHING COOL AND
GROOVEY HAS TO BE PRENTITIOUS.
IT JUST HAS TO
 DON'T LEAVE ME ALONE AGAIN)
MISS YOU MISS YOU MISS YOU. I SOMETIMES
WISH I COULD FEEL SOMETHING
DIFFERENT COS LIKE I SAID I
CANNOT COPE WITH THE PROSPECT
OF REJECTION. ITS KINDDA HARD
TO DESCRIBE AND I HAVE NOT

GOT THE WORDS TO SAY THINGS
PROPERLY.
    RELAPSE 3 / - ABOLISH ALL FORMAL
TIES ie COMMAS, SEMI-COLONS.
THEY JUST STOP THE FLOW OF WORDS-
JUST BURN BURN BURN THE BLOOD
OF POETS SHOULD FLOW.
    HO HUM THESE RELAPSES ARE STARTING
TO ANNOY.
    BACK TO MUTED OBEDIENCE.
ANYWAY - I AM 20 - I HAVE BEEN
SWIMMING WITH THE RUMBLEFISH
FOR 20 YEARS. NOW I MAY HAVE
THE CHANCE TO WALK ON LAND.
THE PROSPECT IS SO SCAREY. I DON'T
THINK ANYONE REALLY UNDERSTANDS
THIS. TO SURVIVE THIS LONG I
HAVE HAD TO DEVELOP RESERVES OF
SELF-RELIANCE AND SELF-CONTENT-
MENT. CONSEQUENTLY I HAVE
ELEVATED EVERY TINY EVENT TO
PEDESTAL STATUS. LIKE WHEN
I SPOKE TO YOU WAS A CLIMBING-
MOUNT-EVEREST-SORT-OF-ACHIEVEMENT.
D'YOU SEE?? I HAVE NEVER HAD
TO SHARE ANYTHING, EXPRESS MY
FEELINGS TO ANY-ONE - ONLY MY
PAPER AND PEN. AND NOW -
WHEN I REALLY WANT TO EXPLAIN
THINGS THE MUSE HAS FLOWN.
THIS LETTER IS NOT JUSTIFYING
MY FEELINGS. AND THAT HURTS.
WORDS ARE MY ONLY WEAPON -
NOW THEY ARE BLUNTED. THERE
IS NO LOVE. MORE IMPORTANTLY
THERE IS NO HATE.
    RELAPSE 4 / (NOT AGAIN) - HATE
IS VITAL - LOOK AROUND - "LIFE
IS IN RUINS" - WHY - COS THE
WORLD IS A BASTARD AND LIKES
IT THAT WAY. WHEN I WAS IN
COLLEGE I HATED EVERYONE,
CONTEMPT, SCORN - YOU NAME
IT. SECRETLY I LONGED TO

GO TO SAY THE CUCKOO BUT I
KNEW I COULDN'T AND THAT'S
JUSTIFIED — YOU HAVE TO DIFFERENTIATE
BETWEEN GOOD AND BAD. THEY
ALL HATE ME AND I HATE THEM,
AT THE END OF THE DAY THEY
NEEDED OTHER PEOPLE TO SURVIVE —
COULDN'T SEE THROUGH A YEAR
WITHOUT A BOY/GIRLFRIEND. ME —
I ONLY NEEDED MYSELF. NOW
WHO'S INADEQUATE?? DOES A
RELATIONSHIP MEAN YOU CAN'T COPE
WITH LIFE — TOO AFRAID, TOO WEAK?!
I DUNNO. ALL THESE QUESTIONS
ARE IN MY HEADS TEARING ME
APART. IF I HAVE A GIRLFRIEND
AM I JUST LIKE EVERYONE ELSE.
WILL I BE HAPPY WITH DULUX,
DOGS, 2-3 KIDS, MORTGAGES, OLD
SCHOOL TIES BLAH BLAH BLAH?!
I DUNNO.
 I NEED YOU BUT NOT IN SOME
STUPID REACTIONARY MEANING.
I NEED YOU BECAUSE I CARE
NOT BECAUSE I NEED A
RELATIONSHIP OUT OF HABIT. AND
THAT IS WHY I THINK MOST PEOPLE
GO OUT TOGETHER. FOR SOMETHING
TO DO — A LAUGH, A GIGGLE.
LAUGHTER IS THE REALITY OF
ILLUSION. PEOPLE GO OUT WITH
EACH OTHER TO PARADE, GUILTLESS
SEX AT PARTIES, PAH!
 I NEED YOU FOR MYSELF NOT
FOR THEM. I WISH I WISH YOU'D
UNDERSTAND BUT THE WORDS ARE
DYING ON ME.
 I AM NOT ARROGANT — I JUST
THINK EVERYONE SHOULD OPEN
THEIR EYES A BIT MORE, GET
SOME DEPRESSION IN THEIR SOULS.
YOU KNOW WHEN I GO DOWN THE
CUCKOO AND RED LEON I SEE
PEOPLE SO SELF SATISFIED AND

CONTENT, REGARDLESS OF WHATS
HAPPENING. I AM NOT ADVOCATING
MASS SUICIDE.
     I WANT AWARENESS.
LISTEN TO OLE WILLY BURROUGHS

"(HE WALKED ON, LOOKING AT EVERY FACE
HE PASSED, LOOKING INTO DOOR-WAYS AND
UP AT THE WINDOWS OF CHEAP HOTELS. AN
IRON BEDSTEAD PAINTED LIGHT PINK, A SHIRT
OUT TO DRY ... SCRAPS OF LIFE. LEE
SNAPPED AT THEM HUNGRILY, LIKE A
PREDATORY FISH CUT OFF FROM HIS PREY
BY A GLASS WALL. HE COULD NOT STOP
RAMMING HIS NOSE AGAINST THE GLASS
IN THE NIGHTMARE SEARCH OF HIS
DREAM."

HOPE THAT CLEARS EVERYTHING UP.
ITS JUST SO HARD. SOMETIMES I
JUST WANT TO BANG MY HEAD
AGAINST A WALL. WATCH MY
BLOOD FLOW - BLEED BLEED BLEED.
MAYBE THEN SOMEONE WILL
UNDERSTAND. LAST TIME I WENT
DOWN THE LION I SAW SOME
PEOPLE FROM COLLEGE AND
BASICALLY THEY WERE PART
TIME PEOPLE. THEY WORK ALL
WEEK DOING CYNICAL THINGS,
THINGS THEY DESPISE AND ALL
FOR MONEY. WHAT DOES THAT
ENABLE THEM TO DO - GET PISSED,
SORDID AND DENIED SEX - I
SEE THEM AND I HATE THEM -
SLUTS. AND IT WAS THE SAME
IN COLLEGE (AND UNIVERSITY)-
PEOPLE JUST LIVING FOR THE
WEEKEND; LIVING FOR BEER
AND SEX. (I DRINK ALCOHOL)
AND ITS JUST NOT ENOUGH.
I DON'T MIND WHAT THEY DO
I JUST WISH THEY'D SEE A
BIT MORE. THERES SO MUCH

GOING ON AND NO ONE SEEMS TO
CARE, WHY.
  LAST TIME I WENT TO CARDIFF
I SAW THE DRUNKS OUTSIDE THE
MARKET. I HEARD LIPSTICK GIRLS
SAYING "THATS DISGUSTING".
I DID NOT SEE THE SAME THING.
SAW A VICTIM OF SOCIETY, I
SEE MY RESPONSIBILITY, I ACCEPT OF
THE BLAME. I SPENT HOURS
ASKING MYSELF WHY WHY WHY LIFE
AND THEN I SPENT HOURS ASKING
MYSELF WHY THOSE GIRLS DIDNT 'X'
CARE.
  AWWWW LOOK — IM SORRY
THIS LETTER IS GOING ALL SELF
INDULGENT AND DEPRESSING BUT
I SEE NO OTHER WAY. I HATE
ALL THIS 'I OPEN MY WINDOWS,
THE SUN IS SHINING, I SKIP
THRU THE PARK, LOLLIPOPS AND
CHOLOTE - SYNDAE KISSES, A FISH
JUMPS UP, MY RADIO BELLOWS
SOUP ORACIONS BABA BA"
  IT CAN FUCK OFF AND DIE.
ITS NOT ENOUGH. I JUST WANT
EVERYTHING TO MEAN SOMETHING
AND I THINK IN 1988 THATS
ASKING TOO MUCH. I WISH I
COULD CHANGE FOR YOUR SAKE
BUT I HAVE TO FEEL LIKE
THIS. NOW YOU SAID YOU HATE
JASON AND SO SOON YOU WILL
HATE ME
  RELAPSE 5 — WHITE MAN SPEAKETH
TRUTH
  I DO NOT MEAN TO ANTAGONISE
YOU; I WAS SO SORRY I DEPRESSED
YOU THAT SATURDAY BUT I'M
AFRAID ITS INEVITABLE. THATS WHY
SOON YOU WILL HATE ME. I DONT
WANT YOU TOO BUT YOU WILL.
A DARKENED CREVICE OF BOY-HOOD
SPIRALS IN MY HEAD. LOOK

HIGH
I AM
LOST
BUTTON
ON
THE
FRENC
JACKET

303

BABEY I DONT MEAN IT. ITS
JUST THAT I ULTIMATELY DEPRESS,
REDUCE THINGS TO NEGATIVE
FACTORS. I WANT TO MAKE YOU
HAPPY. BUT I CAN'T DO IT
LIKE I KNOW YOU WANT. I MEAN
I CAN'T BE ALL HAPPINESS AND
SMILES LIKE YOUR HEROES
(BUN, FRAZER............). I JUST
CAN'T. I TRIED — HONEST.
SORRY SORRY SORRY. ITS JUST — I'M...
I GUESS I DON'T SEE HOW YOU CAN
BE REALLY HAPPY UNLESS YOU'VE
EXPERIENCED SADNESS. AND I DON'T
MEAN THE SADNESS OF PERSONAL
EXPERIENCE, RELATIONSHIP FAILURE.
I MEAN SADNESS AT SEEING
SOMEONE BUY A DAMNED RECORD,
LAUGH AT A CRIPPLE, WALK
PAST A DIRTY CRUMBLING BUILDING.
OH GOD YOU'RE GONNA HATE
ME. I AM THE LAUGHING
STOCK OF SOCIETY — A CHEAP
HEAL, A BUM, A FOOL.
I'M SO SO SORRY.
   I THINK I'LL SHUT UP.
      FOR NOW.

   I MISS YOU BABEY BLUE

         Richey

PS. KISS KISS KISS
PPS TOUCH THE SKY AT MIDDAY ON
   SUNDAY — I'LL THINK OF YOU
   BY DOING THE SAME THING
PPPS DROP YOUR LIFE AND PICK UP
   YOUR SOUL
PPPPS I MISS YOU xxxx

304

Letter to Scottish pen-pal Alistair Fitchett. Richey and Alistair would often write to each other about poetry and music.

DEAR ALISTAIR,
            THANKS FOR THE LETTER. EVERY
DAY I SEEM TO GET MORE AND MORE ENCOURAGED
BY FINDING ANGELS IN THE SCRAPHEAP. THIS
GODDAMN DECAY OF A COUNTRY IS FALLING
BUT IT IS SPITTING OUT ANSWERS EVERY DAY.
EVERY DAY. WE STARTED OFF, GENUINELY BELIEVING
JUST IN OURSELVES, THAT NO ONE ELSE HAD
ANYTHING ELSE TO OFFER, OR EVEN WANTED TO
LISTEN. I AM GLAD TO SAY I WAS WRONG.
THERE IS SO MUCH TO BE ANGRY ABOUT IN THIS
LAND AND, ONLY NOW, I CAN SEE THAT SOME
PEOPLE ARE ANGRY. AT THE MOMENT THO
EVERYTHING IS UNDERGROUND, EVERYTHING JUST
A BIT TOO SMALL SCALE. I WANT IT TO
GROW OUT OF CONTROL. I WANT TO HEAR SONGS
BURNING ACROSS RADIO ONE AIRWAVES, I WANT
ATTITUDE AT NO/1 IN THE CHARTS, I WANT
TO SEE THE STUPID, CRASS BULLSHIT OF SO-
CALLED POP SOLUTIONS SUCH AS DARLING
BUDS, ETC BEATEN TO DEATH, I WANT TO
SEE KIDS IN SCHOOL READ BIG SUR, WATCH
BIRDY AND CUCKOO'S NEST, I WANT TO SEE
KIDS RESPECT LIFE OVER ESCORTS, I WANT
TO SEE YOUTH FIND ANSWERS BY THEMSELVES
AND NOT THRU THE MORALLY BANKRUPT
DESIGNER BULLSHIT OF THE I.D/FACE STYLE
FASCIST BRIGADE. IF HITLER WAS ALIVE TODAY
HE WOULD WEAR A HUNDRED POUND SHIRT
AND MEIN KAMPF WOULD HAVE A GLOSSY
COVER.
       AT THE MOMENT IT DOES SEEM LIKE
SOMETHING IS HAPPENING. I HAVE NEVER HEARD
THE CLAIM OR HELLFIRE SERMONS BUT THEY
DO SEEM TO BELIEVE PURITY CAN TRANSCEND
ANY OPAQUE BARRIERS. ALSO KEVINS TOTAL
BELIEF, AND YOUR WRITING — WHICH WE ALL
LIKED, IT ALL SEEMS TO BECKON SOME KIND
OF HOPE. THE PRESS AT THE MOMENT

KINDA HAVE THEIR HOPES PINNED ON BIRDLAND
AND ALTHO THEY MAY WELL HAVE SOME
KIND OF BAND IDENTITY, SOME HATE IT IS
JUST DISTILLED, THEN WATERED DOWN INTO
SOME GODFORSAKEN ROCK AND ROLL MYTH.
I MEAN I HAVE NOTHING AGAINST
THE ~~AUTO DESTRUCT~~ AUTO-DESTRUCTION
OF INSTRUMENTS AS LONG AS THIS NAIVE
ANGER IS BACKED UP WITH THOUGHT MOST
BANDS THO JUST FALL INTO THE TRAP OF
ROCK AND ROLL DICTATORSHIP. NO ONE
SEEMS TO HAVE ANYTHING TO SAY, I JUST
HAVE A MILLION THOUGHTS A SECOND. I
DO THINK THAT FOR A BAND TO
BREAK THE CELL OF FOREVER BEING
SMALL THEY HAVE TO SORT ~~OF~~ INDULGE IN
SOME KIND OF BAND-CLICHE-ATTITUDE BUT
 AS LONG AS IT IS MATCHED BY INTEGRITY
AND WANTING TO CHANGE THINGS THEN IT IS
FINE. LIKE YOU CAN ~~SMASH~~ GUITARS BECAUSE
TOWNSHEND DID IT OR YOU CAN SMASH
GUITARS TO SHAKE UP THE AUDIENCE, TO
GO THRU CATHARSIS, TO RIP THEIR APATHY
UP, TO DESTROY THEIR ACCEPTANCE BY
HUMILIATING THEM, BY MAKING THEM LOOK
EMBARRASSED AS YOU SMASH THE GUITAR, BY
MAKING THEM FEEL GUILTY FOR NOT
LISTENING. I OBJECT WHEN PEOPLE
DO NOT LISTEN — NOW YOU CAN EITHER WALK
AWAY AND LEAVE THEM OR YOU CAN MAKE
THEM LOOK, YANK THEIR ATTENTION. BASICA-
LLY WE, AS A MASS CONSCIOUSNESS STRETCH-
ING FROM STRATHCLYDE TO KENT TO
BLACKWOOD, HAVE TO CHANGE THE WHOLE
COUNTRY. AND IF WE, AS A BAND, HAVE
TO INDULGE IN A ROCK AND ROLL SMASHING
OF GUITARS TO BREAK UP THE SYCOPHANTIC
DOUBLE-STANDARD MORALS OF BRITAIN
THEN IT IS A PRICE ~~ONE~~ WE WILL ~~B~~ PAY.
REPRESSION IS A SYSTEM, IT TELLS US
TO OBEY, OBEY — NOT TO DO THIS, NOT TO
DO THAT, TO FEEL LIKE A FOOL TO JUMP
ON STAGE, NOT TO SHOUT AT THE EVER APATHIC
AUDIENCE, THAT TO CARE IS WRONG — AND

MOST BANDS GIVE IN. AND THEN EVERYTHING CARRYS ON. FUCKING GREAT. IF PEOPLE LAUGH FINE. IF PEOPLE THROW BOTTLES AT US FINE. AT EVERY CONCERT WE HAVE CHANGED SOMEONE → IT HAS COST US A LOT, MOST NOTABLY A DESTROYED P.A AND A BROKEN JAW BUT IT IS WORTH IT. IF PEOPLE DON'T ACCEPT IT THEY CAN STEW IN THEIR OWN JUICES. WE ARE A STATE OFFENCE BECAUSE WE CARE. NO ONE WANTS TO GIVE US A CHANCE BECAUSE WE THREATEN THEIR EXISTENCE. ALL WE NEED TO DO IS PUT FEELING OVER REASON, BELIEF OVER COMPUTERS ETC. ONCE YOU START ACCEPTING WHAT YOU ARE TOLD THEN WHERE CAN YOU GO?? ONLY INTO A HOLE CALLED CIVILISATION, ONLY INTO STANDARDS THAT JUDGE LIFE THRU A SUIT AND CAR. I AM IN MY FINAL YEAR AT UNIVERSITY AND THE COMPANYS ARE AROUND BUYING UP EAGER YOUNG SOULS AND EVERYONE IS JUST TAKING IT ALL, SELLING THIS COUNTRYS (AS IF ITS THEIR TO SELL) FOR A SEX-CAREER BULLSHIT CAREER IN A BANK. WHEN I GET OUT IN JUNE WE WILL SEE YOU IN SCOTLAND, WE WILL SEE KEVIN, WE WILL SPIN THIS COUNTRY, WE WILL PLAY EVERYWHERE. WE HAVE NOT SENT THIS RECORD TO ANY COMPANY OR RADIO STATION. COME JUNE WE WILL DO IT ALL FAST - THE EXTREME SENSE OF NOW, A TOTAL HOWL OF IMMEDIACY. PEOPLE TELL ME NOT TO BOTHER, TO GIVE IT ALL UP FOR A MANMADE NEED, A CONSUMER DREAMLAND MYTH.
   "DON'T EAT AWAY AT MY MIND WITH YOUR
    IDEAS OF DECENCY COS I'LL BE IN SUICIDE
    ALLEY WHERE I CAN BE WHO AND WHAT
    I WANT TO BE"
ANYWAY THANKS FOR LISTENING BUT MORE IMPORTANTLY THANKS FOR WRITING - IT WAS BRILLIANT AND ENCOURAGING.
             LOVE Richey

DROP YOUR LIFE AND PICK UP YOUR SOUL.

References

The publishers will be happy to make good any omissions in future reprints. Only the first instance of a cited work has been included.

Introduction
'Teenage Rampage', *Sounds Magazine*, 1991
'Blackwood Calling?', *Select*, 1992
'Boys from Blackwood', *Spiral Scratch*, 1991

Chapter One
'From Despair to … Despair', *Deadline*, 1993
'Pathetic', *Q Magazine*, 1992
'Bangkok Sucker Blues', *NME*, 1994

Chapter Two
'Manic's Depressive', *NME*, 1994
'Depression = Drink = Mutilation', *Kerrang*, 1994

Chapter Three
'Dead End Street', *Vox*, 1993
'Drags to Riches', *Melody Maker*, 1992
'Manic Sheep Teachers', *NME*, 1993

Chapter Five
'It Couldn't Be You', *Select*, 1998
'Five Years Gone', *Kerrang*, 2000
'Not So Manic Now', *Guardian*, 2004
'Love Will Tear Us Apart', *Esquire*, 1998
In the Beginning: My Life With The Manic Street Preachers, Jennifer Watkins Isnardi, Blake Publishing, 2000

'The Search for Richey Manic', *Vox*, 1996
'The Last Time I Saw Richey', *Guardian*, 2000
'I Think We've All Tried to Deny it at Some Point, but Being Unhappy and Dissatisfied is Part of Our Make-Up', *Volume*, Autumn, 1994
'Parental Guidance Advised', *Melody Maker*, 1991
'Gorgeous in Spite of Himself', *The Times*, 1994
'Attention All Pathetic, Unloved Sluts', *Check This Out*, 1992
Impact Magazine, 1988

Chapter Six
'Road Hogs!!', *RAW*, 1994

Chapter Seven
'Going 4 Gold', *Metal Hammer*, 1993
'Glam Racket', *Select*, 1993
'From Sneer to Maturity', *NME*, 1993
'Don't Give up the Deity Job', *NME*, 1994
'It's Not A Question of Compromise; It's Just a Question of Clarity', *Pop Matters*, 2005
'Nicky Wire: Prime Minister,' *NME*, 1997
'Handjobs and Holy Bibles', *Kerrang*, 1994
'The Record That Changed Our Lives', *NME*, 2014

Chapter Eight
The Hiding Place, Trezza Azzapardi, Picador, 2000
'Archives of Pain', *Melody Maker*, 1994
'James Dean Bradfield of the Manic Street Preachers on a year of hospital horror', *Select*, 1995
'Manic Depression', *Melody Maker*, 1994
'One Foot In The Past', *The Word*, 2005
Sacred Sex: Erotic Writings from the Religions of the World, Robert Bates, HarperCollins, 1994
'Manic Street Preachers - The Revolutionaries', *Q Magazine*, 2009
'Something Just Flipped In His Head', *RAW*, 1994
'Rapid Mood Swings', *Sky*, 1994
'Manic Street Preachers Interview Part 2', *NME*, 2009
'We Shall Overcome', *Select*, 1996

Chapter Nine
'Rant for Cover', *RAW*, 1994
'Manic Street Preachers: There's just so much hate within this band. Why are we still like this?', *Uncut*, 2014
'Manic Street Preachers on The Holy Bible', *NME*, 2014
'Manic Street Preacher', *Music Life*, 1995

REFERENCES

'Manics New Testament', *Melody Maker*, 1994
'Rant For Cover', *RAW*, 1994
'Blood, Sweat and Tears', *The Face*, 1994
'Smile, It Might Never Happen', *Q Magazine*, 1994
'Richey Edwards of the Manic Street Preachers chooses his Men of the Year',
    Melody Maker, 1993
'All That Glitters', *Melody Maker*, 1994
'B Side: Manic Street Preachers', *MOJO*, 2001

Chapter Ten
'Everything Must Go ... On', *NME*, 1996
'Culture, Alienation, Bordeaux and Despair', *Melody Maker*, 1994
'We've Never Quite Walked It Like We've Talked It', *NME*, 1998
'Manic Street Preachers Interview Part Three', *NME*, 2014
Suede: Love and Poison, David Barnett, Andre Deutsch Ltd, 2003
'Ooh, Aaah, Street Preach-Ah', *Melody Maker*, 1994
'How we made Manic Street Preachers' Everything Must Go', *Guardian*, 2016
'Everything Must Go Interview', *NME*, 1996
Impact Magazine, 1988
'Did Someone Order Gloom Service?', *The Face*, 1998
'And If You Need An Explanation: Manic Street Preachers interviewed', *The Quietus*,
    2016
'Everything Must Grow Up', *Q Magazine*, 1998
'Manic Street Preachers', *Music Life*, 1995
'This Album Could Seriously Damage Us', *Guardian*, 2009

Chapter Eleven
'It Was The Best Of Times', *Q Magazine*, 2016
'The Point of No Return?', *The Sunday Times*, 1995

Chapter Twelve
The Denial of Death, Ernest Becker, Souvenir Press Ltd, 1974
'Manic Street Preachers', *EP Magazine*, 1991
'Manic Street Preachers Rewind The Film', *WalesOnline*, 2013

Chapter Thirteen
'Missing', *Independent*, 1998
'The Search for Richey Manic', *Vox*, 1996
O'Hara's Fundamentals of Criminal Investigation, Charles C. Thomas
    Publisher, 2013 edition
Love & Death: The Murder of Kurt Cobain, Ian Halperin and Max Wallace, Allison
    & Busby UK edition, 2014
Disasters on the Severn, Chris Witts, Tempus Publishing, 2002
Paint it Black: The Murder of Brian Jones, Geoffrey Giuliano, Virgin Books, 1994

Brian Jones: Who Killed Christopher Robin? The Truth Behind the Murder of a Rolling Stone, Terry Rawlings, Helter Skelter Publishing, 2005

'Manic Street Preachers: Sublime and ridiculous', *Independent*, 2004

'From Despair to ... Where?', *NME*, 1995

Index

INDEX

Edwards, Ivor (great-grandfather) 13
Edwards, Nick (cousin) 16, 18, 48
Edwards, Paul (cousin) 16
Edwards, Rachel (sister) 77
  Apocalypse Now, on RE's love of 194
  Asperger's, on possibility of RE having
      207, 211
  Bethune suicide, on RE's reaction to
      128–9
  birth 16
  childhood/RE's childhood and 17–25,
      28–9, 30, 33, 34–5, 33, 36, 37, 40,
      41, 42
  Christmas before RE's disappearance and
      202, 203
  '4 Real' incident, on 98
  Manic Street Preachers and 45, 67, 73,
      82, 84, 91, 94, 96, 98, 106, 117, 120,
      140, 164, 168, 170, 175, 185, 186,
      190, 198, 199, 201, 272–5
  RE's Cardiff flat, on 124
  RE's degree, on 79–80
  RE's disappearance and ix–xi, 4, 6, 218,
      220, 221, 222, 223, 224, 237, 239,
      243, 244, 246–7, 249–50, 251–77
  RE's drinking, on 74–5
  RE's interest in religion, on 188–9
  RE's job with Islwyn Borough Council,
      on 81
  RE's relationship with family, on x, xi, 8,
      12, 13, 14, 15, 57, 211
  RE's suicide attempt, hospitalisation and
      132, 134, 135, 136, 137, 138, 139,
      140, 147, 148, 149, 155–6, 157
  RE's tattoos, on 199
  Snoopy (RE's dog) death, on RE's reac-
      tion to 204, 206
Edwards, Richey:
  academia, love of 2, 25, 42, 48, 54, 79,
      209
  acne 32, 36, 60
  address books 36–7, 131–2, 142, 222
  alcohol and 4, 56, 60–1, 74–5, 93, 123,
      126, 142, 145–6, 152, 153, 156, 160,
      187, 203, 206–7, 265
  Alcoholics Anonymous Twelve Steps
      programme and 142, 145–6, 156
  ambition 2, 5, 90, 94, 96
  androgyny 30, 39, 62, 145
  animals, love of 21, 60, 158, 202,
      204–5, 206
  anorexia 4, 30, 141, 150, 162, 264
  anti-love credo 64–6, 75–6, 129,
      168, 217
  anxiety first creeps into behaviour 32–3
  Asperger's syndrome (AS) and 207–11

Bangkok, time in with Manic Street
      Preachers 12, 125–8, 130, 175,
      237, 239
bangs head against brick wall 198, 234
Bethune suicide and 128–9, 130
birth 16
body, embarrassment about 32, 49–50
Borderline Personality Disorder, diag-
      nosed with 152–6
Cardiff, buys flat in 123–4, 130
charisma 5–6
childhood 2, 7–8, 9–10, 16–35, 37
class consciousness 9–10, 33–5, 38, 46–7,
      50–1, 52, 169, 177–8, 237, 238
Cobain suicide and 122–3, 201
collages 39, 49, 61, 73, 84, 87, 113, 171,
      192, 221
comic books, love of 20–1
conspiracy theories and 94, 101–5
Crosskeys College 36–47
'Cult of Richey' 6, 190
current affairs/politics, interest in 41–2,
      46–7
depression 134, 136, 138, 152, 153, 156,
      190–1, 233, 249
diaries 21, 48, 202–3, 204, 241, 255
disappearance
  ATM cash withdrawals and 217–18,
      223–4
  CCTV and ix, 260–2
  childhood writing on escape over the
      Severn Bridge and 28–9
  Cobain suicide and 122–3, 133, 138,
      202, 259, 263–4, 274
  copy-cat suicides and 256–7, 260
  conspiracy theories surrounding
      259–68
  declared dead 269–70
  Embassy Hotel stay and 218, 219,
      220–1, 225, 237, 242, 251, 253,
      262–3
  gift box addressed to girlfriend, Jo left
      in Embassy Hotel 221–2, 225,
      237–47
  immortality, exile and disappearance,
      fascination with heroic ideas and
      narratives of 3–4, 7–8, 13, 15, 89–91,
      113–14, 115, 158, 172–3, 184, 193–5,
      199, 214, 232–49
  Israel, wish to visit and 243, 244–5
  Jim Morrison myth and 114–15, 202,
      265
  last documented week 217–19
  Manic Street Preachers and
  see Manic Street Preachers *and indi-
      vidual band member name*

315

INDEX